FRANK LLOYD WRIGHT

FRANK LLOYD WRIGHT

AN INTERPRETIVE BIOGRAPHY

BY ROBERT C. TWOMBLY

HARPER & ROW, PUBLISHERS

NEW YORK, EVANSTON, SAN FRANCISCO, LONDON

B
Wright

Portions of this work previously appeared in *The Wisconsin Magazine of History* and in *American Quarterly.*

FIRST EDITION

STANDARD BOOK NUMBER: 06–014467-X

LIBRARY OF CONGRESS CATALOG CARD NUMBER: 72–9248

C.2

CONTENTS

ILLUSTRATIONS

PREFACE

My arrival in Frank Lloyd Wright country in 1962 aroused my curiosity about a body of work I had seen represented only by the Guggenheim Museum in New York and the Morris Gift Shop in San Francisco. A midnight visit to a Unitarian church, a dinner engagement at a semicircular fieldstone house, and a list of Wright's local designs in a Milwaukee newspaper sparked an investigative journey that culminated several years later in a summer spent in various unscholarly attitudes on the Wisconsin River near Spring Green, within earshot of Taliesin, the architect's home. There were two major outgrowths of that long process: a strong emotional attachment to his work and to the valley in which he lived, and this biography, which I trust has not been impaired by that attachment. Since prefaces are supposed to be personal statements, I here record my hope that construction can somehow be stopped on the year-round resort designed for the Spring Green area by Wright's heirs, the Taliesin Associated Architects. The landscape he loved most is a peaceful and beautiful place, needing only to be left alone.

My interest in Wright evolved from an avocation to a research problem to a doctoral dissertation at the University of Wisconsin. The work could not have proceeded without the immense local newspaper files at the State Historical Society in Madison; without the proximity of greater Chicago, where I scrutinized and photographed Wright's buildings more times than I can remember; and without the tolerant advice of Professor E. David Cronon, my mentor. Other Wisconsin people whose help was substantial are: Alan Mast, now of Augusta, Maine; Thomas S. Hines, Jr., now at UCLA; Leslie H. Fishel, formerly director of the State Historical Society, now president of Heidelberg College (it is not that everyone leaves Wisconsin, simply that academic communities tend to be transient); Professors William O'Neill (now at Rutgers), David Lovejoy, William R. Taylor (now at Stony Brook), and Joseph Elder; Madison architect John Buschke, who opened to me his extensive collection of Wright memorabilia; editor William C. Haygood of *The Wisconsin Magazine of History*; and the staff of the Historical Society, a most congenial and resourceful group of people. Cynthia Merman and Hugh Van Dusen at Harper & Row also gave invaluable assistance.

There are still others who deserve special thanks, including the many owners of Wright homes who permitted me entrance and described their experiences. Edgar Kaufmann, Jr., of Columbia University offered valuable suggestions and support for turning the dissertation into a book, Professor Robert H. Moore of the University of Maryland considerably improved my prose and my ideas, and Professor Richard H. Kohn of Rutgers gave so unstintingly of himself that the final product bears his imprint: my debt to all three is great.

The most tenacious and insightful critic, however, was Alice Jacobs Twombly, who traveled many a mile, advised on many a photograph, struggled through many a draft, and in spite of it all remained an unquenchable source of ideas and inspiration. Much of the analysis, in fact, originated with her. One of her greatest achievements was a cosmic happening totally beyond my comprehension: as promised, she delivered Jonathan Dana, our firstborn, on June 8, 1969, Wright's one hundred second birthday. Since then I have occasionally questioned the viability of the open floor plan, but never the power of a liberated woman.

ROBERT C. TWOMBLY

FRANK LLOYD WRIGHT

For while objectively a social reality, the work of art is, in its genesis, a projection of a deeply personal process, and any approach that ignores the personal at the expense of the social is necessarily incomplete.

Ralph Ellison, *Shadow and Act* (1964)

1. NEARLY EVERYTHING TO LEARN

[1867-1893]

Frank Lloyd Wright's early years were nomadic and unsettling. Before he was eleven he had lived in six towns in four states, from Massachusetts to Iowa, while his restless father searched for a better situation. In his early teens he worked summers to help his family financially, and when his parents divorced he quit high school to take a job. He started college, but after two uneventful semesters left for Chicago, where he switched employers four times in a year. A week before his twenty-second birthday he married his eighteen-year-old fiancée, his first romantic attachment. But despite his provincial background and his lack of formal training, Wright had by his mid-twenties acquired the social and architectural tools necessary for entrance into Chicago's professional upper middle class.

Like the wandering pioneer of American folklore, Frank Lloyd Wright's father willingly subordinated family stability and familiar surroundings to a relentless search for personal fulfillment. William Russell Cary Wright, a minister, was born a minister's son in

1825 in Westfield, Massachusetts. Obviously a precocious child, he entered Amherst College in 1839 at the age of fourteen to study music and law, but left after two uncompleted years. Upon graduation from Madison University (later named Colgate) in 1849, he took his first job as a music teacher in Utica, New York, and there in 1851 married Permelia Holcomb, a native of the region. In short order the newlyweds moved to Hartford, Connecticut, where he continued to teach, resumed his study of the law, and was admitted to the bar in 1857. But after six years in Hartford his wanderlust asserted itself, and William C. Wright joined that inexorable westward migration, arriving at Lone Rock, Wisconsin, to hang out a lawyer's shingle sometime in 1859.[1]*

His choice of residence was an apt one, for Lone Rock immediately recognized him as a potential leader, a well-educated man possessing skills useful to the community and conducive to personal success on the frontier. He was ambitious, aggressive, made friends easily, and elicited confidence and respect. Within a year he was appointed commissioner of the Richland County Circuit Court, testimony to his political as well as his legal sagacity, and then announced his candidacy for county school superintendent, winning the enthusiastic endorsement of a local newspaper. "Probably no better man could be selected," the editor contended. "His friends speak very highly of him. . . ." Wright lost, but tried again and won in 1863. His wife died during his two-year tenure in April 1864, leaving him a widower with three children, but before long he met Anna Lloyd Jones, who lived just seven miles away, in Hillside.[2]

Frank Lloyd Wright's mother was born in Wales in 1842. Her family migrated to Ixonia, Wisconsin, in 1845 and two years later moved to the Helena Valley, to Hillside, a tiny farming settlement across the Wisconsin River from Spring Green. The Lloyd Joneses, a tightly knit Unitarian clan, soon became one of the most numerous and prosperous families in the south-central part of the state. The reverence in her home for books and learning

* Source Notes begin on page 307.

4

probably directed Anna to teaching, one of the few socially accept-
able careers for young ladies, and one that had already attracted
two of her sisters.[3] Since the county superintendent interviewed
job applicants and lectured at the annual Teachers' Institute,
Anna may well have met her future husband in his professional
capacity. The mature, widely respected, and well-educated superintendent must have impressed the bookish, comparatively sheltered but strong-willed Anna, for they were married on August 17,
1866, when he was forty-one and she twenty-four. By this time
Wright had entered politics, but his brief career as a minor official
in the Union (Republican) party and as a deputy United States
revenue collector was even shorter lived than his legal practice, for
Wright had become a preacher and was establishing a reputation
as an orator. During his first marriage he had begun to ride the
thirty-five miles round trip each Sunday to preach at the Richland
Center Baptist Society, which had ordained him in August 1863.
In May of 1867, when his new wife was eight months pregnant,
the Wrights left Lone Rock to preside over the construction of the
Society's first building. Just as they were settling in, Anna gave
birth to the first of her three children, her only son Frank Lloyd,
on June 8, 1867.[4]

Throughout his life Frank Lloyd Wright consistently maintained that his architectural career had somehow been prenatally
chosen for him by his mother, who did not consult William in the
matter. Yet the younger Wright freely admitted that his lifelong
reverence for Bach and Beethoven was instilled by his father, who,
he recalled, had taught him the structural similarities between
music and buildings. William's relationship with his son was never
close and terminated early, but his impact was profound and lasting. Indeed, in the architect's last magazine article, published in
1957 when he was ninety, he recounted—as he had many times—
his love-hate attraction for his father: love for William's music
and the esteem in which his peers held him, hate for his authoritarian manner as a parent.[5] Although young Wright owed his
interest in the arts to his father as much as to his mother, William

C. Wright's career and influence on his son have never received the attention they deserve.

For one thing, while in Lone Rock the Reverend Wright had established a local reputation for excellence in public speaking at a time when skillful oratory was universally admired. The prize of delivering the eulogy for Abraham Lincoln in April 1865 was presumably given to him as the town's most able spokesman, and, according to one observer, Wright made "an appropriate and eloquent address which . . . was highly praised by all who heard it."

Then, after January 1866, when his tenure as superintendent ended, he devoted himself entirely to the Richland Center Baptist Society. A month after his son's birth in 1867, he gave his first local concert, for the benefit of the building fund, establishing himself as both musician and preacher, a pattern that characterized his later associations with other communities. His "musical attainments [were] well known," the town's newspaper reminded its readers, and the concert was "equal to the best entertainment ever given here."[6]

Despite widespread appreciation of his diverse talents, however, William Wright found the center too confining, perhaps too unprofitable. Community largesse dispensed at occasional "donation parties" held to supplement his meager salary was hardly sufficient recognition of his worth. To salvage his pride, and with an eye toward greener pastures, the Wrights moved to McGregor, Iowa, in March 1869.

Hoping that commerce would be more remunerative than preaching, Wright went to McGregor as part owner of the music department in a general store. But the flattering reputation that preceded him had little to do with mundane business matters: "Our city has reason to be glad," the editor of the McGregor Times commented, "that so valuable a gentleman has been added to its religious, musical, and social lists." Wright quickly became active in civic and religious affairs, preaching "very acceptably when requested to do so," directing a musical group, and contributing to the Thanksgiving Festival.

He excelled at everything but turning a profit, and even though everyone knew he was "not professionally a clergyman," he delivered a much-admired funeral oration over the body of a locally prominent citizen and within a short time was made temporary pastor of the Baptist Church, a position he held for the next two years. His congregation respected him immensely, "as unassuming and plain a Christian as walks or talks," and his sermons were "highly commended by those who are competent to judge. . . ." People had come to "expect something original, practical, and unhackneyed from Mr. Wright," his friend the newspaper editor wrote. "He is a plain speaker and for that we like him." To most people in McGregor, the Wrights were "valued friends," and they were therefore disappointed to learn in May 1871 that their minister was leaving:

There are few clergymen who have so strong a hold upon their congregation as the reverend gentleman has, and we happen to know that there are none who do not rejoice at the success which his people have met in persuading him to remain.

So when the Wrights actually left McGregor two months later—in July 1871—everyone felt the loss:

The people . . . have not submitted willingly to the decision which takes from us this excellent man. They love him . . . and separate from him with regret, and will ever follow him with their kindest wishes to whatever field of labor he may be called.[7]

Frank Lloyd Wright depicted his father as a moody man, subject to frequent periods of depression. "Failure after failure added to failure," he wrote, produced "the inveterate and desperate withdrawal on his part into the arid life of his studies, his books, and his music, where he was oblivious to all else."[8] This was certainly true in the 1880s, when the young man was old enough to notice the deterioration of his parents' relationship, but during the 1860s and 1870s William Wright was admired by his fellow townsmen, beloved for his preaching and music, and welcome in community affairs. On the surface, at least, he seemed happy enough. His "desperate withdrawal" developed later, after considerable social and financial frustration.

The Wrights left McGregor as optimistically as they had left Richland Center. After spending the next few months with the Lloyd Joneses near Spring Green, they moved to Pawtucket, Rhode Island, where William assumed the pastorate of the High Street Baptist Church in December. He undertook his difficult responsibilities enthusiastically, for the next two years presiding over what seemed an endless series of fund-raising efforts designed to rescue the congregation from an embarrassing debt. But the church was apparently beyond salvation, for shortly after Wright resigned and left the city in January 1874, its building was put up for auction. Nevertheless, he was applauded as "a workman that need not be ashamed—earnest, unwearied, successful, as far as circumstances permitted."[9]

In Pawtucket Wright again displayed the varied talents and amiable personality that had made him popular elsewhere. His public lectures—some religious, some not—revealed a continuing interest in politics when he thanked God for President Ulysses Grant's reelection, and a moderate interest in reform when he discussed "the responsibility of public carriers for human life and safety." He gave his first addresses on temperance and on ancient Egypt, dependable lecture topics thereafter, and was elected assistant clerk of the Providence Baptist Association, reading his circular letter to the 1873 convention on "How may our efficiency as churches be increased?" Not the least of his accomplishments was the composition of " 'Tis Sweet to Meet, and Each Other Greet," a song published as sheet music and sold as a supplement to *The Social Times*, a church paper he edited briefly.

By late 1873 Wright had decided to leave Pawtucket, perhaps because as in Richland Center he had had to rely on handouts. At a surprise party, for example, the gentlemen of his congregation suddenly presented him a "quantity of greenbacks," embarrassing him almost as much as did the subsequent newspaper account. As usual, his decision was unpopular. Having been impressed by his energy, his perseverance, and his "admirably" conceived and delivered sermons, the High Street Baptist Society voted unanimously not to accept his resignation. But despite its wishes Wright left in January 1874 to disappear from the historical record until the following August, when he preached a trial sermon at the First Baptist Church in Weymouth, Massachusetts, entering the pulpit there on September 6.[10]

Wright's Weymouth career followed the usual pattern. He quickly established a reputation for excellence in music, befriended the local newspaper editor, and helped form a literary circle. He associated himself with the Massachusetts Total Abstinence Society and the Weymouth "Reform" Club, more than likely another temperance organization. He convinced the Baptist Church to install a pipe organ, paid for by the wealthy parishioner who had been instrumental in his coming. "He had some wonderfully interesting musical Sundays at his church," one Weymouth resident remembered, but they were "not entirely to the satisfaction of his congregation." Perhaps his habit of "seat[ing] himself at the piano, and throwing back his head, with its snow-white hair, sing[ing] and play[ing] to us some song of his choosing" disquieted church members sensitive to ministerial decorum, especially on the Sabbath. The chroniclers of local history do not agree whether Wright resigned in October 1877 or was fired, but when he left the pulpit the church took up a special collection, since during the national depression it had been unable to pay his salary.

Wright then turned to lecturing and music as alternate sources of income. His talk on temperance at the Universalist Church was his first foray outside the Baptist fold, while his addresses to the Women's Christian Temperance Union on "Curiosities of Egypt" and "Reigns of the Ptolemies and Cleopatra" were as well attended as his musicales, one of which was "the most brilliant display of home talent ever witnessed in town." But his triumphs

9

left him unsatisfied, and William Wright decided to return to Wisconsin, perhaps at his wife's urging. After a farewell sermon at the Universalist Church and a testimonial dinner at the Reform Club, in April 1878, the Wrights were accompanied to the railroad station by a large group of well-wishers, citizens of another town that wanted him to stay.[11]

The William C. Wrights traveled directly to Wisconsin to spend the spring and summer with the Lloyd Joneses, substantiating Frank Lloyd Wright's recollection that he was eleven when he first worked on his Uncle James's farm. Although the date of his move to Madison is uncertain, William was cited in a rural newspaper in August 1878 as a resident there and as pastor of the Liberal (Unitarian) Church of Wyoming, a settlement near Hillside. He had probably secured this position and its associated responsibilities through the influence of Anna's brother, Jenkin Lloyd Jones, a prominent Chicago clergyman and the missionary secretary of the Western Unitarian Conference. "The State work," Jones wrote in Unity, the journal he edited, "has been put in the hands of Mr. Wright who has energetically pushed missionary enterprises, ministering fortnightly to the little society at Wyoming, and visiting other places"—Edgerton, Richland Center, Lone Rock, and Bear Creek. Before the year was out Wright, who had been "recruited" from the Baptists sometime after May 1878, was appointed secretary of the Wisconsin Conference of Unitarians and Independent Societies.

Although his services were "heartily" commended to the officers of the American Unitarian Association, Wright did not find his new affiliation any more financially rewarding than the Baptist Church. Even with proceeds from the music studio he had opened in Madison by March 1880, Wright could not support his family, and was forced back to the lecture platform and the pulpit in other denominations to supplement his income. In October 1881 he opened a series of meetings in the Spring Green Congregational Church. "As a lecturer, Mr. Wright is one of the best," a local newspaper observed, "and none should fail to hear him." But

Frank Lloyd Wright's family. Clockwise from lower left: Aunt Jane Lloyd Jones, Sister Jane, W. C. Wright, Anna Wright, Uncle James Philip, Cousin Elsie Philip, Sister Maginel, Frank Lloyd Wright

apparently many did, for although his talk on Ireland "was without doubt one of the best we ever attended," the turnout was "very small," ending the projected series after the first session. Nevertheless, Wright spoke to the Congregationalists periodically until late 1884, and continued his Unitarian functions through the summer of 1885.[12]

Meanwhile, Frank Lloyd Wright entered the Second Ward Grammar School. His boyhood years in Madison, as he described them, seem normal enough. He and his closest friend, Robert M. "Robie" Lamp (for whom he designed a house in 1904), engaged in the usual boyish activities. They "invented" things, flew kites, published a one-sheet neighborhood newspaper, and found themselves in the inevitable adolescent imbroglios. Predictably, given his parents' interests, he enjoyed reading and music, and from his father learned to play viola in the family orchestra. He was shy around girls but popular with young people generally, had a tendency to fantasize, and especially liked to paint and draw. In 1885 he quit Madison High School to take a drafting job with a University of Wisconsin professor of civil engineering, Allan D. Conover, who was also the city engineer and a consultant to the State Railroad Commission. Conover had just opened an architectural office and hired Wright as one of his first assistants.[13]

Young Wright apparently left high school because of the financial difficulties resulting from a dramatic change in his family's situation. In April 1885 William C. Wright filed for and received a divorce, without any contest whatsoever from Anna. Claiming she was insulting, extravagant, ignored her duties, and was money hungry, Wright objected most when she refused "me intercourse as between husband and wife" by deserting him for two years in every way but physically removing herself from home. She had told him she hated the very ground he walked on, that she would never again live with him as a wife. Although his suit concentrated on the period after 1883, he contended that "our married life has been unhappy from the start," since she was jealous of her three stepchildren, who had long since left home. Anna made no defense, and after winning William left Madison. His son never saw him again.[14]

The roots of the tension between William and Anna were deep. She had come from a prosperous, tightly knit immigrant family. Her husband, who had settled far from his old-line New England parents, could not recreate for her the sense of camaraderie and united purpose that had characterized her youth. It was difficult for her to adjust to frequent moves from one small town and one poor church to another, waiting for her husband—who was entering middle age when they married—to find what he wanted. Her teaching career had been abandoned, and she found herself in an alien denomination, the stepmother of three older children. Her husband's restlessness contributed to an uncertain family atmosphere, in sharp contrast to what she remembered from childhood. Even her return to Wisconsin did not save her marriage, but, indeed, might have made it seem worse in comparison to life at Spring Green.

The family economic situation was another factor contributing to its eventual breakup. The Wrights' move to Madison may have been prompted in part by a promise of financial assistance from the Lloyd Joneses. (Undoubtedly it was, as already indicated, Jenkin Lloyd Jones who secured Wright's position with the Unitarians.) The summers that Frank Lloyd Wright and his entire family spent with his uncle were presumably designed to ease money problems. (After the divorce, Anna's family was willing to support her.) In Madison William Wright had held three jobs simultaneously—music teacher, Unitarian missionary, and lecturer—but still he could not provide the financial security Anna had grown up to expect and demand. It was not that the Wrights were poverty stricken, but that Anna's aspirations were high. Undoubtedly this contributed to her hostility and to his feeling that she was extravagant, thoughtless, and overly critical.

A kind of tragic pattern emerges from even the little that is known of William Wright's story. He was never able to stay where he was most appreciated; every small town in which he lived praised him enthusiastically and counted him a welcome asset, but they could not satisfy his own sense of worth. He believed that his talents warranted a larger and wealthier audience, but he never lived up to his own expectations. A proud and talented man, he probably felt that his status and income should have been greater than they were. The inability of small midwestern towns to satisfy him led him back East, but further financial disappointment— church bankruptcy and the depression of the 1870s—took him on a second westward migration, not with the optimism of youth this time but with the burdens of family, old age, and defeat. By 1885, at the age of sixty, he knew that success had passed him by. He had disappointed Anna, but more important he had disappointed himself. William Wright lived in a world of unfulfilled ambitions, reaching for elusive dreams, his daughter Maginel wrote, "that refused to take shape." His life was poignant proof that the safety valve of the American West was sometimes closed.

Children often detect uneasiness between their parents. If there was discontent in the family, the sensitive Frank Lloyd Wright was probably aware of it. He could not have been oblivious to the breakdown in parental relations after 1883, when he was sixteen. He must have noticed that his mother "hated the very ground" his father walked upon. He must have been puzzled by William Wright's behavior—his moodiness and withdrawal. But his questions about his father's disappearance were probably answered satisfactorily by his mother, with whom he continued to live and whose version of the episode he accepted without reservation. After years of suffering through financial uncertainty, William's self-absorption, and his lack of interest in her and the children, Anna told her son, she reluctantly asked him to leave, secretly hoping he would not. Taking advantage of the opportunity, he walked out, leaving her "deeply grieved, shamed." Emotionally broken, Anna suffered the public disgrace of a divorce, in court and forever after. She never stopped believing William would return, and wondered what "crime" she had committed to be "punished" so cruelly. In actuality, of course, Anna had been the defendant against a lonely and frustrated husband who had apparently clung to a deteriorating marriage long after it was salvageable. But Anna—unsympathetic, proud, and unwilling to share responsibility for the breakup—told her son that *she* was the plaintiff, charging William with desertion in a desperate attempt to save the rest of her family.

Frank Lloyd Wright accepted this view for a variety of reasons. He never saw his father again after 1885, but since, except for periods of a few months at a time, he continued to live with or close to his mother until her death in 1923, he had ample opportunity to learn her interpretation without his father's countervailing explanation. Indeed, he had a need to accept Anna's version because it so easily (and so perfectly) came to function as a psychological buttress in his own life.

In 1926, when he wrote the sections of his autobiography dealing with his parents, Wright was a fugitive avoiding arrest under the Mann Act. Since 1909 he had been involved in a continuing series of highly publicized love affairs; he had been divorced once, married twice, linked with three mistresses, and was living with yet a fourth companion. Far from apologizing or feeling remorse for his behavior, Wright felt persecuted, and accused society of intolerance. Until she died, his mother was one of the few sympathetic persons who seemed to understand him and who remained loyal and supportive. Not only had she given him land to build a home for his first mistress, but she later shared that home with him and his second "soulmate." Just as Anna had suffered through her "persecution," so had he been publicly condemned for doing what he felt was right. Just as she had been "punished" for her courage, so had he been ostracized for acting openly and honestly. As Wright saw it, he and his mother had suffered similar unjust fates, and the parallel between their lives gave him a certain solace. Identifying with Anna's interpretation of her marital difficulties gave him a crutch to lean on during his own predicaments.[15]

Despite Anna's continuing presence, William C. Wright had a considerable impact on his son. Much has been inferred about the influence on Wright of the pictures of English cathedrals placed in young Frank's nursery by his mother, and of the "basic forms, simple materials, and true colours" of the Froebel blocks she gave him to play with in Weymouth, after discovering them at the Philadelphia Centennial Exposition in 1876 during a family excursion. Those who have analyzed the early influences on Wright's architecture have particularly stressed the Froebelian system of programmed building exercises, partly because Wright acknowledged this influence himself and partly because of the geometry of his designs. There can be little doubt that the Froebel experience was every bit as crucial in Wright's development as his later contact with Louis Sullivan, yet the critics invariably overlook Wright's obligation to music, which in his autobiography he discussed before any other source of inspiration. Position on a page may not indicate priority of importance, but it seems quite evident that Wright's sensitivity to structure and composition owed as much to music as to other influences. In adult life it was a constant means of relaxation, and he inevitably compared it to architecture ("an edifice—of sound!" he remarked once). There are obvious parallels between the horizontal progression of his designs—"plasticity," he called it—and the rhapsodic flow of Beethoven, whom he especially admired, and between his geometric precision and Bach's musical symmetry.[16]

The influence of William C. Wright's music must have been immense if in the 1950s the architect could tell his sister: "Strange . . . I dreamed of Father during my nap. Just this afternoon. I was in a dark place . . . the little chamber behind the organ in the Weymouth Church, . . . for the organ bellows. I was pumping away and pumping away. Father was playing Bach. I heard it, Sis, in the dream, very distinctly, every note as he used to play it. My God, Bach required a lot of air! I had to pump like the devil[!] and woke up tired!" Although the negative associations of paternal authority and back-breaking labor remained throughout Wright's life, it was overshadowed by the joy of hearing the music he helped create, and of playing viola and piano in the family orchestra. Even more exciting, Wright remembered, were Victor Hugo's comparisons of Gothic cathedrals to musical forms, comparisons he might not have appreciated but for his father. Thus, while Anna Wright's blocks were undoubtedly a significant factor in her son's attraction to architecture, William Wright's music was at least of comparable importance.[17]

The fact that William C. Wright's legacy to his son partly derived from his failures as a parent, and from his absence, not his

presence, in the household, does not make it any the less profound—and the fact that the boy had his mother to reinforce him
did not obviate the father's negative impact. While William
Wright's scholarly habits, along with Anna's inclinations, may
have encouraged his son to take intellect seriously, it was his
frequent withdrawal into himself that forced young Frank (not
unwillingly) to rely on his own resources. Letting his imagination
wander, he began to develop his talents, and early in life learned a
sense of personal responsibility and independence. The atmosphere William Wright created, furthermore, was probably as
influential as his personality. His authoritarian manner helped
destroy family mutuality, and his constant wandering in search of
opportunity compounded its instability. Later on, Frank Lloyd
Wright's architecture made obvious and sustained attempts to
correct these very conditions.

After the divorce in 1885, perhaps with the encouragement of
his employer, Professor Allan D. Conover, Wright entered the
University of Wisconsin as a special student without a high school
diploma, remaining for two semesters, from January through
March and from September through December, 1886. According
to his transcript he was enrolled in the "scientific" curriculum, but
in his first semester took only French, for which he was not given a
grade. In the fall term he received "average" marks in descriptive
geometry and drawing, the only courses he carried. He also joined
the Phi Delta Theta fraternity, but his brief association with it
ended when he left the university in December. Wright often
claimed to have quit in the spring of his senior year, a few weeks
short of graduation, disgusted with the university's irrelevance.
The fact is, however, that his needs and its usefulness never
coincided.[18]

During 1886 Wright received very practical architectural training from an important source close to the Lloyd Joneses: Joseph
Lyman Silsbee, a prominent Chicago builder of Queen Anne style
residences, who had recently designed All Souls Church for
Wright's Uncle Jenkin. Early in 1886 Silsbee produced a plan for

UNITY CHAPEL, HELENA, WIS.

Unity Chapel, 1886, near Spring Green, Wisconsin, by J. L. Silsbee

Jones's Unity Chapel at Helena, Wisconsin, which was completed by August. When the rendering was published it bore the inscription "F. L. Wright, Del[ineator]"; he had, however, more important responsibilities on the project than that. According to William C. Gannett, a noted Unitarian divine, the chapel's three-room interior had been "looked after" by "a boy architect belonging to the family."[19] Though it is indeterminable whether Wright designed the interior or simply supervised its construction, it is probable that when he moved to Chicago a few months later—presumably early in 1887, after his fall semester in college—he knew where to find a job.

In his autobiography Wright claimed that, reluctant to exploit a family connection, he took a position with Silsbee only as a last resort—and even then, he said, his employer did not know who he was. But at nineteen, with college not to his liking, with little by way of accomplishment, and with an entree into the profession, there is every reason to believe that Wright exploited his connection with Silsbee, who knew exactly who he was—for why should a prominent architect hire an unknown quantity? If he had absorbed only a smattering of his mother's pride, his father's ambition, or the Lloyd Jones sense of achievement, he would have been impatient to begin his career. And indeed, no sooner had he taken this initial step than he was moving rapidly along the clearly marked path to recognition. Probably through Silsbee's influence, Wright published a sketch for another of his employer's Unity Chapels (at Sioux City, Iowa) in the June 1887 *Inland Architect and News Record* (Chicago). To meet the deadline he must have submitted it immediately after his arrival at the firm or even, perhaps, while working for Silsbee in Wisconsin. In any case, as his signature on the drawing attested, he was already thinking of himself as "Frank L. Wright, Archt."

Except for a few weeks at Beers, Clay and Dutton, where he went for higher pay, Wright remained with Silsbee approximately a year before joining Dankmar Adler and Louis Sullivan. Those first few months in Chicago proved to be excellent training. Silsbee, who undoubtedly awakened Wright's interest in residential architecture, was a skilled practitioner, producing eclectic but beautifully drawn designs, the influence of which continued to appear in Wright's work through the 1890s. Silsbee allowed his young draftsman plenty of latitude, permitting, perhaps even encouraging, him to seize any opportunity for advancement. The apprentice published three renderings under his own name during 1887, and one—a house and school combination for his aunts Jane and Ellen at Hillside—was erected by November, partly because his employer gave him time off to supervise construction.[20] At twenty, still a draftsman, Wright had executed his first commission, bearing witness to the quality of the training he had received from Conover and Silsbee.

Wright remained at Silsbee's at least until November 1887, leaving shortly after that to join the firm of Adler and Sullivan as

The Hillside Home School, 1887, near Spring Green, Wisconsin

one of several new apprentices hired to develop drawings for the Chicago Auditorium (1887–1889), which Sullivan was designing at the time. Having already completed a number of commercial structures, which had made him one of the nation's most respected architects, during Wright's tenure Sullivan went on to produce some of his best commissions: the Walker Warehouse (1888–1889), the Getty Tomb (1890), the Schiller Building (1891–1892), the Transportation Building at the 1893 Columbian Exposition, all in Chicago; and the Wainwright Building (1891) in St. Louis. These were exciting and supremely creative days for Sullivan and a fortunate experience for Wright, who acquired invaluable knowledge from extensive conversations with his "Liebermeister," as well as from analyzing his system of ornament and his skyscraper designs.

Like Silsbee, Sullivan recognized Wright's talents, allowing him unusual freedom, for example, to work on small portions of the auditorium without supervision, and in 1890, due to the press of business, to design the few residential commissions the firm accepted to please its commercial clients. As chief draftsman with a private office, Wright produced about six houses from 1890 to 1892, one of which, for James Charnley (1891) in Chicago, was remarkable for its strikingly simple, horizontally oriented facade with broad, flat surfaces. The success of this venture, his rapidly increasing interest and skill in residence architecture, and the payments on the home he had built for himself in suburban Oak Park in 1889 encouraged him to moonlight. From 1891 to 1893 he designed approximately ten houses without his employer's knowledge, but when Sullivan discovered the "bootlegged" ventures, as Wright called them, he fired his assistant, probably early in 1893, whereupon Wright opened his own office in the Schiller Building,

James Charnley House, 1891, Chicago. Enclosed porches added later

a recent Sullivan opus.* For a time he shared his suite with Cecil Corwin, former manager at Silsbee's, and did his drafting in Oak Park, where he built a studio in 1895.

The twenty-five-year-old architect launched his independent practice with impressive credentials. As a former apprentice with Silsbee, one of Chicago's most popular artists, and with Sullivan, then at the top of the profession, Wright had designed about twenty-five buildings, of which twenty had been executed, including seventeen houses, a hotel remodeling, a school, and a boathouse. Two of his homes—for Charnley and for Allison Harlan (1892) in Chicago—were remarkably fresh, featuring broad, clean surfaces, a straightforward simplicity, and a mastery of Sullivanian ornament.[21] His entrance into the widely advertised competition for the Milwaukee Public Library and Museum in November 1893

* The relationship between Wright and his mentor has been analyzed by Grant C. Manson, "Sullivan and Wright: An Uneasy Union of Celts," *The Architectural Review* 118 (November 1955): 297–300. Wright's version is in *An Autobiography*, pp. 89–104, 107–109, 110–111.

It is still not known exactly when Wright opened his own practice. His friend, Robert C. Spencer, Jr., reported in 1900 that Wright secured the commission for the William H. Winslow House (River Forest, Ill.) "in the third year of his independent practice" ("The Work of Frank Lloyd Wright," *The Architectural Review* 7 [June 1900]: 65). Most sources date this commission 1893, which would mean that Wright opened his office in 1890 or 1891 (perhaps Spencer was referring to Wright's office in Sullivan's suite). Actually, the commission for the Winslow House was first announced in June 1894 in *The Inland Architect* 23: 56 (and in the Oak Park, Illinois, *Reporter*, June 8), pushing the start of Wright's career ahead to late 1891 or early 1892. Even this date seems too early, yet Spencer was in a position to know.

Grant C. Manson, who has done the most thorough research on these early years, presents evidence that Wright launched his own practice in 1893. In 1890 he was first listed in the Lakeside City Directory of Chicago at 1600 Auditorium Building—Adler and Sullivan's. In the 1893 directory Wright's address changed to the Schiller Building, his office in independent practice (*Frank Lloyd Wright to 1910: The First Golden Age* [New York: Reinhold Pub. Corp., 1958], 215). When his drawings for municipal boathouses won the competition in Madison, Wisconsin, in May 1893, Wright was described as "a former Madison boy, now a Chicago architect," without mention of Sullivan (*Wisconsin State Journal*, May 12, 1893). The conclusion seems to be that by May 1893 Wright had opened his own offices at 1501 Schiller.

also brought him useful publicity.* Wright's buildings were frequently derivative in grammar and style, but they had a reputation for thoughtful design and careful execution. If he had accomplished little before 1887, his architectural career in 1893 looked promising indeed.

Wright's social life also acquired new dimensions after his arrival in Chicago. At Silsbee's he had met Cecil Corwin, like his employer and the other draftsmen a minister's son. Wright later remembered that Corwin had the air of a cultured and sophisticated gentleman, qualities that attracted the youngster from Wisconsin. Perhaps the boy who had grown up with Bach, Beethoven, and books could not escape the finer things of life, for with Silsbee as a model and Corwin as a mentor Wright began to attend concerts, to improve his wardrobe, and, when he could afford it, to dine in more expensive restaurants. Cecil's culture was "similar to mine," Wright remembered, "yet he was different. And so much more developed than I. So I began to go to school to Cecil." At his Uncle Jenkin's All Souls Unitarian church, which he attended regularly, he was introduced into the liberal Unitarian upper middle class, the source, as it turned out, of several early clients. In church he also met Catherine Lee Tobin, daughter of a prosperous businessman who lived in the fashionable Kenwood district of the South Side. After a year or more of Wright's persistent wooing, the couple married on June 1, 1889, when he was twenty-one and she eighteen, and moved into his newly designed home in a relatively unsettled section of Oak Park, immediately west of Chicago.

Wright's marriage to Catherine is not without significance beyond the usual importance attached to such events. As his background indicates, Wright had come to Chicago as something of a rube. If he was not without a feeling for music and literature, he

* Young Wright, who thought "the site and purpose of the [Milwaukee Library and Museum] afforded a most excellent opportunity for the exercise of the highest skill in architecture," struck a dissenting posture in his first major interview when he "expressed surprise at the inexperience shown by many of the plans" (The Milwaukee Journal, November 21, 1893).

was, nonetheless, socially inexperienced. He had never traveled in upper-middle-class circles as Sullivan, Silsbee, Jones, and Corwin had done, and, as far as women were concerned, Wright was less than a beginner, if that is possible. In his autobiography he recalled his lack of social poise—indeed, his colossal bumbling—at a college dance where he was so shy that "the sight of a young girl would send him like a scared young stag, scampering back into his wood." In later years Wright may have considered himself something of a lady killer, and in his autobiography exaggerated his early shyness to dramatize the rapidity with which he had acquired rapport with the opposite sex (or to point out, in view of his several affairs, that he was not entirely a cad). Yet there is much truth in his claim to unfamiliarity with the ways of women.

For one thing, he apparently rushed into marriage with the first girl he had ever seriously considered. Toward Catherine, it seems, it was love at first sight, and having made up his mind to marry her Wright could not be deterred. Despite his inexperience and her youth, Catherine was a particularly appropriate choice. She understood the rules of etiquette and the social conventions of the upper classes who were, after all, the patrons of architecture. If the "social instinct" had been "left out of my education," as Wright correctly remembered, it was hardly so with Catherine, who, as an independent girl, had long been trusted by her parents with considerable freedom. "Everything revolved around her," he noted. "Not only was she accustomed to having her own way but to having it without any trouble whatever." If the beginnings of social poise involve learning to manipulate one's family, Catherine was well schooled. Furthermore, as "a very sensible girl," she forced Wright to save money, and even before their marriage helped manage his finances. "She was sensitive and careful about things," which he was not. "Where people were concerned," Wright admitted, "I had nearly everything yet to learn." To all indications, Catherine was just the person to navigate him through the unfamiliar waters.[22]

With Catherine to guide him socially, and with excellent architectural contacts and credentials, Wright launched his career in a rapidly growing metropolitan area, an ideal place for a young man with manifest skills in domestic, and a background in commercial, design. By 1893 his buildings demonstrated that his apprenticeship with Silsbee and Sullivan had been fruitful; his plans were carefully conceived and executed, and at least two—the Charnley and Harlan houses—showed verve and unusual talent. Little about Wright at this time suggested rebelliousness or eccentricity; to most people he was simply a "rising young architect of Chicago."[23]

2. THE ART AND CRAFT OF SUCCESS

[1893–1901]

In the years after he opened his practice Frank Lloyd Wright took the prescribed avenues to professional recognition. He was realistic enough to know that he could not launch a career by antagonizing influential colleagues, and, while he may have been critical of the architectural establishment at times, he was hardly rebellious. The eccentricities later associated with him developed only after the appearance of that sense of confidence accompanying success and fame. He followed a prudent course during the 1890s, but the two overriding intellectual interests that dominated his attention—the nature of the family and a philosophy for architecture—indicate that his objectives were not limited to acquiring wealth and fame. In 1901—when he integrated his design concepts with his metaphysical probings, his technical knowledge with his understanding of family life—he produced the creative synthesis called the "prairie house," which ultimately carried immense consequences for international architecture.

Consciously or unconsciously, Frank Lloyd Wright had chosen a wife who could guide him through the intricate social conventions and priorities imposed by his profession. Similarly, by instinct or design, he had moved to an expanding upper-middle-class community of professionals who needed and could appreciate his services. Wright accurately described Oak Park, Illinois, as a suburb "which denies Chicago." The community held a high opinion of itself: its residents were Oak Parkers, not Chicagoans, though many worked in the city. Their activities centered in their churches, their schools, and their civic organizations. Oak Parkers were white, Protestant, provincial, exclusive, and prosperous; they shunned urban political corruption, happy that Austin Street, which separated the city from their "dry" suburb was the point, as Congregational minister Bruce Barton put it, where "the saloon stops and the Church steeples begin."[1]

In 1893, about the time Wright opened his practice, his immediate neighborhood was singled out as an example of Oak Park's progress and expansion. Houses had never been at such a premium, a local newspaper commented; they were occupied so fast there were practically none to be had. One of Wright's own designs, in fact, was mentioned as typical of the community's dramatic growth. Indeed, his buildings were soon very typical in Oak Park, where by 1901 he had built eighteen and by 1909 twenty-nine.[2] The houses that line the streets of his neighborhood today constitute a museum of his architecture; at the time they were excellent advertisements in a profession ethically bound not to solicit commissions.

In suburban Oak Park Wright faced certain social obligations that he could not, and chose not, to ignore. He was careful, in fact, to observe the important upper-middle-class conventions. He lived in a fashionable suburb, and joined the tennis club in adjacent River Forest, even more fashionable. The year after he opened his practice he began speaking to civic organizations, and in 1900 he appeared in print for the first time.

He contributed to Oak Park's newspapers, competed in the annual Chicago Horse Show, dined at the best restaurants, and frequented expensive clothiers. He became an art connoisseur, loading his home with rugs, vases, and hangings, particularly from the Orient. He patronized the theater, concerts, and museums, often in parties with wealthy clients, some of whom traveled with the Wrights to Japan in 1905, on their first trip abroad. Wright joined the esoteric Caxton Club, devoted to the admiration and preservation of rare books and bindings, and was a charter member of Daniel H. Burnham's and Hamlin Garland's Cliff Dwellers, a "congenial Chicago club," Wright called it, for artist and literary folk. He owned the latest automobiles and kept expensive riding horses.[3] In view of his later antiurban diatribes it is important to note that, during these years and for a decade more, no one enjoyed metropolitan pleasures more than Frank Lloyd Wright.

Catherine Wright gave teas, luncheons, and afternoon musi-

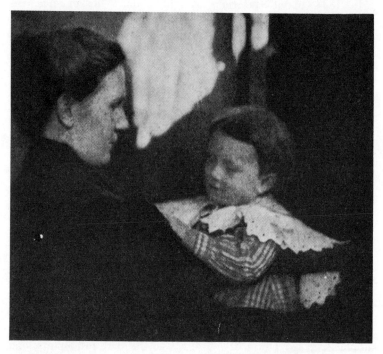

Catherine Wright and her son David

cales. She joined and spoke to local literary associations, operated a neighborhood kindergarten—then something of an "avant-garde" endeavor—and with her husband was a member of All Souls Unitarian Church. As fashion dictated, she summered in Wisconsin, where Wright joined her via the weekend commuter circuit, and of course she sent some of her children to Hillside, the progressive boarding school run by the Lloyd Joneses. She was known locally as an excellent entertainer.[4]

Indeed, the Wrights' most signal observance of the social amenities—a ritual that maximized their good name in the community—were their parties. Years later their son John remembered that Father had "clambakes, tea parties in his studio, cotillions in the large drafting room. . . . From week to week, month to month, our house was a round of parties. There were parties somewhere all of the time and everywhere some of the time." Wright liked to have people around him, and there is little doubt that he was popular. As a local newspaper remarked in 1901, "Mr. Wright is held in high esteem by his neighbors."[5]

So, too, was his architecture. Far from being ridiculed and rejected, as he often wrote later, his buildings were well received. Indeed, the prestigious *Architectural Review*, commenting in 1900 on photographs of Wright's work published in *The Inland Architect*, praised it as "extraordinarily interesting. One may condemn," it added, "but one is driven to admire. Here is originality and unquestionable genius. Good or bad . . . the work is full of intense personality."[6] From 1893 through 1901 Wright produced seventy-one designs, of which forty-nine were built, an average of eight commissions and five and one-half completions a year. Among the latter were three apartment projects in Chicago, a golf clubhouse for River Forest, and a scattering of stables and boathouses. Although most of his work were residences in the greater Chicago area and in Wisconsin (summer homes for Chicagoans), he received commissions from as far away as Buffalo, Los Angeles, and Texas. His reputation was primarily regional in these years but his publication in 1901 of two articles in *The Ladies' Home*

Journal indicated that this would not for long be the case, and that he was developing an interested following on the East Coast.[7]

From the beginning Wright took the preferred route to the top of his profession. Talent aside, he played the architectural game according to the rules. He began his speaking career in 1894 before the Evanston, Illinois, University Guild, where he outlined the possibilities for increased practicality, beauty, and honesty in residential design.[8] Organizational activity was important for any aspiring professional, and in the same year Wright joined the Chicago Architectural Club, a chapter of the Architectural League of America, where immediately he was put on the judging panel of its subdivision, the Architectural Sketch Club, to select the best drawing for an "Art Club" house in classic or Renaissance style.[9] Like many other young aspirants, Wright was eager to display his work, and so he participated in the club's annual exhibitions in 1894, 1898, 1899, and 1900.[10] Newcomers to the profession traditionally entered competitions in the hope of instant fame. Although his 1893 entry for a Milwaukee library and museum failed to win, he was chosen that year to design two boathouses in Madison, Wisconsin. In 1898 he submitted a drawing to the Luxfer Prism Company's $2,000 contest for an office building, but withdrew it when he, along with Daniel H. Burnham, W. L. B. Jenney, and William Holabird, was placed on the judging panel. Nevertheless, his scheme was published anonymously in *The Inland Architect*, where illustrations of his work appeared on the average of once a year.[11]

If the notion that Wright consistently avoided professionalization is not exactly accurate, neither is the companion assertion that he always worked alone. After he left Sullivan and Adler, he shared Chicago offices with his friends Cecil Corwin and Robert C. Spencer, Jr., although he did his drafting in Oak Park. Whether he ever collaborated with them, especially Spencer, with whom he held many ideas in common, is unknown. In 1898, however, Wright, Spencer, and George R. Dean were chosen by the Central Art Association to design a ten-room, $10,000 home for the Trans-Mississippi Exposition.[12] In 1898 and 1899 Wright collaborated on a new All Souls Church for Jenkin Lloyd Jones with Dwight Heald Perkins, although the building was later completed without Wright's assistance. Early in 1901 he and Webster Tomlinson "entered into copartnership with offices in Steinway Hall and studios at Oak Park." Scholars disagree on whether the two actually designed together during their brief association, but since they shared a studio the possibility is a good one. Finally, in 1906, Wright and two other members of the River Forest Tennis Club designed a new clubhouse, replacing one recently burned down.[13]

Wright's professional upward mobility reached a significantly high plateau in 1900 and 1901. He contributed to the Chicago Architectural Club's annual exhibition in 1900, when he also appeared in print for the first time, in May: his letter on the debate over whether architects should place "progress before precedent" was included in an article by his friend George R. Dean in *The Brickbuilder*. In June *The Brickbuilder* published his speech, "The Architect," delivered in Chicago before the second annual convention of the Architectural League of America. The most important event of the year as far as he was concerned, however, was a feature article by Robert C. Spencer, Jr., in the June 1900 issue of the prestigious *Architectural Review* entitled "The Work of Frank Lloyd Wright." Dozens of plans and illustrations showed his efforts in their very best light, and the text praised him exuberantly. "Few architects have given us more poetic translations of material into structure than Frank Lloyd Wright," Spencer noted. "To those who understand and know him best," he was, though barely thirty-three years old, "a perpetual inspiration."[14]

Such high praise in a leading professional journal was hardly detrimental to Wright's reputation. Indeed, it may have led in 1901 to the publication in *The Ladies' Home Journal* of two illustrated articles by him on residences, and of a third—a design for a small bank—in *The Brickbuilder*. He also spoke at Jane Addams's

Hull House, where in March 1901 he delivered his important speech, "The Art and Craft of the Machine," since reprinted many times and translated into several languages. This lecture and *The Home Journal* articles were widely discussed, leading one scholar to note "the authority with which he already spoke in these early years."[15] If "authority" overemphasizes Wright's influence, it is nevertheless clear that by 1901 he was a bright light among the younger midwestern architects.

Wright's growing reputation was not based simply on making speeches and publishing articles, for behind those speeches and articles—giving them a substance that compelled attention—was a body of work and a creative mind that made an impressive leap forward in 1901. For it was then that Wright announced the "prairie house," pronounced it a functional and aesthetic breakthrough, and proceeded to build it. Nineteen-one was the year in which many of his ideas, beliefs, even guesses, jelled in a remarkable synthesis, signaling the beginning of a new episode in his life and a new era in American architecture. This episode—a decade of artistic and intellectual ferment that has been called Wright's "golden age"—produced his first significant solution to problems he confronted repeatedly during the 1890s: how to design residences that would preserve and strengthen proper family living, and how best to utilize modern machinery in that effort. Because his notions on the nature of the family were confused during the 1890s, his early homes sometimes contradicted themselves and each other. Yet his work in that decade foreshadowed what was to come.

Although Wright is one of the giants of architectural history, he did not build his reputation with cathedrals, palaces, famous skyscrapers, and monuments of state. Le Corbusier had his government buildings in India, his Marseille housing block, and his chapel at Ronchamp; Mies van der Rohe his Chicago Lake Shore Apartments and his New York Seagram Building; and Walter Gropius his Harvard University and federal government edifices. In Wright's canon, however, it is not a handful of magnificent structures that is most noteworthy (although to be sure that hand-ful is a large one) but a continuous and almost compulsive attempt to build the perfect house.

During his seventy-two-year career, an overwhelming number of his almost eight hundred designs—close to six hundred, in fact—were residences. His first executed building, in 1887, was a "home school," and virtually his last commission, accepted a week before he died, was for a meager $3,000 summer cottage.[16] After the early 1940s Wright had little new to contribute to the theory of residen-tial design, and with his numerous multimillion-dollar commis-sions in the 1950s certainly did not need the small fees. The reason for his continuing interest—despite his international reputation and the lucrative projects offered to him—lies elsewhere, and can only be explained as an autobiographical as well as a professional imperative.

His early and perpetual fascination with residential architecture had several sources. J. L. Silsbee's encouragement and Louis Sulli-van's decision to turn his few house commissions over to Wright may have awakened an interest compounded by later successes, and the growing demand for homes by Chicago's upper middle class in the 1890s when he was starting out may have influenced him as well. But he was also motivated by "psychological" im-pulses as well as by tactical considerations: his own family history played a central role in his attraction to domestic design. It is very likely that his disrupted childhood helped originate his interest in the nature of the family and that his later marital frustrations kept that interest alive.

Frank Lloyd Wright's childhood was a contradictory mixture of family patterns and relationships. In his immediate family, his minister father seems to have been a stern disciplinarian of the Victorian mold, insisting in order, decorum, and dignity at home. Both of Wright's parents, with their strong religious bent, be-lieved in the sanctity of the household. But their divorce during Wright's midteens dramatized the hostilities—even hatreds—that lurked beneath the surface, hatreds the Victorian family consistently denied. This experience, probably illuminating as well as shattering for Wright—who may have been forced even then to contemplate the nature of the institution—was entirely in keeping with the character of his family, however, for as a group it did not seem particularly close.

In the first place, Wright's father apparently devoted increasingly greater attention to his career than to his wife and children, leaving his son relatively free to pursue his own interests. A second notable characteristic about the Wrights was their lack of solidarity. Although Frank had two sisters and three stepsiblings, he hardly mentioned the former and never mentioned the latter in his autobiographical writings. His family, as he described it, had only three members: a distant, stern father, a sympathetic, loving mother, and himself. His parents seemed to exist only for him. While this may be nothing more than another example of Wright's overblown ego (in the 1920s when he wrote his autobiography), it also reveals that he remembered his family as a fragmented collection of individuals (and as loci of authority) rather than as members of a group.

The principal lesson Wright seems to have learned from his early years was self-reliance. In his autobiography he describes things he did, alone or with friends, but hardly anything his family did together, a significant omission for what it tells about Wright's childhood. After his parents' divorce in 1885 he and his mother grew closer, working, with the aid of relatives, to keep alive financially. After he moved to Chicago and until her death in 1923, Anna Wright depended upon her son for food and shelter, forcing him prematurely to assume adult responsibilities as the only male in his household. In so doing he developed a sense of self even stronger than when his father's real and symbolic absences from home left him to his own resources. His youthful independence may have enabled him at times to withdraw from family tensions, but he recognized that it also needed curbing lest it develop into the kind of reclusiveness he believed had cut William C. Wright off from his children. The young architect tried to avoid this danger in his early homes by emphasizing the importance of group solidarity.

Fortunately, there was another kind of family with which he had had intimate contact in childhood, one that emphasized the sense of togetherness lacking at home. The Lloyd Joneses, with whom he spent his summers (probably from 1878 to 1886), were a large, prosperous group with vigorous Welsh traditions and a strong sense of camaraderie. They valued their individuality, but not at the expense of group loyalty. As free-thinking Unitarians of decided intellectual bent on the American frontier, they were forced into a collectively defensive posture, symbolized by their motto: "Truth Against the World." The Lloyd Joneses became political and economic leaders in their part of Wisconsin, working, worshiping, and living so closely together that both they and their neighbors (sometimes enviously) referred to them in Old World terms as a "clan." Wright believed that his summers in Spring Green and the influence of his uncles had been the high point of his youth, of crucial importance in his later development. Until 1909, when personal difficulties forced him into isolation (at Spring Green, significantly), he maintained close and frequent ties with his maternal relatives, whose jealously guarded individuality was nevertheless subordinated to the interests of the family unit as it confronted man and nature.[17]

If Wright called upon his childhood experiences (as he undoubtedly did, though probably unconsciously) when he turned to residential architecture, he had two models to draw upon. The Lloyd Joneses offered the security, happiness, and individuality made possible by mutual respect, common purpose, and group harmony: a fellowship among equals, insofar as that was possible in Victorian America.* His own family, on the other hand, warned him of the disintegration that could occur when group needs were

---

* Many elements in Victorian America working against equality of sex and generation were in the case of the Lloyd Joneses somewhat minimized by the family's strong intellectual bent, its Unitarianism, its frontier situation, and its members' insistence on asserting their individual aspirations.

overshadowed by individual aspirations and hostilities. The house he built for himself and his bride in Oak Park (1889), and his first significant residential commission, the William Winslow House (1894) in River Forest, Illinois, were responses to both legacies. The Oak Park home was set back on its lot as far as possible, emphasizing the detachment and privacy that both families had cherished. But on the inside Wright made ample provision for the kind of group events that had characterized the Lloyd Joneses. Indeed, in the early homes, which permitted him the most self-expression, Wright emphasized family togetherness more than personal independence, as if assuring himself that the breakup of 1885 would not be repeated. He was apparently trying to recreate architecturally the positive attributes of the Lloyd Jones experience, while minimizing the negative aspects of his own family background.

When the visitor enters the front door in Oak Park, he immediately confronts an inglenook with seats on either side. There at the heart of the house is a fireplace core, acknowledging the traditional nineteenth-century hearth where the family gathered. But in Wright's house the recessed fireplace with seats was hardly a family corner: it was too small, too centrally located, too conspicuous. It was more a symbol than a functional requisite, and like the inglenook in the Winslow House certainly an important one. As Norris Kelly Smith has perceptively noted, the Winslow reception hall "affirms the sacredness of hearth and home. The room seems hardly to have been designed for family use. . . . Yet it is the most formal, the most carefully articulated room in the house. Behind a delicate wooden arcade, [something like] a rood screen before an altar," is a large fireplace. "It looks as if it were intended for the celebration of some solemn family ritual," Smith concludes, "affirming the sacramental nature of the institution of marriage."[18]

Both these entryway-inglenooks were symbolic affirmations of an old important value: family togetherness in a specific and benevolent place.* Wright often referred to the fireplace as the "heart" of the house, and by that he meant the spiritual as well as the control center. But in Oak Park and River Forest he did not intend these areas for use; they were designed to make a point. Calling up memories of the farm and the close-knit traditional family, these sacramental inglenooks reminded hustling suburbanites of the love and holiness marriage and the family represented.

A second immediate impression obvious in both these houses is the impossibility of moving straight ahead; the inglenooks block forward progress, forcing the visitor to the right or to the left, where, in the Winslow House, there is a library. To the right the living room, like the library an airy open space with large windows, is separated from the entrance hall by sliding double doors. At Oak Park Wright provided a similar organization, except that he placed an open dining room–parlor area to the left and a side entrance–stairwell trimmed with an elaborate sculptured frieze on the right. In both buildings spaciousness, light, and a sense of adventure draw visitors into and around the house, through unusually wide doorways, encouraging participation in family activities. Leaded windows, panels of ornament, rich wood trim, and excellent craftsmanship made it clear that the inhabitants had well-developed tastes and life-styles. The balance right and left suggested orderliness, as well as preordained patterns of motion with specific places for specific functions, thereby acknowledging traditional family organization. But the free-flowing space, the variety of vista, and the uniquely personal design aspects indicated a degree of experimentalism and a public statement of individuality unique for the period—an individuality of the family as a unit, however, not of its several members.

During the winter of 1896 and 1897 Wright and William

---

* Wright and Winslow were personal friends, and therefore this home and the architect's own were commissions on which he had greater opportunity to incorporate his own notions, one of which was the fireplace and/or inglenook combination that appeared at the physical center of almost all his designs in the 1890s.

Winslow published a limited edition of William C. Gannett's *The House Beautiful*, a book that, if read carefully, further illuminates the young architect's objectives in residential design. Gannett was a Unitarian minister Wright greatly admired, a close family friend since childhood, and it is clear from his prefatory remarks, and from his elaborate, hand-drawn page decorations, that he was sympathetic to the author's philosophy. *The House Beautiful* urged its readers to make their homes simple and unpretentious. It abhorred gaudiness, materialism, and conspicuous consumption, advocating functional beauty and unity in decoration and design. A gracious, beautiful home, Gannett had written, would foster self-respect and encourage an atmosphere of love and warmth for its residents. The house, fundamentally a spiritual entity, was a "building of God, not made with hands." Obviously agreeing with the author's domestic philosophy, Wright wrote Gannett in December 1898 that his labors on the special edition had been "our first work for the sake of the work yet to be undertaken."[19]

In the last chapter of *The House Beautiful*, "The Dear Togetherness," Gannett enunciated views that were central to Wright's own thinking. The atmosphere of the house, the author contended, should be "like a constant love-song without words, whose meaning is, 'We are glad that we are alive together.'" It was an atmosphere made possible by "many self-controls, of much forbearance, of training in self-sacrifice. . . ." Such discipline led not to domestic austerity, but to cheer, peace, trust, delight, and finally to "a higher beauty . . . swiftly wrought by love within each soul,—the enlargement of powers, the enhancement of attractiveness, the virtues greatened, the meanness abated, and that unselfishness of each one for the other's sake, which really makes one a stronger, nobler self." Love was the shaping force in Gannett's ideal home, but it was both a cause and a result of family happiness, "since home relations [were its] wellsprings. . . ." In such a loving environment, "the sunrise of a new life breaks." This romantic, idealized, Victorian clarion call for therapeutic domesticity touched the exposed nerve of Wright's family deficiencies at precisely the time he was beginning his own household and opening his practice in residential architecture.

Despite his propensity toward purple prose, Gannett was not entirely a rank sentimentalist. He urged his readers to use the latest in building techniques: pressed stone exteriors, fibrous slab interiors instead of laths and mortar, and iron ribbing instead of floor beams and rafters. The modern house should get its steam heat directly from the municipal boilers, should have electricity and "telephones" piping music from "a distant capital." Equally important was family life-style. Only fresh food shipped in daily would suffice. "Taste" should be apparent everywhere—in pictures, flowers, music, color schemes, draperies, table decorations, furniture arrangements, service, and the homeowners' clothes. Gracefulness, too: a harmony of colors, a song to children before bed, a good morning to God. Superfluousness should be removed and the "verys" banished.

Books should also be pervasive: introductions to "the noblest company that all the generations have generated," books were excellent furnishings. A quality newspaper that reported politics, business, thought, knowledge, and humanity, but not divorce, murder, prizefights, or "the shames of low city life"—a good newspaper was the truest house furnishing. Also necessary were an encyclopedia, a dictionary, and an atlas. And then there were the guests—"as important a part of the furnishings as their chairs. . . . People must look forward to going there; true hospitality is not in the effort made to entertain but in the depth of welcome. Guests love to come for people, not for things." Gannett's suggestions closely resembled Wright's personal and architectural values, and his goals were very much his young admirer's. There is little doubt that the clergyman had articulated many of the architect's incipient feelings, and that his influence on Wright's early work was strong.[20]

Despite his attraction for Gannett's book, however, Wright was not completely satisfied with its philosophy. Gannett's emphasis on family togetherness understated its individuality vis-à-vis the larger community. Wright's rapidly developing artistic and intellectual sensitivities would not permit him to wallow in the clergyman's obvious sentimentalities, nor could he allow his family uncritically to accept community norms. Even in his early buildings it was clear that, if Wright revered graciousness, hospitality, and sacred rituals, he also understood that families engaged in their own particular activities without reference to their neighbors. The Winslow House and his own home expressed these considerations.

From the street, both are classically balanced and formal, paying tribute to orderly and traditional patterns of activity, clearly expressed in the interior as well by their modified cruciform floor plans. But the face shown to the public in a facade is not necessarily the one known to the family, as the rears of these houses demonstrate. In back, the Winslow House is ordered and orderly, to be sure. A broad central chimney overlooks a porch, the services, the dining and bedrooms, from which extends on cross-axis a ground-floor bay, all of which repeat the balance of the front. But to the left of the porch is a freestanding wall extending into the back yard to shelter a patio. To the right, almost as tall as the chimney, is a three-story octagonal stairwell, articulated on the exterior, and by no means balancing the dormer window that pierces the attic roof on the left. The street facade is notable for its simplicity and cleanliness of line, but the rear is busy and active—almost fussy—in its menagerie of geometrical shapes, its protrusions, and its asymmetry. One thing is clear, however. The face—the self-image—the Winslow House shows the street is entirely different from that reserved in back for the family. The facade promises visitors an orderly placid interior, and is indeed exceptionally inviting; the rear, by contrast, acknowledges the functional diversity of family life.

Wright's Oak Park home makes similar statements. Facing the residential side street it is simple, orderly, and somewhat conventional, but on the rear parking area it is a study in contrast and

William H. Winslow House, 1894, River Forest, Illinois

William H. Winslow House rear, 1894. Sliding glass doors added later

complexity. Wright seemed to be bowing to community expectations in the front, while letting random family movements dictate the arrangement where it was more private. When he built his multifaceted and irregular studio in 1895 it faced busy Chicago Avenue, not his neighbors. He also expanded his home about this time, including an unusual barrel-vaulted playroom and larger dining facilities. His articulation in this instance is also important. He could have added to the front, where there was much more space, but chose to preserve the orderly facade, tucking the additions to the limited area at the side and rear. Since the studio soon dramatically altered the house's appearance Wright could not have been concerned with preserving the original aspect. It seems, therefore, that he thought it proper to express to the neighborhood an image of the orderly family. In so doing he further com-

Frank Lloyd Wright's house, 1889, Oak Park, Illinois

plicated the rear arrangement, another way of saying that the simplicity of life diminished as his household grew in number.

Most of Wright's early houses reflected the influence of J. L. Silsbee and the conventional wisdom of the 1890s, although virtually every one was in some way uniquely his.* It was in the more adventuresome and the more interesting houses, like his own home and the Winslow House, however, that Wright most seriously confronted the nature of the family. But even the Winslow House, his best effort of the decade, was not a complete success. After three-quarters of a century it is still the most noteworthy building in its upper-middle-class neighborhood, but it is jarring and inharmonious in its parts, has a strangely stark facade, and lacks the repose characteristic of Wright's later work. Largely because his purposes were quite different when designing its front and rear, he made it almost two separate buildings—dazzlingly beautiful but thematically dissonant.

Like most of his domestic architecture in the 1890s, the Winslow House revealed impressive thought but fundamental confusion about how best to provide architecturally for the family. When Wright created dichotomous front and rear facades he was in effect giving passers-by an interpretation of interior events entirely different from the "truth" reserved for insiders; in the process he sacrificed architectural harmony for unnecessary detail, visual stimulation, and vaguely dishonest posing. When he combined simple classical exteriors with more complicated asymmetrical interiors, or united the quasi-religious with the avant-garde, he wavered between orthodox and progressive conceptions of family functions. And when he opened interior space he expanded the possibilities for informality and random movement, but his geometric shapes, luxurious accessories, traditional room designations, and cruciform floor plans assumed orderly and conventional activity. Separate articulation of functional units—stairwells, play-

---

* As late as 1900, with the S. A. Foster House in Chicago, one may see the dominance of conventional styles in a Wright design, but here, as in his every effort, there is something obviously and totally his own.

rooms, dining bays, libraries—indicated certain places for certain things, or a procedural quality to life, but stating the importance of each function so clearly also pointed the family toward a mélange of activities without enumerating priorities.

Despite their contradictions and shortcomings, these early efforts reveal the development of Wright's thinking. Drawing on the experiences of the William C. Wrights and the Lloyd Joneses, influenced by *The House Beautiful*, and aware of his own growing family, the young architect considered it more important to provide for group solidarity than for individual concerns. Whether it was a symbolic inglenook, an extraordinary playroom for his children, or one of a number of exquisite dining or living rooms, his most careful attention went to areas of group activity; he devoted less thought than he would later to individual retreats and private corners. Obviously the Lloyd Jones model had been paramount. Wright conceived of the family as a tightly knit group within a larger community from which it withdrew occasionally (but did not reject) for its own sustenance. More deeply concerned at this stage of his career with family unity than with personal freedom, he assumed that the one made the other possible.

If Wright leaned heavily on his own past when confronting the nature of family life, he looked decidedly to the future when he dealt with a second consuming interest that competed for his attention as the twentieth century opened. Believing that machinery would radically alter the appearance of buildings and the nature of the profession, Wright found it necessary to explore the complex interrelationships among family structure, construction methods, and technological developments in order to work out a philosophy of architecture and a companion theory of aesthetics. His first two important speeches that have survived—"The Architect" (1900) and "The Art and Craft of the Machine" (1901)— chronicle his rapidly maturing ideas and, supplemented by two brief articles—"A Home in a Prairie Town" and "A Small House with 'Lots of Room in It' " (both 1901)—illustrate with word and picture the practical applications of his theories. By 1901 Wright had assembled the philosophical and architectural weapons necessary to launch a devastating assault on the contemporary residence.

"The Architect" described the doldrums in which Wright found his profession, while "The Art and Craft of the Machine" offered an alternative. In the earlier speech, delivered in 1900 to the second annual convention of the Architectural League of America in Chicago, Wright told his colleagues that in this country commerce had triumphed over art. The lust for money had reduced the American architect to the status of servant to the business community. Unwilling to sacrifice certain profit for the less tangible benefits of individuality and experimentation, he slavishly reproduced European styles, catering to uninformed public demand. Having "degenerated to fakir," Wright charged, the architect "panders to silly women his silly artistic sweets." In years gone by he had been the master of creative effort, making "imperishable record of the noblest in the life of his race in his time," but now he modeled commercial buildings after Greek temples and luxury homes after Louis XIV palaces, all because the businessman and his wife "knew what they wanted." No longer an independent force, the architect had become a salesman, peddling pre-packaged "styles" for huge firms ("plan-factories"). At the height of the Industrial Revolution in America, Wright was painfully aware that the status and self-determination of his profession had been eclipsed by the triumph of business values.

Still, there was hope. Common sense—that hallowed American attribute—would prevail. The public would gradually learn that a bad American original was preferable to a good European copy because it was authentic. As the taste and the artistic appreciation of the nation matured—and at this time Wright was sure it would—America would develop a native architecture. In that noble effort he and his young colleagues would play a central role. They would

help the people to feel that architecture is a destroyer of vulgarity, sham, and pretense, a benefactor of tired nerves and jaded souls, an educator in the higher ideals and better purposes of yesterday, to-day, and to-morrow.

Such an art only is characteristic of the better phase of commercialism itself, and is true to American independence, America's hatred of cant, hypocrisy, and base imitation.

When once Americans are taught in terms of building construction the principles so dear to them at their firesides, the architect will have arrived.

To interpret the best in national ideals, to transcribe them into buildings, and to instruct the public in its own heritage was a large order for any profession. But it would be done when the rush for money gave way to a spiritual and aesthetic renaissance.[21]

Wright's optimism in 1900 was based on instinct, on faith in America's good sense and capacity for growth, and on the missionary potential of the younger architects. His lecture was, consequently, general and lofty. By contrast, "The Art and Craft of the Machine"—delivered in March 1901 at the opening of the Arts and Crafts Society in Jane Addams's Hull House—was programmatic, although it sacrificed little by way of rhetorical flourish. In 1900 Wright had prophesied that architecture would improve, and now he told how. "In the Machine lies the only future of art and craft," he assured his audience. Artists must end their protest against technology; instead of blaming it for the destruction of traditional skills, they must seize the machine as the characteristic tool of the age, and with it create a new art, vital to the life of the times.

Architects had thus far totally misconceived and misused machinery. Instead of exploring new techniques to create an architectural aesthetic appropriate to the twentieth century, they used technology to design buildings suitable only for classical Greece and Rome, Tudor England, or Renaissance France. Fakery, imitation, and sham, Wright charged, flooded the land, bearing absolutely no practical relevance to modern living. "Badgered into all manner of structural gymnastics," wonderful new materials were forced to "look real," that is, old. Steel beams, for example, the structural reality of the commercial edifice, were buried under tons of decorative marble and dysfunctional granite, so that the whole might resemble a Greek temple. Lying about its purpose and its construction methods, such a building used the latest technology symbolically to reject the modern age. Wright also cited mass-produced wood carving as a further illustration of technological chicanery. By substituting an imitation for the genuine article, manufacturers debauched an honored skill and negated the machine's capacities. Used to produce myriads of "elaborate and fussy joinery of posts, spindles, jig-sawed beams and braces, butted and strutted, to outdo the sentimentality of the already over-wrought antique product," nineteenth-century skills were being transformed into twentieth-century frauds.

The time had come, Wright insisted, to learn from the machine, to assert control over it. The central and primary lesson of modern technology was "simplicity." New methods reemphasized old truths, for example, that "the beauty of wood lies first in its qualities as wood," not in how it could be carved and twisted to approximate something else. "No treatment that did not bring out these qualities . . . could be plastic," he continued. "The machine teaches us . . . that certain simple forms and handling are suitable to bring out the beauty of wood and certain forms are not; that all wood-carving is apt to be a forcing of the material, an insult to its finer possibilities. . . ." Intrinsically, wood had unparalleled artistic properties—markings, texture, color, grain—that the machine, "by its wonderful cutting, shaping, smoothing, and repetitive capacity" had "emancipated." Modern methods could create "clean, strong forms that the branch veneers of Sheraton and Chippendale only hinted at, with dire extravagances."

Recent technological developments had also liberated iron and steel, which, possessing a beauty of their own, should be allowed unadorned expression. And cement—a plastic covering—enabled the architect "to clothe the structural form with a simple, modestly beautiful robe where before he dragged in . . . five different kinds of material to compose one little cottage. . . ."

Multitudes of processes—metal-casting, electroglazing, and more— "are expectantly awaiting the sympathetic interpretation of the master mind. . . ." Already the emancipator of the creative person, the machine in time would also be "the regenerator of the creative conscience." New techniques, Wright thought, would for the first time reveal the essential nature of building materials, opening to the perceptive architect unlimited potential for new designs. The resulting aesthetic breakthrough made possible by the machine would be "organically consistent," that is, "in conception and composition . . . the essence of refinement in organization."[22]

To suggest the machine as the solution to architectural problems was, for 1901, provocative but, as Wright stated it, vague. A month before the Hull House speech, however, he had published in The Ladies' Home Journal the floor plans and renderings of a new kind of residence embodying the techniques he described, followed in July by another illustrated article. Next, the same month, came his announcement that he would build eight demonstration homes, proving the efficacy of his ideas. Although the project never materialized, he began construction on the first prairie buildings before the year was out. What he was beginning to call "organic" architecture was actually taking form in wood, stone, and mortar.

"In keeping with a high ideal of family life together," Wright offered "a simple mode of living" to the February 1901 readers of The Ladies' Home Journal. The exterior rendering of "A Home in a Prairie Town" showed a low, decidedly horizontal, two-story building. Seemingly without flourish, it was actually highly decorated by its windows, screens, flower boxes, and contrasting colors and shapes, but all the trim was functional. Wide, overhanging eaves and low terraces emphasized the influence of the prairie. "Firmly and broadly associated with the site," Wright explained, the proposed home "makes a feature of its quiet level." Interior perspectives revealed that every aspect—including custom furnishings, built-in accessories, and decorations—could best be made by the new machine techniques Wright had been mastering. In the text of this and the following article for the July issue—"A Small

House with 'Lots of Room in It'"—he listed the innovations, refinements, and simplicities possible with intelligent application of technology. Moldings, paint, varnish, drainpipes, and many other "necessities" had been eliminated. After specifying plans and costs, Wright declared himself ready to accept orders.[23]

Simultaneously with the publication of the second article, Wright announced that money had been obtained to implement the "quadruple block" scheme included in "A Home in a Prairie Town." On both of two four-hundred-foot-square blocks in Oak Park, Illinois, Wright said he would design four houses, each commanding an entire side, and sharing common acreage with its three neighbors to the rear and in the center. The eight-home "colony" would be erected, Wright said, to show that his ideas were practical. Serving as a model for his attempt to integrate buildings with site and with each other "in a community where everything will be in harmony and where nothing offensive to the eye shall exist," this "architectural surprise" would incorporate the best of the city and the country. The experiment was intended as a showcase for the ideas of "The Art and Craft of the Machine" illustrated in *The Ladies' Home Journal*.[24]

Unfortunately for Wright, the project was never launched. But his proposals were taken up in 1901 by, among others, Frank Thomas, who wanted a prairie house at the far end of Forest Avenue, the architect's own street, and by Ellen and Jane Lloyd Jones, who had decided to expand their Hillside Home School at Spring Green.* During the next decade Wright refined and im-

---

* It might be useful here to correct the dates of two Wright designs at Spring Green: the Romeo and Juliet Windmill, consistently given as 1896, and the second Hillside Home School building, usually attributed to 1902, but also to 1903 and 1904. The windmill was actually designed and constructed around September 1897: see *The Weekly Home News*, September 23 and 30, 1897.

The Hillside Home School's second building was designed in 1901. "The plans have been drawn and sent from the studio of Frank L. Wright, architect, Chicago," *The Weekly Home News* reported on October 17, 1901, "and . . . construction will begin at once." The cornerstone was laid in April 1902 and the building completed approximately April 1903. See ibid., April 24, 1902, and February 19, 1903.

proved the experiment begun here; 1901 was only a beginning. But in a very fundamental way it was also an end, to eight years of architectural wandering. During the 1890s it had been unclear just where Wright's ideas were taking him, but it was certainly a place he himself did not know. In 1887 his Wisconsin relatives had given him his first opportunity, and in 1901 their needs and his again coincided. The prairie house—that great synthesis of art and science, theory and practice, that ultimately won Wright international fame—owed a considerable debt of gratitude to a neighbor down the block and to two maiden aunts in rural Wisconsin.

3. A RADICALLY DIFFERENT CONCEPTION

[1901–1908]

In less than a decade Frank Lloyd Wright's prairie designs brought him European plaudits and as many commissions as he could fill. No one in 1901 could have anticipated the philosophical maturity and the architectural achievements that had become his by 1908. The heady feeling of success enabled him to speak with an authority he never lost, and his corpus of impressive structures gave him the confidence to be bold and audacious. Although the public associated Wright with a group of progressive midwestern architects known as the Prairie School, "as far as we can tell," writes historian Vincent Scully, "all the significant ideas were his, the innovations were his own, and the development of their common style was wholly dependent on him."[1] It is hardly surprising, therefore, that when Wright published a retrospective article in 1908 he admitted being proud of his achievement.[2]

The twentieth century in America opened amidst a wave of national self-scrutiny. The muck that had given a protective covering to political corruption, corporate malpractice, and urban decay was being raked away. Protest and reform drifted into literature, where the social realism of Stephen Crane, Jack London, and Theodore Dreiser exposed the brutalization of the working man, and into painting, where George Bellows and John Sloan of the Ashcan School depicted the seamier side of life. Even though Frank Lloyd Wright's houses were designed for the upper and middle classes, they too were considered "reformist," since everything about them implied discontent with the status quo. And there was much to be unhappy about. The typical turn-of-the-century house for the prosperous—the sort of building that set the styles and attracted attention in professional literature—had lost touch with fundamentals. In an age of opulence and unrestrained acquisitiveness its significance had changed dramatically. Once primarily a shelter, a dwelling place, and a family center, it had become a status symbol, a stage for entertainment, and a measure of wealth. The socially conscious were frequently as concerned with public opinion as with their own needs and comfort when they built homes. Social pressure in the urban East could force an upwardly mobile businessman, as Edith Wharton remarked in one of her novels, to build a "complete architectural meal; if he had omitted a style, his friends might have thought the money had given out."[3] The Victorian home of the upper classes had lost the home's original purpose: for the elite and those clamoring to join its ranks a house was not a place to live but a social investment.

Patrons of architecture were apt to lavish money on reproductions of medieval castles, ornate mélanges of European styles, and inharmonious displays of "artistic" forms totally unrelated to local environment or to the national ideals of practicality and egalitarianism. The Vanderbilt family, for example, ordered French Gothic mansions—testaments to their emergence as American commercial aristocrats—from the society architect R. M. Hunt. His town house for W. K. Vanderbilt in New York City (1881), a fussy, elaborate chateau on Fifth Avenue, was surpassed in pretentiousness and grandeur only by his Loire-type castle for G. W. Vanderbilt in Asheville, North Carolina (1895).[4] The not-quite-so-rich, in their envy and haste, could be even gaudier. The incredible Carson House (1886), designed by Joseph and Samuel Newsom, in Eureka, California, thrust dormer windows through mansard roofs, filled every available space with trim, sculpture, and pillar, threw in more angles, peaks, and gables than can fully be appreciated, and capped it all with an enormous top-heavy tower encircled by a modified widow's walk. The Carson House, write two authorities, adds insult to insult "until its swagger betrays a man of wealth who wistfully hoped to acquire prestige through foreign forms, no matter how grossly mishandled. . . ."[5]

Chicagoans were not as crude perhaps as some of their West Coast counterparts (who differed from their surreal Hollywood descendents only in degree), but they too expressed their aspirations in architecture. Aware that theirs was not the first among American cities, that Chicago trailed New York in wealth, status, power, and influence, the Lake Shore plutocrats pursued social equality with their own extravagant paeans to Victorian eclecticism. The Mary Wilke House (1889) by M. E. Bell, for example, combined Richardsonian materials and forms with Middle Eastern domes and French roof lines, a sodden mass of clutter, the antithesis of restraint.[6] In the European-oriented East, American eclecticism—which randomly combined Continental styles—had a certain authenticity. But in the Middle West—the heartland of America—it was conspicuously inappropriate and noticeably foreign. The houses of Chicago, as Wright himself exclaimed, "were fantastic abortions . . . tortured by features that disrupted the distorted roof surfaces from which attenuated chimneys like lean fingers threatened the sky." The interiors were chopped up into "box-like compartments . . . and the 'architecture' chiefly consisted in healing over the edges of the holes that had to be cut in the walls for light and air" and egress. As long as their buildings were "fashionable," most people cared no more about them than horses did stables. The typical Chicago home at the turn of the century, Wright concluded, "lied about everything."[7]

Another characteristic of contemporary midwestern houses—

one that disturbed Wright when he analyzed them—was their alienation from environment, something other commentators also noticed. Norwegian immigrant Ole E. Rölvaag wrote that the ubiquitous gabled frame house "seemed strangely conspicuous on the bare, level landscape; one could not help wondering if they really belonged here." Willa Cather also expressed serious reservations. She remembered a house with "sharp-sloping roofs to shed the snow. It was encircled by porches, too narrow for modern notions of comfort, supported by the fussy, fragile pillars of that time, when every honest stick of timber was tortured by the turning-lathe into something hideous." In order to build "suitable to the prairie," a Sinclair Lewis character observed, one would need an "entirely new form of architecture."[8]

Wright's new forms had their roots at least as far back as 1891. With considerable backing and hauling he had struggled for the better part of a decade to create an alternative to Victorian eclecticism. In retrospect it is easy to trace a direct progression from the James Charnley (1891) and William Winslow (1894) houses to the prairie house, as if Wright was moving straight toward a predetermined goal (a view he repeatedly offered in his writing). This analysis, however, reduces his achievement to a mechanical process and minimizes the considerable difficulties he faced. During the 1890s it was clear that Wright disliked prevailing styles and was disturbed by what he saw around him, but no one, least of all he, knew where his efforts would lead. No one in 1894 or even in 1900 could have predicted the mature prairie house. Not until after 1901, when the new designs dominated his work, did the distance he had traveled become clear.

As late as 1900 Wright continued to lean heavily on precedent, directly utilizing the architecture of J. L. Silsbee, Louis Sullivan, Henry Richardson, and the Orient. There was, for example, the Frederick Bagley House (1894) in Hinsdale, Illinois, depending on the authority either Dutch Colonial or Suburban Richardsonian, with its detached octagonal library, gambrel roof, gables, inset porch with Ionic columns, and elliptical attic window, a feature of many Richardson buildings. In 1895 Wright built a Tudor half timber for Nathan Moore in Oak Park, and in River Forest he pierced Chauncey William's steeply pitched roof with dormer windows high above an exposed foundation lined at the entrance with uncut boulders. His Oak Park house for George Smith (1899) was one of several with precipitous roofs and sharply skirting eaves, to which he added flaring ridgepoles in the decidedly Japanese S. A. Foster House (1900) in Chicago. Wright continued to borrow from traditional styles even after the turn of the century, but never in a slavish manner.

Mixed with the more conventional efforts of the 1890s were a number of designs that in retrospect seem prophetic. Lacking the coherence of the prairie house, they nevertheless included many of

George W. Smith House, 1899, Oak Park, Illinois

its elements. The James Charnley House (1891) in Chicago, for example, was notable for its smooth brick facade, completely encircled by a concrete string course under the third story's widely spaced windows. In 1892 the Chicago home for Allison Harlan featured a slightly overhanging, gently peaked roof, numerous windows in rhythmic series, and a plain brick wall—itself a part of the facade—enclosing the front yard. At the Municipal Boathouse (1893) in Madison, Wisconsin, Wright painted the underside of the broad eaves to match the building and edged them in contrasting trim. The William Winslow House (1894) in River Forest emphasized the widely flaring hip roof and brought the horizontal string course from the Charnley House down under the second story windows. These and other structures made little reference to prevailing styles, showed mastery of Sullivan's ornamentation, and demonstrated Wright's unusually original thinking.

In the next few years he relied on these devices with increasing frequency. William Winslow's stables, 1894 projects for Orrin Goan in La Grange, Illinois, and A. C. McAfee in Chicago, his own 1895 Oak Park studio, the 1896 Heller House and Devin project in Chicago, the River Forest Golf Club in 1898, and the 1900 Joseph Husser House and Robert Eckart project in Chicago and River Forest, were all horizontally oriented with gently sloping roofs, overhanging eaves, and contrasting trim around the upper story, where there was sometimes a frieze-fenestration combination. Eliminating foundations by resting on water tables, they featured broad expanses of unadorned surfaces and dispensed with projecting encumbrances. Along with other early commissions, like the 1900 Harley Bradley and Warren Hickox houses in Kankakee, Illinois, they were distinctive enough to bear the architect's own "signature," as historian Grant Manson has put it.[9] But rounded arches, detailed friezes, sculpture-ornament, the Spanish flavor of the Husser House, the ominous loggia at the Heller House, and the sharp peaks and heavy-handed trim at Kankakee, clearly distinguish them from the harmoniously resolved prairie houses they anticipated.

Wright's new residential concept grew out of his own architectural experience and personal history, jelling into a brilliant synthesis after a decade of trial and error. According to his autobiography, which describes the prairie house as well as anything else, Wright based it on his conviction that buildings should serve human needs and reflect human size, not be showplaces, status symbols, or museums (which ironically his have since become). So, he wrote, "I brought the whole house down in scale. . . . Walls were now started at the ground on a . . . water table that looked like a low platform under the building . . . [and] stopped at the second-story window-sill to let the bedrooms come through above in a continuous window series below the broad eaves of a gently sloping, overhanging roof." The climate being what it was, he continued, "violent in extremes. . ., I gave broad protecting roof-shelter to the whole. . . . The underside of roof-projections was flat and usually light in color to create a glow of reflected light that softly brightened the upper rooms. Overhangs had double value: shelter and preservation for the walls. . ., as well as this diffusion of reflected light. . . ." Usually two or three levels, prairie houses looked lower than that and longer than they were. Unbroken sweeps of horizontal trim in contrasting colors, low-pitched or flat roofs, and extended walls, terraces, and overhangs thrust it laterally beyond its confines. "The house began to associate with the ground," Wright noted, "and became natural to its prairie site." He often placed a large urn with plantings at the front, indicating an integral relationship between architecture and nature.

The outside of the house, he wrote, "was all there, chiefly because of what happened *inside*." The wall, redefined as a screen, was no longer an obstacle to the flow of space. Rejecting what he described as "boxes beside boxes or inside boxes, called rooms," he declared the "whole lower floor as one room, cutting off the kitchen as a laboratory, putting the servants' sleeping and living quarters next to the kitchen but semi-detached, on the ground floor. Then I screened various portions of the big room for certain

domestic purposes like dining, reading, receiving callers." He reduced the number of doors, except in the upper stories, where he
retained his sleeping "boxes." Interior trim took on psychological
as well as decorative importance. "The ceilings . . . could be
brought down . . . by way of the horizontal bands of plaster on
the walls themselves above the windows and colored the same as
the room-ceilings," he explained. By bringing the "ceiling-surface
and color down to the very window tops," he increased the sense
of lowness, intimacy, and warmth, and by running continuous
bands of contrasting trim around the room above the doors and
windows he added a feeling of movement, spaciousness, and flow.
Whenever possible, he built in the furniture and fixtures.[10]

Wright continued to design this new kind of residence until
1914, becoming increasingly more excited by unusual and dramatic
sites, so that prairie houses were not always built on the prairie
(suggesting, perhaps, that a more accurate nomenclature is in
order). He easily adapted his plans to the gently sloping shores of
Lake Delavan, Wisconsin, where he built five homes from 1900 to
1905. One of his best efforts was the 1905 Thomas P. Hardy
House in Racine, Wisconsin, a pavilion residence in the Mediter-
ranean tradition, jutting out dramatically from the steep bluffs
overlooking Lake Michigan. For another challenging situation that
year he perched the W. A. Glasner House in Glencoe, Illinois, on
the edge of a plummeting ravine, with a bridge and teahouse
projected over a subsidiary crevice. He also began to use materials
native to their region, a factor he repeatedly stressed later. The
second Hillside Home School building (1901) in Spring Green,
Wisconsin, relied on local timber and fieldstone, but generally,
throughout the prairie period, Wright's designs called for wood,
brick, or stucco regardless of locale.

As time passed, and as Wright grew more certain of his abilities, his architecture—clients permitting—became bolder and
more dramatic. Several of the early prairie houses tended to be
rather squat, to terminate abruptly, and to sit steadfastly, even
broodingly, on their sites, lacking flair and adventure. The F. B.

Frank Thomas House, 1901, Oak Park, Illinois. One of the first executed prairie houses

Henderson House in Elmhurst, Illinois, and the Frank Thomas House in Oak Park (both 1901), for example, seem cramped and confined in comparison to the first *Ladies' Home Journal* design to which they are thematically related. A number of early houses, with short overhangs and relatively inconspicuous windows, had somewhat blocklike, uninviting facades; they seem introspective, tentative, afraid to reach out literally or symbolically beyond the safety of their sturdy walls, although the tendency is there. They are static rather than active, reserved rather than outgoing. They represent trial balloons for a new idea rather than the confident statement of a proven thesis.

In contrast, several of Wright's later designs reveal a confidence, a daring, a willingness to take calculated risks. The Illinois houses for Avery Coonley in Riverside (1907), Isabel Roberts in River Forest (1908), and Frank J. Baker in Wilmette (1909) are among those uninhibited by the hesitancy of inexperience. With eaves overhanging further, with walls and terraces flung wider, with a greater number of windows more emphatically and rhythmically articulated, and with contrasting trim more explicitly stated, the mature homes reach beyond their physical and psychological boundaries. Yet, longer and lower than their predecessors, they nestle into the ground for strength and protection. Their successful resolution of a number of architectural paradoxes, moreover, further contributes to their maturity. For example, they are at once active and static: while firmly and obviously rooted to site, they also reach into space. Anchored resolutely to the ground—looking as though nothing could rip them from their moorings—they offer a safe and secure harbor to the family battered about on the unchartered seas of modern life. With their extensions and openings embracing man and nature, they face life optimistically and accept uncertainty without fear.

A comparison of the Arthur Heurtley House (1902) in Oak Park and the Frederick C. Robie House (1907) in Chicago illustrates the growth of Wright's confidence and skill. The Heurtley House is a simple rectangle, the alternately projecting brick bands on the facade create the impression of solid stone, making it seem even more self-enclosing than it actually is. A second level veranda under brief eaves and behind substantial corner piers; first-floor front windows hidden to the rear of a loggia, itself recessed behind a low wall; and an entrance tucked in the dark alcove of a Sullivan arch do not, even on the sunniest days, relieve the blocklike, apparently impenetrable facade. The house guards its opening jealously and, with its limited overhangs and heavy appearance, seems to withdraw within the safety of its walls, a precaution hardly necessary in the refined, upper-middle-class Oak Park of 1902. In view of the fact, however, that the Heurtleys' marriage was not particularly happy,[11] the house's inwardness may have been Wright's attempt to strengthen the weak bonds of matrimony with brick and mortar. Or its social conservatism may simply have reflected his architectural progress at this early stage of the prairie genre.

The Robie House, at an intersection one block from Chicago's busy Midway Plaissance, could easily have retreated from its urban distractions, but unlike its predecessor, reaches out to accept all possibilities. At a time when Wright was eagerly participating in city life, he designed a house that transformed its banal setting into an aesthetic playground, a building still infrequently rivaled in architectural drama and adventure. The Robie House appears even longer and lower than it actually is, primarily because its roofs—cantilevered so impossibly beyond its walls—unite with sweeping, uninterrupted trim to create an overwhelmingly horizontal attitude, and because the extended fenestration, running the length of the second story, is divided by emphatic vertical mullions that accentuate and contrast perfectly with the whole. The house leaps out beyond its confines and, with its incredible cantilevers, soars off into space, yet its insistent horizontal lines keep it securely earthbound.

With these contradictory tendencies the Robie House remains in a state of perpetual tension. Its almost unbounded energy, and the aggressive individuality of its several members, threatens to

Arthur Heurtley House, 1902, Oak Park, Illinois

Frederick C. Robie House, 1907, Chicago

tear the building asunder, yet its parts are subtly and resourcefully woven together. The light and shadow of its complex facade, for example, at first glance only a complicated assortment of forms, inevitably resolves itself into a kind of semicubist composition of supremely sensible proportions, an architectural chorus made even more harmonious when roof snow highlights the several components. Another unifying device is the broad central chimney, which acts as a massive stave anchoring the building to site and the pieces in place. The Robie House is clearly an active structure, one that changes unexpectedly with the seasons and from various angles of vision, a reflection of the ebb and flow of natural and urban life.

And yet the house is obviously a safe, secure family place— strong, sheltering, and protective. With a long wall guarding the terrace from intruders but permitting social intercourse, and with the family and bedrooms on the second and third stories overlooking the street, it stipulates independence without withdrawal, group solidarity without rejection of the community. As Frederick Robie himself remembered: "I wanted to . . . look out and down the street to my neighbors without having them invade my privacy." The hovering roofs, the overhangs and enclosed terraces, even the nooks and crannies forcefully articulated on the exterior, state clearly that deep within this architectural tour de force was a family sturdy enough to cope with its stimulating effects. The Robies were that kind of people, and years afterward remembered the excitement of living there.[12] This house, one of the most successful in Wright's entire career, was not a building he could have designed in 1902. It was the bold, confident statement of a mature artist, vivid evidence that he had fully exploited the implications of his initial conceptions.

Of course, not all the early prairie houses were outwardly cramped, stolid, or conservative, nor were all later ones far-flung, expressive, and open. Many Robie House characteristics had indeed appeared before, in the Ward Willitts House (1902) in Highland Park, Illinois, for example, and the Darwin C. Martin

House (1904) in Buffalo, while by the same token, not a few of the later homes—for P. D. Hoyt (1906) in Geneva, Illinois, for Stephen Hunt (1907) in La Grange, Illinois, and for G. C. Stockman (1908) in Mason City, Iowa, to name three—are boxy, squat, and self-contained after the Heurtley fashion, although broader eaves and more vigorous trim give them a livelier, less restricted appearance. But an evolution had occurred, for between 1902 and 1907 Wright discovered and devoted considerable attention to a difficult problem: how to express the relationship between form and function. Whereas the Heurtley House had understated that relationship, the Robie House is based on its precise comprehension. By 1907 Wright's buildings were reiterating the message that interior events governed exterior arrangements, that life-style, in other words, dictated architectural organization. Although he never completely abandoned the cruciform plan (which he had virtually introduced into American residential architecture), he found it increasingly necessary after mid-decade to rely on other means of expressing function more accurately.

Around 1905 Wright began applying Louis Sullivan's dictum, "form follows function," to longitudinally oriented plans organized linearly end to end, not centrifugally. The Ward Willitts House (1902), although an outstanding early prairie design, was the kind of composition he began gradually to abandon. Unlike the Heurtley House of the same year, the Willitts had wide sheltering eaves and low wings reaching out from a two-story central core, but it was rigidly conceived nonetheless. Its single-level cross axis, culminating at one end in a porch and at the other in a porte cochere, was a classically balanced, perfectly proportioned foil to the taller cruciform it bisected. These wings, essentially nonfunctional, were apparently intended to ease what would have been rather abrupt terminals, to relate the building more comfortably to the ground, and to further emphasize the overall balance. By way of contrast, the facade of the W. A. Glasner House (1905) in neighboring Glencoe, with no obvious center of gravity and no purposeless members, was functionally economical

Ward W. Willitts House, 1902, Highland Park, Illinois

from end to end—pictorial to be sure, but organized around the internal arrangement of space. The building, as Wright liked to put it, was designed "from inside out."

The Glasner House, one of his most exciting commissions, was perched atop a steep ravine. In the original plan, only partly executed, Wright included an octagonal library at one end, a matching teahouse at the other—reached by bridge over a subsidiary ravine—and a third, separately articulated octagon, a sewing room affixed to a corner of the bedroom, itself projecting slightly off center from the building's main axis. The plan's single thrust, from library to teahouse—there is no cross axis—is tempered by the suggestion of a diagonal movement: the living room and adjacent bedroom, oriented toward and culminating in the sewing room, seem about to plummet into the ravine but for the two octagonal extremities that pin the whole firmly to the bank. The Glasner House achieves its orderliness abstractly, not with left balancing right in classical fashion, but because the separately articulated members agree with each other in mass and proportion, and because of the spatial relationship of library and teahouse to the sewing room, which, though slightly off center, becomes the focus of the entire scheme. The independently stated members are harmoniously incorporated into the whole by consistent grammar and sensible proportion. The shape, character, and definition of the facade is governed by interior requirements. The house looks the way it does, in other words, because its internal arrangement of space dictates external appearance. Wright had come to the conclusion that classical organization was not the best vehicle for accommodating the less formal and sometimes unpredictable ebb and flow of modern life.

Except for the magnificent but unexecuted residential complex for Harold McCormick (1907) in Lake Forest, Illinois—Wright's closest contact with the new corporate elite—the Coonley Estate was his most ambitious implementation during these years of "form follows function." In 1907, on a large, elliptical plot rising gently from the Des Plaines River in Riverside, Illinois, Wright

W. A. Glasner House, 1905, Glencoe, Illinois. Bridge and pavilion never executed

designed three buildings for Avery Coonley, whose inherited fortune provided his architect with unusual opportunities. The spacious Coonley living room, one of Wright's best creations, overlooks a large pool from the center of the more arresting half of the main axis. Two flanking gallery-loggias lead in one direction to a separately articulated dining unit—almost a building in itself—and in the other to the bedroom section, the lesser half of the dominant axis. With a guest wing branching off to form an L, the bedrooms are obviously an extension of the living area, but their architectural expression underscores their functional differentiation. Servant quarters, perpendicular to the living room and parallel to the guest wing, enclose the third side of a utility court that extends beyond the main building as a sunken garden, bounded on one side by a garage-stables-chicken house combination, behind which is a small gardener's cottage.

Although the two outbuildings are interesting enough, Wright achieved his greatest successes, of course, in the main house, where the functional requisites of living, not a preconceived format, governed plan, organization, and external appearance. The beautiful living room, the aesthetic high point and social center of the Coonley Estate, dominated but did not overpower the entire scheme; the dining room, wherein occurred the most carefully planned social functions as well as the formal family gatherings, received its own special and stately attention; equally important with dining, but of less architectural and public interest than the living room, the sleeping area was expressed as a clearly subordinate element of the facade; and finally, of course, the guest and servant wings were left to the periphery. The several divisions and units, separately stated because they contained different functions, were integrated by controlled spatial relationships, by proportions that reflected functional significance, and by the overall horizontal orientation in which scale and arrangement reflected the flow of human activity. At the Coonley Estate Wright demonstrated that architecture was best organized around life, not academic, styles.

The prairie houses were exercises in architectural elimination. If

Avery Coonley House, 1907, Riverside, Illinois

the facade of the Willitts House foreshadowed Piet Mondriaan's semicubist paintings, the organization of the Coonley Estate anticipated later developments in transport design. Much as the form of an airplane, a racing car, or a submarine is a pure expression of its function, so were the Coonley subdivisions determined by their internal requisites. To achieve this Wright was forced to spread his structures over the surface of the land. Like the National Capitol in Washington, the Willitts House had held two opposing tendencies in unnatural tension: "that toward central authority and union" evident in the central stack, as Vincent Scully has stated it, and "that toward horizontal expansion and dispersion in the proliferating wings." The Glasner, Robie, and Coonley Houses, however, and many others, exploded that tension; freed from preconceived notions of architectural organization, they expressed the life patterns of the modern family more closely. Of course, there had been a certain safety in the classic, where everything was orderly, logical, and rational—very middle class. But one of its limitations, as Scully has noted, was an inability to integrate "a rigidly geometric exterior envelope [with] an interior which came to demand more and more functional and visual variety."[13] To move across the land, to follow life's lead, to shake off authority, were all risky without doubt, but they were central to American ideology.

When Wright moved away from the classic tradition, however, he did not leave psychic voids. The prairie house was every bit as emotionally reassuring as the Victorian residence for it had, as Wright put it, an "elemental law and order" of its own. Its fireplaces, its low intimate ceilings, its rich primary colors and natural materials, and its supreme common sense, all fulfilled a deep psychological need to feel at ease in knowable surroundings, while its close association with Mother Earth tapped the perpetual human impulse to live close to the soil. Wright was fully aware that the literal and symbolic harmony between his buildings and nature evoked sympathetic cultural memories. "The horizontal line," he wrote, "the line of domesticity," enabled his houses to "lie serene beneath a wonderful sweep of sky," circumventing the age-old struggle between man and his environment that had made the nineteenth-century residence a battleground. Wright proposed a working partnership with nature—"a more intimate relationship with out-door environment."[14] Therefore, he increased the number of windows, using only casements that swung out in a gesture of embrace and, under overhanging eaves, could remain open even in the rain. Striking horizontal trim, the antithesis of "artistic" embellishment, paid homage to, and interpreted, the lay of the land. Window boxes and urns made greenery a permanent part of the facade. Gentle hip roofs cherished the snow for its insulation. And instead of raping the earth with a cellar excavation, the prairie house left it essentially unscathed with a concrete slab.

Embracing nature was a crucial architectural objective, but it was not paramount. More difficult to contend with, as Wright well knew, were the tensions, the personality clashes, the disappointments—the unpredictable intangibles of interpersonal relationships—that could disrupt a family and that had destroyed his own. During this decade Wright developed two particularly important buttresses against familial disintegration, both of which had their origins and drew their significance from psychological as well as architectural factors. His concept of shelter, something he often wrote about in connection with the prairie house, meant protection from inclement weather, of course, but it also implied a psychologically healthy atmosphere. And his open floor plan, a reaction to residential overcompartmentalization, was manifestly intended to strengthen group solidarity. The vision of a close-knit family living joyously in emotionally therapeutic surroundings was undoubtedly informed by his childhood experiences at Spring Green with the Lloyd Joneses.

Wright remembered in his autobiography that he especially "liked the *sense of shelter* in the look of the [prairie house]" (his italics).[15] It is particularly noteworthy that he remarked on the sense of shelter, not on shelter itself, for a feeling, an atmosphere—something captured in the "look" of a place—has to do principally with nonphysical stimuli. Since his homes made friendly overtures to the environment, their numerous symbols of self-protection were undoubtedly intended to be psychologically as well as physically reassuring. For example, upper level living rooms under broad eaves may have been drier and warmer than others, but they also increased privacy for inhabitants, who could observe their neighbors without themselves being observed. Doorways in Wright houses hardly ever opened directly to the street; usually tucked behind a wall, out of sight around a corner, or in a secluded alcove, they discouraged casual approach. Open porches, verandas, and terraces were generally guarded by walls, roofs, or arbors, minimizing exposure. Casement windows opening out, increased one's sense of control over the environment. The inevitable dark recesses, the shadowed facade, even the complexities of surface, suggested there was more to the building than met the eye, that deep inside was a family approaching the outside world on its own terms. Unlike Wright's residences of the 1920s and 1930s, however, prairie houses did not turn their backs on the community. Built for businessmen—not glad-handing Babbitts, of course, but dignified Coonleys and reserved Robies—who courted public favor, they faced the street and, like manor houses for urban gentry, projected an image somewhere between hospitality and indifference. Their inwardness indicated group mutuality, sheltered symbolically by the same architectural devices that offered physical security.

Inside, Wright opened up floor space. By eliminating doors, reducing walls, and increasing vista, he declared the main floor—except for the kitchen, utility rooms, and servant quarters—a large undivided space, architecturally screened according to function. Two examples illustrate Wright's method. In the Edwin Cheney House (1904) in Oak Park, he simply abolished rooms on the first floor front. The entire street side became one large space, at intervals of one-third partially divided according to use by low walls extending a few feet toward the center. The dining and living areas, the library and recessed fireplace alcove, therefore, all merged into one. In the Frank J. Baker House (1909) in Wilmette, Wright was even more dramatic. With its unusually "low center of mass and its striking horizontality," Grant Manson writes, the Baker residence stretches out well over 150 feet.[16] Nevertheless, it is possible to stand at the further end of the porch and look through the long dining room, the large entry, the two-story living room, a second porch, and out the other end for an incredible sweep of uninterrupted vista that joins the immense whole together. "Sense of shelter" in this house meant visual and spiritual unity—despite physical dispersal—accomplished architecturally.

Merging the downstairs into one large entity had significant sociological consequences: it could encourage parental authority and/or promote family mutuality. Unless children went outside or into their bedrooms, for example, they were observable everywhere; easier supervision enabled parents to extend their control, from the younger generation's point of view, perhaps, an unfortunate by-product of increased efficiency. On the other hand, opening the main floor improved its accessibility, facilitating contact among family members. Children could involve themselves more easily and for longer periods in their parents' affairs. The dining room, for instance, could hardly be closed off and might be used all day for reading, sewing, or play; the living area could not remain empty of children for long.

The open plan reflected changes in American family life of which Wright must have been conscious. Recognizing a shifting relationship between time and place—there was no longer a fixed time to use a certain room or a fixed place to do a certain thing—the open plan encouraged informality and the broadening of family activities to include younger members. By bringing the group together more often in such a way as to reinforce its ties, the prairie house fought the centrifugal impact of suburban, industrial society. It pursued even more determinedly an objective first introduced in the Winslow House reception hall: the preservation of sacred family unity—now allowed greater informality—from the disintegrating forces of modern civilization.

Architectural historian Norris Kelly Smith agrees that Wright wanted to solidify the family, but argues forcefully that he was unsure of how to do it. He seemed to waver, according to Smith, between preference for a regular and formal family structure and an irregular, informal one, an indecisiveness particularly evident in the dichotomy between his living and dining rooms. As Smith correctly shows, Wright found dining—where the family gathered for a single, clearly defined purpose (or perhaps even ritual)—easy to manage architecturally. "Dining is . . . always a great artistic opportunity," Wright admitted. Smith has perceptively noted that Wright "consistently treats the occasion as if it were liturgical in nature." Severely rectilinear furniture in severely rectilinear settings made prairie house dining rooms "more like stately council chambers than the gathering places for the kind of intimate family life usually associated with [his] name." Smith concludes that these rooms "declare unequivocally that the unity of the group requires submission and conformity on the part of its members."

By contrast, Wright's living rooms were more informal but harder to design; since they were used for a multitude of purposes, behavior there was variable and unpredictable. The problem, Smith notes, was to reduce social chaos to architectural order. "Human beings must group, sit or recline, confound them," Wright wrote perturbedly in reference to the living rooms. "Arrangements for the informality of sitting in comfort singly or in groups still belonging in disarray to the scheme as a whole: *that* is a matter difficult to accomplish." Smith argues that Wright's inability to reconcile informality with order was also apparent on exteriors—for example, in the difference between the rigidly classical J. Kibben Ingalls House (1909) in River Forest, and the asymmetrical Robie House. At stake was the problem of freedom versus order, Smith says, of providing for patterns of authority and submission within the family, while at the same time preserving individual liberty. And, he concludes, Wright failed to hold the two poles of the dichotomy apart, ultimately allowing the symbols of order and formality to dominate his work.[17]

But Smith overlooks Wright's familiarity with contemporary social convention. A recent study demonstrates that most of his clients were businessmen whose conservative political and religious views undoubtedly carried over into their social relationships.[18] Since his practice depended on commissions from the upper middle class, whose tastes, desires, and life-styles were hardly avant-garde, Wright did not—contrary to legend—browbeat his clients into accepting his ideas against their will. Often he was happy to take their suggestions. And hard-headed businessmen, who did not buy homes for the sake of architectural experiment, could be quite insistent. Wright's achievement was to maintain his integrity while designing buildings even more congenial to the social and private lives of his conservative clientele than the prevailing styles. Before the days of the cocktail party, the buffet, and the barbecue, dining was the crucial expression of social form. The dinner party—the most elaborate ritual for the hostess—was planned with meticulous care; her ability to perform with finesse and to direct her servants with grace was often the measure of her standing. Great efforts were made to have things "just so." The intricate rules and procedures for the affair were well known to participants and, of course, to their architects. Wright frequently gave dinner parties himself, and thoroughly understood that dining rooms were obliged to express the sociology of dignified and orderly entertainment.

On the other hand, vests that had been straightened at the table were often unbuttoned afterward when guests retired to the living room, perhaps breaking up into small groups (by sexes) for conversation, musical entertainment, political discussion, or liquid refreshment. Accommodating a multiplicity of events simultaneously, living rooms often played a less stately role than dining rooms in the dynamics of early twentieth-century social life. Accordingly, Wright designed them for more informality, to provide for the less ritualized aspects of a family's public and private existence. What Smith interprets as Wright's uncertainty in architectural expression—the order versus freedom dichotomy—may simply have indicated, therefore, his grasp of social reality.

Taken by themselves his dining rooms imply formality, order, and traditional family organization, but in the context of the open plan they are an aspect of his concern with the sharing and accessibility of household activities, and in the light of the disintegrating pressures of urban life on the family, they obviously emphasize group cohesion. Wright had no particular commitment to the authoritarian family or to the submissiveness of children; indeed, his social consciousness and his own history suggest that the mutuality and solidarity lacking in his childhood were of higher priority. He may not have formulated a precise model of the modern family, but he probably understood that urban pleasures and the absence of the father fractionalized it, making the architect responsible for reuniting it in any way he could.

In stressing Wright's domestic architecture it would be an oversight to ignore one of the most important and lasting achievements of the prairie years. By basing his designs on formats machinery could best produce, he developed an architectural grammar entirely adaptable to public as well as residential buildings. He found it possible, as a result, to rely on the same materials, construction methods, ornament, and parti—to create the same look, in other words—for domestic and nondomestic designs. Both were informed by an attitude toward social organization— with a set of expressive symbols, and a concept of the proportion of members, units, and spatial arrangements—that could be articulated by the machine, for in Wright's view of things, private and public buildings were not so very different and were not required to appear so. Thus in his commercial designs he sometimes expressed internal organization and authority relationships with architectural analogies to the family. The Larkin Administration Building (1904) in Buffalo and Unity Temple (1905–1906) in

Oak Park, for example, were conceived as part-time homes for extended families, as, of course, was the Hillside Home School.

The similarities in appearance, style, and expression between Wright's public and private prairie buildings are obvious. The River Forest Tennis Club and the Pettit Mortuary Chapel (both in Belvidere, Illinois, 1906), the Lake Geneva (Wisconsin) Inn (1911), and even something as small as the garage for George Blossom (1907) in Chicago are so similar on their exteriors to prairie houses that the uninformed might take them for residences. The Yahara Boat Club project for Madison, Wisconsin (1902), and the City National Bank and Hotel (1909) in Mason City, Iowa, are grammatically quite close to the W. H. Freeman residence (1903) in Hinsdale, Illinois; the 1907 "Fireproof House for $5,000," published in *The Ladies' Home Journal;* and the home for Elizabeth Gale (1909) in Oak Park. The significance of Wright's achievement was that it was no longer necessary for him to shift styles each time a new architectural problem arose. He understood that, while the similarities between public and private life were all grist for the machine's mill, their differences were not sacrificed by a common appearance. The fact that his mortuaries and hotels bore a striking resemblance to his homes did not mean that Wright was unable to differentiate among living, dying, and visiting, or that his was a limited architectural vocabulary, but simply that he had created a kind of Esperanto of design, a language comprehensive enough to speak to many possibilities.

The three most famous nonresidential buildings Wright executed before he closed his practice in 1909 were the Hillside Home School (1901), the Larkin Administration Building (1904) in Buffalo, and Unity Temple (1905–1906) in Oak Park. The Hillside School particularly resembles the prairie houses, and while all three illustrate the diverse possibilities of his grammar, they also indicate the widespread praise and admiration he received during these years. The Hillside Home School, fashioned out of local timber and fieldstone for his Aunts Jane and Ellen Lloyd Jones

The Hillside Home School, 1901, near Spring Green, Wisconsin

near Spring Green, Wisconsin, was one of the first prairie buildings. Nestled into a gently sloping site, and with overhanging eaves almost touching the ground at points, it emphasized the relationship its students would have with their environment. The long parallel lines of horizontal roof and trim, the open spacious interior, and the native materials, all of which symbolically recapitulated the surrounding topography, were enhanced by excellent craftsmanship, modern furnishings, leaded windows, and careful planning—which, with the many architectural innovations, stressed the appreciation of art, culture, and intellect the school sought to instill.

Clearly, Wright's purpose here was to link art and nature for residential and pedagogical advantage. Far from being too avant-garde (or too "radical," as Wright claimed of his designs) for rural

Spring Green, the Hillside Home School was welcomed as "a beautiful and ideal building," applauded precisely because it was "something out of the ordinary." Its planning and construction were followed eagerly each step of the way, and in a short descriptive column in the local weekly, the reporter used the word "beautiful" seven times, as well as "delightful," "elegant," and "convenient." If a structure's worth can properly be measured by the response of those who use it, the Hillside Home School was an overwhelming success, for it was, as one man commented, "a great joy" to be in.[19]

In common with Unity Temple, the controversial five-story Larkin Administration Building bore its greatest resemblance to the prairie house in the interior, where its trim, lighting fixtures, stairwells, and other embellishments suggested that the touchstones of work life were not totally dissimilar from those at home, or, in more modern parlance, that the roles man performed should not divide him into unrelated segments. With a large main floor for the clerical help lit artificially and by skylights high overhead, and with balconies around the perimeter providing office space for the managers who could look down on the work force, the Larkin Building reinforced traditional notions of employment and familial authority. Indeed, the architect's stated intention was to create a "family-gathering under conditions ideal for body and mind," a simulated "family home" that would uplift the workers and be profitable for the owners. The structure was sealed to shut out noise and dirt from adjacent industry and railroads, featured custom-made metal office furniture, and was air-cooled and fireproofed—most of which were Wright's own innovations. Its freestanding stairwells—a fire safety measure—were articulated as massive pylons on the four corners of the exterior. Russell Sturgis, a leading architectural critic of the period, acknowledged that the Larkin Building was comfortable, forward looking, eminently utilitarian, and unusually well planned, but deemed it hopelessly ugly. On the other hand, *The Architectural Review* considered it "about as fine a piece of original and effective composition as one

Administration Building for the Larkin Company, 1904, Buffalo, New York

could expect to find." Three directors of the Larkin Company must have agreed when they commissioned Wright to design their homes.[20]

Unity Temple consists of two massive cubes, the larger an auditorium connected by an entrance loggia to the smaller, which houses the church's community and secular functions. Its poured concrete exterior left "natural" was one of the first uses of that material in that way in a public building. The symbolic impor-

Interior of the Larkin Administration Building

tance of the cubes and the relationship of their functions was clearly stated: the spiritual activities of Unity took precedence over the secular, which were housed in the smaller subdivision, but the two were inseparably linked into a greater whole by the sturdy bond of the entrance loggia. The reporter for *Oak Leaves*, a local paper, congratulated Wright on Unity's "indescribable beauty." "The eye and the mind were rested and the soul uplifted," he wrote, and then exclaimed, in a paean of unrestrained praise, "it

Unity Temple, 1905–1906, Oak Park, Illinois

has the magic of grandeur to steal the carnal sense and inspire the spirit of reverence and desire for larger service." Most of the parishioners were perhaps unaware of these nobler and more esoteric aspects of Wright's accomplishment, but they agreed that Unity provided "superb surroundings" for their affairs, "an edifice in which all can take pride. . . ."[21]

Even Wright's most provocative designs met enthusiastic approval in both urban and rural America. Although his work looked different and was constructed differently from anything before, although it was indeed radical, it was not incomprehensible to an intelligent layman. Like many another intellectual breakthrough,

Sanctuary of Unity Temple

Wright's complex ideas were arduously arrived at, but their practical application made immediate common sense. His houses were, in other words, more efficient than the prevailing types—inside and out. They appealed to a generation of Americans whose heroes—businessmen and reformers—had successfully eliminated obstacles to personal achievement, and had simplified political and industrial processes. A perusal of the architectural journals indicates that Wright's prairie buildings were not ridiculed and abused, as he later claimed, but were favorably commented upon and widely imitated. *The Inland Architect*, for example, published over a dozen of his designs from 1901 until its demise in December 1908. Leading articles in the June, July, and August 1906 issues of The House Beautiful were devoted to him, and, in their surveys of Chicago buildings, The Brickbuilder (September 1903) and The Architectural Review (April 1908) praised him most effusively. In a July 1905 analysis of Wright's work, The Architectural Record noted that he "stands more prominently than any other Western architect . . . designing residences. . . . Whatever [his] influence has been in the past, it will be even more efficacious in the future."[22]

Wright's first feature-length publication in a major journal also substantiates his considerable influence toward the end of the decade. "In the Cause of Architecture," appearing in the March 1908 issue of The Architectural Record, included, in addition to eighty-seven illustrations, a number of specially composed advertisements featuring his buildings. The widely read text was praised as "practical idealism" by another magazine, which urged its readers to digest Wright's very important concepts.[23] Shortly before, in 1907, his first solo exhibition at the Chicago Art Institute had generated considerable discussion. Some critics disliked his work, of course. S. W. Fitzpatrick dismissed it as "simply exotic," with the reservation—revealing his own incomprehension—that the more recent buildings were "far saner" because of their "artistic daintiness." If Russell Sturgis thought the Larkin Building a "monster of awkwardness," Harriet Monroe considered the Unity Temple to be "without grace or ease or monumental beauty."[24] But this seems to have been the minority position; the consensus ranged from tolerant acceptance to enthusiastic approval. One New York critic thought Wright's ideas "absolutely in the line of creative architecture." And a small-town midwestern editor wrote that his "well known devotion to the horizontal as well as his cardinal principle of 'bringing outdoors indoors' " made him "one of the most distinctively American architects of today. . . ."[25]

Wright's steadily growing practice burgeoned after the introduction of the prairie house. Only twice prior to 1901 had he received more than eleven commissions a year, a figure he never failed to equal or surpass, however, before he left Oak Park in 1909. From 1901 to 1909 he executed approximately ninety of one hundred thirty-five commissions, an average of fifteen designs and ten completions a year, compared to averages of about eight and four respectively from 1893 to 1900. From 1901 to 1904 he built eight of twelve buildings yearly, while from 1905 to 1909 his output rose to eleven of seventeen. If anything, the prairie houses became more popular as they grew more distinctive. Although a vast majority of his commissions were from the Midwest, especially the greater Chicago area, they also came in from California, Montana, Tennessee, New York, and Quebec. His architecture in fact and in the name was regional, but it could have been built anywhere, and was. Shrewd businessmen, practical-minded Unitarians, and his own country relatives were all attracted to his "radical" new ideas.[26]

The development of prairie architecture had involved a considerable investment of time, thought, and energy. Much more than a commodity peddled for profit, it was fundamentally for Wright an extended intellectual exercise. It was not unnatural therefore that he should have published a kind of retrospective essay—a long, illustrated review of his work since the turn of the century—in The Architectural Record of March 1908. "In the Cause of Architecture" was optimistic and self-congratulatory. His most comprehensive philosophical statement since the Hull House speech of 1901, it was another building block in the edifice later known as "organic architecture."

"Radical though it may be," Wright began his essay,* my work "is dedicated to a cause conservative . . ."; it is "a declaration of love" for the spirit of that "elemental law and order inherent in all great architecture," a law and order most readily observed in natural forms, particularly plant and animal life. Since great buildings had always been based on nature's motifs, he claimed, their careful study would yield "a sense of the organic," by which he meant at this time "a knowledge of the relation between form and

* The punctuation has been slightly altered.

function." Nature's secrets, however, could only be discovered by diligent contemplation. Like many of his contemporaries in letters and the arts, Wright believed that reality and truth were not to be found on the surface of things, which at best was an illusory, superficial manifestation of essence, and at worst a deception. The truth of a thing was hidden, requiring extensive probing, but it was discernible and it yielded valuable lessons.[27] For the architect, the patient analysis of nature would reveal the true meaning of function and structure. Japanese artists were among the very few who had learned to derive building forms from a close observation of nature's principles. Louis Sullivan had also been aware of her bounty. Wright would only admit, therefore, to three sources of inspiration: the art of Nippon, his "liebermeister," and nature itself.

Good architecture, of course, was not the literal reproduction but the translation of natural principles into form and method. In the broadest sense, Wright meant that a design might be "deduced from some plant form that has appealed to me," such as the sumac at the Susan Lawrence Dana House (1903) in Springfield, Illinois; a house might "flare outward, opening flowerlike to the sky," while another "droop[s] to accentuate artistically the weight of the masses." Or, more specifically, just as nature's creations—flowers, birds, the human hand—were all perfectly functional and carried their own decoration, so architectural trim ought not be applied but should grow organically from the structure itself, in the form of doors, windows, and other functional requisites. The incorporation of natural principles into architecture would be even more difficult than it was, Wright thought, were it not for technology—the "modern opportunity." Never before had the architect so many tools, materials, and processes capable of reproducing and preserving natural characteristics.

Wright's emphasis on nature in this essay and in later writings in no way contradicted his earlier emphasis on machinery. On the contrary, the two became companion cornerstones of his philosophy. Depending upon each other for their integrity, nature would inform and machinery execute a totally new architecture in a historically unique synthesis. Indeed, the machine's capacities were best utilized when they transformed natural principles into architectural forms.

Extensive contemplation of nature and the machine had led him, he wrote, to formulate six architectural propositions upon which he had based his prairie houses. Simplicity and repose, he noted first of all, characterized works of art as surely as they did natural forms. For architectural art this meant that a building "should contain as few rooms as will meet the conditions which give it rise. . . ." Doors and windows should be "integral features of the structure, and if possible act as its natural ornamentation"; too much detail turned houses into "mere notion stores, bazaars, and junk shops." Appliances and fixtures should be designed into the building, pictures incorporated into the general scheme as decoration, and furniture built in. "The whole," he wrote, "must always be considered as an integral unit."

Wright's second proposition was that "there should be as many kinds (styles) of houses as there are kinds (styles) of people and as many differentiations as there are different individuals." Thirdly, "a building should appear to grow easily from its site and be shaped to harmonize with its surroundings. . . ." If they were not particularly interesting, the structure should be "as quiet, substantial, and organic" as possible. The prairie, of course, had its own natural beauty—"a quiet level"—which Wright tried to recognize and accentuate.

Fourthly, he believed that natural colors—"the soft, warm, optimistic tones of earths and autumn leaves"—were easier to live with, "more wholesome and better adapted in most cases to good decoration." Next Wright urged home builders not to force materials but to respect their individual properties and preserve their natural qualities. The sixth and last proposition was more a statement of faith than a rule to live by. "A house that has character stands a good chance of growing more valuable as it grows older while a house in the prevailing mode, whatever that mode may be, is soon out of fashion, stale, and unprofitable." Obviously, Wright considered the prairie house an eternal verity, not a passing fancy.

In a very fundamental sense, Wright thought of his buildings as problem-solving mechanisms, with floor plans the functional, and elevations the aesthetic, solutions to the problem of designing a satisfactory residence for American conditions. The difficulty was to make the elevation and the plan harmonious, to integrate them "organically" (a word—now evolving into a concept—that he used more frequently in this essay than ever before). As nearly as possible, he wrote, a house should be the "grammatical expression" of an "organic integrity," and, insofar as it had style (not a style), it would confront present-day conditions honestly. In other words, a building must be the best possible expression of an idea about how to live modern life, given the prevailing level of sociological, technological, and cultural awareness. Any ideas on this subject carried political as well as architectural implications, as Wright clearly understood.

Analyzing the cultural significance of technology more deeply than he had at Hull House in 1901, Wright maintained that, since machinery now performed so many construction tasks and greatly increased aesthetic consistency, there had arisen a "modern opportunity, to make of a building, together with its equipment, appurtenances, and environment . . . a complete work of art. . . ." Architecture based on the new technology would be "more valuable to society as a whole . . . because discordant conditions [of construction], endured for centuries, are smoothed away." As the "average of human intelligence rises steadily," enabling the individual homeowner to make better choices, the architectural forms he selects would provide for his patterns of living more accurately than the traditional European styles, primarily because the products of machinery truly express, and are expressions of, modern circumstances. As such, they are based on "a radically different conception" of what buildings should be and do. Authentic indigenous architecture, furthermore, could ultimately bring about true democracy, which Wright defined as "the highest possible expression of the individual as a unit not inconsistent with a harmonious whole." The individual citizen therefore bore the same relationship to an organic society as an element in a Wright design to the entire project: his (its) significance could be achieved and expressed only by finding a functional place within the social (architectural) context. In democracy as in architecture, individuality meant "richer variety in unity," a possibility only in America.

"In the Cause of Architecture" was also Wright's most contemporary statement of the way in which the prairie house evolved. He described his thought processes, the development of his architectural notions, the reactions of clients, contractors, and workmen; he listed what he believed were his practical and aesthetic innovations, discussed his achievements, and named his most helpful assistants and draftsmen. He reiterated again and again that his goal was an even more unified and harmonious building. Although he was quite certain that future work "shall grow more truly simple, more expressive with fewer lines, . . . more articulate with less labor, more plastic, more fluent, although more coherent, more organic," he promised to continue the search for better methods of construction, for cleaner and more virile forms of expression. As his "understanding and appreciation of life matures and deepens," his work would "prophesy and idealize the character" of his clients even more acutely. It would become "as pure and as elevating in its humble way as the trees and flowers are in their perfectly appointed way. . . ." If Wright derived intense satisfaction from what he had already accomplished, he fully expected even greater rewards as his skills developed further. He was conquering the profession, early in 1908, and there seemed to be nothing on the horizon, not even a tiny cloud, to indicate that his fortunes might change.

4. AFFINITY TANGLE

$$[1907-1912]$$

And then something went wrong. There came a time for Frank Lloyd Wright when architecture lost its adventure and family life its joy. Believing that marriage, suburban, and professional pressures were conspiring to deny his individuality, he suddenly threw them off in a desperate existential act which perilously threatened his career. After a European holiday with a client's wife he retreated to a rural enclave to take up the artist's life. The ensuing social ostracism—together with his supreme confidence in the wisdom of his moral and architectural positions—intensified his iconoclasm and his disdain for conventional behavior. In 1912 Wright entered his mid-forties with uncertain prospects, on the razor's edge between past glories and future oblivion.

"In the Cause of Architecture" in 1908 was only one indication of Frank Lloyd Wright's growing stature. His third article for *The Ladies' Home Journal* appeared in April 1907, the same month he held his one-man exhibition at Chicago's Art Institute, the first ever given there by a local architect.[1] Most professional appraisal

90

of his work was favorable—very little was overtly hostile—even on the more traditional East Coast, where his reputation was also spreading. In 1906, 1907, and 1908 he designed an unprecedented sixteen commissions a year, surpassed only by his nineteen in 1909.[2] He had finished his magnificent drawings for Harold F. McCormick, the recently completed Robie and Coonley Houses were attracting attention, and Unity Temple had already received touring architectural students.[3] By 1909, when he contributed to the first annual exhibition of the Minneapolis Architectural Club by special invitation,[4] he was well on his way to fame and fortune. Then without warning, and seemingly without cause, he threw it all over. Leaving behind his wife and six children, and entrusting his uncompleted designs to an assistant and a hastily selected colleague, he eloped to Europe with the wife of a client, creating a local sensation. The "prominent Oak Park architect," *The Chicago Tribune* intoned, was responsible for "an affinity tangle . . . unparalleled even in the checkered history of soul mating."[5]

In September 1909 Wright and Mamah Borthwick Cheney left their Oak Park families for New York, sailing from there to Europe. The Wrights and the Cheneys had been a locally familiar foursome, attending concerts and other social functions together after 1904, when the architect had designed the Cheneys' home, a few blocks from his own. The women were members of the same civic organizations, and in November 1907 collaborated on a literary club presentation. It was about this time, when Mrs. Cheney presumably visited the Wrights more than usual, that "the thing happened," as the architect put it, "that has happened to men and women since time began—the inevitable."[6] The love affair had been discussed in Oak Park, where the couple made no attempt to hide their feelings, even from their spouses, but in November 1909, when the urban press discovered the elopement, an open secret turned into a scandal.

Wright had told reporters in September that he was going to Berlin for at least a year to work on a book. He neglected to tell them, of course, that Mamah Cheney would accompany him,

Mamah Borthwick
Cheney

although his family and friends knew his plans. The story came to light only when an enterprising Chicago newsman, aware that Catherine Wright had remained in Oak Park, came across the entry "Frank Lloyd Wright, and wife" in the register of a Berlin hotel.

The activities of the "soul mates" during their year in Europe are unknown, except in broad outline. First they went to Berlin, where the architect made preparations for the portfolio of drawings, *Ausgeführte Bauten und Entwürfe von Frank Lloyd*

Wright, a review of his practice since 1900. Then he moved to Italy where, joined briefly by his son Lloyd, he worked with his assistants in the Villa Fortuna near the Piazzale Michelangelo in Florence, visiting Mrs. Cheney, who remained in a Berlin apartment, for several days at a time when he came to consult his publisher, Ernst Wasmuth. Lloyd Wright remembered that on one of those trips his father met Johannes Brahms, but was disappointed when the composer proved to be a diffident conversationalist.[7]

Wright finished his work on the portfolio by June 1910, whereupon Mrs. Cheney joined him in Fiesole, Italy. Although they may have planned to settle there—Wright sketched a home and studio for the place—they spent most of the subsequent months touring Italian and German art treasures, translating Goethe (the architect's favorite) and Ellen Key (a Swedish advocate of motherhood without marriage), and wandering through bookshops, in essence living the life of wealthy American expatriates. Wright returned to Oak Park in October 1910, leaving his paramour in Berlin and, apparently forgiven by his wife and children, was reinstated at the head of his household. Later in the year or early in 1911 Mamah reappeared, but did not go back to her husband. When she secured a divorce in August 1911, Wright escorted her to "Taliesin," the home he had been building since May near Spring Green, Wisconsin, and left her there. Again he rejoined his family, where his status is unknown, but in December returned to Mrs. Cheney. On Christmas Day, 1911, Wright announced that he and his mistress would live together permanently.[8]

Historians have offered several explanations for Wright's desertion of family and profession. One, which the architect put forward himself, has been readily accepted: he was tired of his domestic situation and in love with another woman. But while these personal factors were obviously of crucial importance, they do not take into account his persistent assertion, stated in various ways, that "I found my life in my work."[9] If he was as consumed

by architecture as he maintained, why then did he leave his practice? In this regard the historical consensus seems to be that
Wright was "a hurt and sensitive genius, driven by the indifference of his countrymen into the arms of appreciative foreigners."
The legend that he had taken a stand "alone in my field," designing buildings "unhonored and ridiculed" with "abuses seldom
described," had been uncritically accepted too long. The related
assertion that Wright left because in 1908 Harold F. McCormick
rejected his magnificent drawings for a gigantic estate in favor of
traditional house plans depends on the untenable assumption that
the loss of a single commission could undermine the work of a
decade.[10] Wright's decision to leave—involving both personal and
architectural considerations—was prompted by a matrix of factors
more complicated than all these suggestions combined.

By no stretch of the imagination was Wright's work abused or
rejected. What bothered him most by 1907 was precisely the
opposite: uncritical acceptance and thoughtless praise. Perhaps his
view of professional criticism was naïve, for he expected searching
analysis from which he could profit, a kind of Socratic dialogue
that would help his ideas develop. What he actually got even from
friendly critics, he insisted, were superficial responses to the obvious aspects of his work—uninformed reactions to his aesthetic and
functional innovations. Wright stated his disappointment quite
eloquently in a long letter to Harriet Monroe, who had sympa-
thetically reviewed his exhibition at the Art Institute for *The
Chicago Examiner* in April 1907.[11] Although she had approved
of his "most interesting experiment," comparing it favorably to
other styles and other traditions, she nevertheless derided its
"unusual, at times even bizarre" appearance. In the letter Wright
accused her of shallow judgment, of not accepting his work on its
own terms, and of failing to probe its underlying philosophy and
its fundamental objectives. But, most important, the letter revealed Wright's dissatisfaction with the manner in which his
buildings had generally been discussed.

"I am hungry," he told her, "for the honest, genuine criticism that searches the soul of the thing and sifts its form. Praise isn't needed especially. There is enough of that, such as it is, but we all need intelligent painstaking inquiry . . . into the nature of the proposition. . . ." Without it, he insisted, his architecture would be "lightly touched up with House Beautiful English for the mob," flattering oversimplifications, that is, for mass consumption. The struggle to create a work of art was difficult enough, he wrote, without prominent voices making it "unnecessarily grim and temporarily thankless" by labeling it a certain "type," thereby negating its uniqueness. Shortsighted analysis would not "harm the inherent virtue of good work," but it could mislead the public and discourage the artist. "When an individual effort to be true to a worthy ideal has the courage to lift its head it deserves something better than the capricious slapstick of 'the type,'" he chided Miss Monroe, "even if the slap appeals to the gallery, in other words 'to our very best people.'" His own architecture, he claimed, had "met little more than the superficial snap-judgment of the 'artistically informed.' I am quite used to it, glad to owe it nothing. . . . But, meanwhile the Cause suffers delay! That is the price the public pays for 'the type' and it is the serious side of the matter."

The objectives of his work and the "cause" for which he fought, he explained, were the rejuvenation of architecture, the creation of indigenous forms to express and suit life in the United States, and the destruction of the "Fakery and Sham [that] rule the day." An American architecture is a possibility and will be a definite probability when it is conceived and executed with "organic consistency and such individuality" as his own work revealed. But "conscientious efforts of this nature" will founder and die unless they "receive the encouragement on their native heath that they already have in conservative England or in France. . . ." There, he noted, but not in the United States, his designs were "accorded the rare virtue of originality without eccentricity." He did not wish to be remembered as the creator of an exotic new style, or indeed of any style, but simply wanted critics to understand that his architecture was first of all concerned with fundamental social and cultural questions. Any analysis—like Harriet Monroe's—that did not approach him on these terms missed the point entirely.

If praise as a substitute for scrutiny was useless, it was positively destructive, Wright thought, when it subverted his identity by forcing him into a group. As his ideas were taken up by others and his buildings widely imitated, there developed a corpus variously known as the Chicago, the Midwestern, or the Prairie Style. Unaware that its distinguishing characteristics—as far as the residence was concerned—had originated with Wright, most critics lumped him with a dozen or more prairie practitioners. Some, like Walter Burley Griffin and William Drummond, had been his apprentices, but none were his equal, although George Maher and one or two others briefly achieved greater popularity. The work of these men—Dwight H. Perkins, Robert C. Spencer, Jr., Richard E. Schmidt, George R. Dean, Irving and Allen Pond, Griffin, Drummond, Maher, and others—was widely applauded. The problem was not their success but his reduction to just another member of just another movement, especially one that depended so heavily on him, and was said to include those—like Beaux Arts traditionalists James Gamble Rogers and Howard Van Doren Shaw—who violated his most fundamental principles. Wright was annoyed and upset when his inspirational role was slighted and his individuality undermined by specious categorization. Somehow he was being swamped by the dimensions of his own success, overrun by a bandwagon he had not intended to create.[12]

An additional irony had risen to plague him. Fifteen years after the fact, observers frequently described him as a "follower" of Louis Sullivan. It became almost a convention to open a description of prairie architecture—including house designs—by reviewing Sullivan who, after creating a new style, as one critic claimed, had passed his legacy on to Maher, Drummond, Schmidt, Wright, and other "pupils." This analysis overlooked the somewhat obvious facts that after 1900 Sullivan had largely been reduced to designing small midwestern banks, that many of the prairie architects had never worked with him, that his influence came from past performances not continuing effort, and that Wright, not Sullivan, had revolutionized the residence. Throughout his life Wright was the first to acknowledge the enormous debt he owed his "liebermeister," paying him eloquent tribute on many occasions, so he was not being an ingrate to resent the erroneous implication that Sullivan was responsible for the prairie house. Sullivan would readily have admitted that he had not taught Wright enough about residential design to account for so great an accomplishment. Indeed, it was almost the opposite: Sullivan designed only two homes between 1892 and the end of his career in 1922, and both—for Henry Babson (1907) in Riverside, Illinois, and for Mrs. Josephine Bradley (1909) in Madison, Wisconsin—were heavily indebted to Wright, who by then had advanced sufficiently to teach the teacher. So to be described constantly as Sullivan's "pupil" only reinforced Wright's belief that he was not being judged on his own merits.[13]

There was yet another important source of his dissatisfaction. The "absorbing, consuming phase of my experience as an architect ended about 1909," he recorded in his autobiography. "I was losing my grip on my work and even my interest in it. . . . [It] seemed to leave me up against a dead wall. I could see no way out. Because I did not know what I wanted I wanted to go away."[14] By 1908 he had completed the Coonley and Robie houses, had supervised the opening of Unity Temple, had finished the McCormick project, and had produced such other notable homes as those for E. E. Boynton in Rochester, New York, Isabel Roberts in River Forest, Illinois, and E. A. Gilmore in Madison. With the exception of the Frank J. Baker and Elizabeth Gale houses in Wilmette and Oak Park, Wright's 1909 ventures lack the conviction, the drama, and the excitement of the preceding four or five years. It may have been, therefore, that he sensed that the prairie genre had reached its limits, that it had been brought to a logical and successful conclusion, that nothing was to be gained from further experimentation.

The great achievement of 1907—the Robie, Coonley, and

McCormick designs—was actually the high point of his prairie era. Their success was partly due to challenging sites, unusually generous budgets, and sympathetic clients, a rare combination of factors that may have stimulated Wright to extra effort. By contrast, the two additional years he remained in Oak Park may have been something like the denouement of a play, when he sensed that the satisfactions of creativity had ended, that the curtain had fallen on his great performance. He came to believe that further exertion was self-defeating. With each of his buildings the "style" gained further popularity and the "school" new adherents who imitated his "manner, rather than the substantial value of his work," as one journal put it, causing the results "generally [to] turn out badly."[15] The longer he remained in Chicago the more he lost his identity. He felt, perhaps, that the introspection of compiling a portfolio might give him a better perspective on what he had already accomplished, and the architectural treasures of the Continent inspire him in new ways and new directions.

Whatever anyone else thought, of course, Wright knew the value of his own work. As he had gained knowledge and confidence—as he came to believe in himself—his self-image began to change, making him even more jealous of his individuality. Increasingly he saw himself as a free spirit, as a creative artist who had earned the right to take liberties with rules and customs. Gradually he realized that his suburban, as well as his professional, situation was too confining. He could never be a truly free and independent person, nor could he be happy in any fundamental way, until he broke certain patterns and boundaries defining his life. The same storm clouds were gathering at home as at work: community and family also took him for granted, threatening his freedom of expression by forcing him into roles and categories that negated his individuality. Happy home and quiet suburb, once ideals to be achieved, were now burdens to be shed.

Earlier in his career, when he had considered it a significant improvement over his adolescence, Wright had adopted the lifestyle of a suburban professional with abandon. Under the tutelage of Cecil Corwin, J. L. Silsbee's chief draftsman, who had be-friended him upon his arrival in Chicago, Wright had acquired a predilection for the "good life." Silsbee and his clients, Sullivan and his, the parishioners at All Soul's Church where Wright had met his wife, and indeed, those who purchased his architecture, were all more or less of a type—his primary reference group for many years. But when he was able to rely on his own judgment and to make choices for himself, he became less enamored with the "proper" behavior and orthodox living that characterized the upper middle class. As his inclinations and habits changed rapidly, suburban life became too ritualized, too predictable, and too stifling. If he kept up many of the appearances—dinner parties and speaking engagements, for example, where he could per-form—his behavior nevertheless grew increasingly "eccentric."

Caring less for community customs as the years passed, he became more individualistic in his personal mannerisms or, as a noted social scientist might put it, less "other-directed." He let his long hair fall over his collar, and his clothes, although expensive, were unusually casual; flowing neckties and smocks, English jackets and riding breeches, and high-laced boots were hardly the suburban norm. He was nominally a Unitarian—in itself a some-what suspect persuasion at the turn of the century—but he rarely attended services, and was sometimes found on Sunday mornings spraying his children with the garden hose while his neighbors on their way to worship looked on disapprovingly. Wright was fre-quently ticketed for driving his custom-equipped automobiles over the speed limit. He made a spectacle of himself at the theater by laughing too loudly. He boycotted Fourth of July celebrations (then the epitome of patriotism), shunned politics, never locked his house, and kept unconventional hours.[16] His most flagrant violation of social propriety, however, was to drive around town in his open car with married women—"purely business trips," his wife insisted. "He was not a mere Lothario," a friend later remembered. "He was a victim of women. They took up more of his time than really was necessary."[17] And after 1904, when he designed her home, an increasing amount of Wright's time was devoted to Mamah Cheney.

Suburban life was made even more tedious by the shortcomings (from Wright's point of view) of his wife Catherine, the socially conscious woman he had courted so eagerly two decades earlier. In their first nine years together they had had five children, and later a sixth. Catherine gave them most of her time—apparently spurning servant assistance—paying very little attention to her husband's architecture. Although she was active in civic affairs, speaking at the local Nineteenth Century Club, the Scoville Institute, and at Unity Temple, where they both were members, she seemed to pattern her activities after her husband, showing little intellectual initiative of her own. For example, she was knowledgeable about Goethe, a favorite of Wright's, and had studied Japanese art, on which he was expert. After they married she had helped him master urban ways, but in the following years she did not—or because of family responsibilities could not—keep pace with Wright's intellectual and artistic development. By the time he left her, Catherine was naïvely, almost obsequiously, devoted—the model Victorian wife, in fact. She claimed to see nothing wrong with his European elopement—he "is as clean as my baby," she declared—and believed so strongly in his eventual return that she refused to grant a divorce until 1921.[18]

Unfortunately, Wright was unsatisfied by Victorian relationships, and by 1909 Mamah Cheney offered him a more stimulating alternative. Mrs. Cheney more closely resembled the two women the architect later married than she did Catherine. Like Miriam Noel and Olgivanna Milanoff, Mamah was artistic, independent, strong willed, and more "exotic" than her predecessor. Like other "liberated" upper-middle-class women of the period, all three were dissatisfied with the social roles custom assigned, looking outside the family for release of energy and talent. They were well read, cosmopolitan, and sophisticated, and each had had children by a previous marriage.

Mrs. Cheney was restless as a suburban housewife. She had

been a librarian after graduating from college, and was more interested in art, literature, and feminism than in her husband or the
daily routine of child-rearing. Unlike Catherine, who supervised a
kindergarten in her own home and was a doting mother, Mamah
left her children with a nurse or at boarding school. With Wright
(the artist) she could explore talents left uncultivated with her
husband (the businessman), whom she had repeatedly rejected
before marrying. She was actively interested in Wright's work—it
was rumored that Edwin Cheney took no part in planning their
home, leaving it entirely to Mamah and her architect—and was
prepared to be his sympathetic comrade. She was completely
willing to abandon the suburbs for a highly individualistic way of
life in Europe and in rural Wisconsin.[19]

Wright was attracted to Mamah in part because she had freed
herself from her children, a second source of his domestic dissatisfaction. In an effort to establish a community of kindred spirits at
428 Forest Avenue, the Wrights had permitted their offspring
considerable independence, which turned out to have had its
disadvantages. In 1893, when the architect had moved his drafting
table to Oak Park from his downtown office, he did so, he wrote,
"to secure the quiet concentration of effort" possible only outside
the "distractions of the busy city."[20] But different disturbances
arose, and two years later he moved again, this time to a studio in
a separate building attached to his house, difficult for the children
to get to. Nevertheless, his second son, John, remembered, "I was
able to discover and find my way. . . . I could get to the balcony
from a hidden stairway . . . [and] throw things over the railing
on the . . . tables and the heads of the . . . men." The children
gave their father no peace. According to John they listened on the
telephone extension and disrupted conversations with clients.
They broke Wright's specially designed house decorations,
squirted him with the hose, sat on his dress hat, and were generally
unresponsive to discipline. "Things began to smash," the architect
himself recalled. "Cries to resound. Shrieks. Quarrels and laughter.
. . . Destruction of something or other every minute." "I often

wonder now," John wrote in 1946, "why he didn't leave sooner."[21]

He did not because "he was preeminently a lover of home and family." He desperately wanted to create for himself the warm atmosphere he had remembered from the Lloyd Joneses. His twenty years of married life and the dominant motifs of his residences seem to confirm that. "He loved fatherhood," John maintained, "he just didn't like . . . everything that goes with it." More than two decades after his departure Wright remembered that "everything, personal and otherwise, bore down heavily upon me. Domesticity most of all. . . . A true home is the finest ideal of man, and yet—well to gain freedom I asked for a divorce." By 1909 personal independence beckoned Wright more compellingly than the security of home and suburb, and the dictates of his artistic temperament far outweighed parental attractions. "The architect absorbed the father in me," Wright confessed, ever mindful of distasteful suburban mores, perhaps "because I never got used to the . . . idea of being one as I saw them all around the block and met them among my friends. I hated the sound of the word papa."[22] Ironically, his successful creation of a united, close-knit family had stifled his individuality. William C. Wright had left home having failed to cement strong group ties; his son fled to escape them.

The dichotomy between the artist and the family man and suburbanite had appeared in Wright's architecture as early as the mid-1890s, when he asserted that his professional aspirations were more unorthodox than his domestic ideals, hoping to maintain a balance between the two by segregating them from each other. In 1895 he had added a studio to his home (1889), partly to accommodate family growth but also as a retreat from rambunctious children. The facade of the house facing the street is classically formal and regular, well within the prevailing "shingle style" defined by historian Vincent Scully, suggesting conventional family behavior and a respect for the community expectations of Victorian America. The interior, however, is flowing and irregular, with unusual vistas and playful events, implying an individualistic, more freewheeling life-style. The studio, on the other hand, is

unmistakably esoteric. Its intricate and complex facades, large sloping windows, broad planes and broken lines, its varying materials,
abstract decorations, contrasting elements, and carefully interrelated parts, all suggest experiment and change. If the facade of the
house hinted to neighbors that family life should be orderly and
simple, and if the interior suggested to guests that domesticity was
more unconventional than they might have expected, the studio
shouted to clients that Wright's practice ignored the usual rules
and formulae.

Undoubtedly, the studio reflected the considerable evolution of
Wright's architectural expression between 1889 and 1895, but it
was also a statement about social organization. Wright chose to
divorce the family and work functions of his life by erecting separate buildings (he might have expanded the residence), making
little attempt to harmonize the two, so that the studio obviously
rejected the middle-class predictability the house so clearly represented. Whereas the house fronted on quiet residential Forest
Avenue, soon to have six more of his designs, the studio faced busy
Chicago Avenue, a main thoroughfare leading directly downtown.
Set farther back from the street than its neighbors, the house
cherished its tranquility, while with precisely the opposite gesture
the studio's steps opened directly on the sidewalk. Obviously, the
buildings had entirely different purposes. In 1895 Wright had
concluded that to avoid conflict his professional activities should
be separate from family obligations: "I didn't see much of him
except at meal time," one of his sons recalled.[23] But this solution
failed: the family continued to intrude. If Wright could not
prevent his private affairs from interfering with his work, perhaps
outside the suburban context and with different living arrangements the two might merge in happier embrace.

Wright hoped that Taliesin at Spring Green would solve the
problem. He built it specifically for Mamah Borthwick,* and as an

---

* After her divorce, Mamah resumed her maiden name. Taliesin is actually
located in the hamlet of Hillside, Iowa County, across the Wisconsin River
from Spring Green, Sauk County.

Frank Lloyd Wright's studio, 1895, Oak Park, Illinois

Partial view of Taliesin I, 1911–1914, Spring Green, Wisconsin

architectural metaphor it reveals more about him in 1911 than anything he wrote. Wright's work and his relationship with Mamah needed a quiet isolation, and in his precarious situation Taliesin was his optimistic attempt to solve the architectural and personal problems that had finally made life in Oak Park impossible. At first glance, however, Spring Green seems an unlikely retreat: Wright could not escape publicity where everyone knew him, within the orbit of the Chicago papers that had made him front-page news. Nor did the disapproval of family and friends lend hospitality to the place. Nevertheless, there were compelling reasons to choose the family seat. Since he expected to lose commissions, building on his mother's land would reduce expenses, while nearby limestone deposits meant cheap materials. He looked for inspiration from the landscape he had loved as a boy. In leaving Oak Park he had rejected family responsibility and violated social norms; the return to Spring Green was a pilgrimage to the safety of childhood familiarities.

Taliesin made provision for all Wright's needs. Intended to be self-sufficient, it included, in addition to living quarters and drafting rooms, an icehouse, recreational facilities, stables, a granary, a power plant, and its own water supply. Unlike the architecturally simpler studio-home in Oak Park, Taliesin was consistent in style, materials, and expression, despite its functional diversity. In the earlier buildings Wright had declared his work more unconventional than his family, but found that the separation of the two preserved the integrity of neither. Placing his faith in new surroundings and happier personal relationships, he now reunited his roles under one roof. Taliesin expanded the central theme of the Oak Park studio by stating unequivocally that Wright alone would define the rules governing his personal as well as his professional life. As much a declaration of independence as his recent actions, and as much an autobiography as the book he later published, Taliesin was an index to Wright's psychological and intellectual attitudes in 1911.

There are several ways to analyze the significance of this famous building. First of all, it was environment-embracing, nestled around and into a hilltop, but not on it; hence its name, which is Welsh for "shining brow," since it was built into the brow, not placed on top, of the hill. Often it was difficult to determine where the building ended and the topography began. Vaguely L-shaped with appendages, including an extended wall garden that rooted it to its site, its long window series and overhanging eaves brought the outside in, while its layers of fieldstone symbolically reproduced nearby rock strata. There were courtyards, fountains, trees, and plantings everywhere, firmly establishing an intimate relationship with the outdoors. But if Wright was maximizing contact with nature—to him friendly and inspirational—he was also minimizing contact with a suspicious and critical world.

From another point of view Taliesin was a kind of stone fortress, overlooking the countryside from its commanding hilltop. Its floor plan and the hill behind made it accessible only by exposed routes. Taliesin's ground-hugging arrangement, its low eaves, sheltered windows, and enclosing courtyards rendered it secure, from both climate and visitors. Its remote rooms and numerous gardens, where privacy was augmented by strategically placed shrubbery, contributed to the retreatlike atmosphere. Taliesin's very complexity was itself a protective measure, understood by inhabitants but disconcerting to outsiders. Many of these defensive motifs had been features in the prairie house (of which Taliesin was an outstanding example) but were developed further here. It is not insignificant, of course, that of all the available sites on the tract of several hundred acres, Wright chose to build on the hilltop rather than in the valley, a decision enhancing Taliesin's psychological strength and its aesthetic success.

There is yet a third way, possibly the most significant, to interpret this building. Wright had written that a successful house would "marry" site so "intimately"—would so accurately express its surroundings, in other words—that it could be built nowhere else. Taliesin performed such a marriage. House and nature—indoors and out—were merged easily and gradually by innumerable architectural symbols and devices. But if the wedding was an artistic success, it was also a social experiment, for Taliesin made overtures to Spring Green, his new community. Unlike most of Wright's houses between 1915 and 1935, Taliesin did not throw up intimidating barriers between itself and outsiders, despite its obvious protective measures. (It was a defensive building, in other words, not an aggressive one.) Taliesin symbolically integrated Wright's private domain with the outside world of the community, a group of farm families—in 1911, some 730 people—he had known for over thirty years. An optimistic prophecy in stone of the social relationship Wright cherished, Taliesin could not in fact have been built elsewhere. Years later he wrote: "There was a house that hill might marry and live happily with ever after."24 He might also have written: "There was a town that I might marry. . . ." Although Taliesin's controlled access indicated that contact would be initiated by the architect and on his terms, Wright wanted to build bridges to his neighbors.

Wright's desire—his need, in fact—to convince Spring Green that his recent actions were purposeful and that his presence was not a threat, led him on Christmas Day, 1911, to call a press conference, and on several subsequent days to issue statements attempting to clarify his position. Another motive behind his outspokenness was a kind of missionary zeal for propagandizing his firmly held but unpopular ideas. Silence about his extramarital relations would probably have been the wisest course, but, instead of letting the affair blow over, he courted a confrontation. His insistence that people listen to him exposed a peculiar symbiotic relationship with public opinion: on the one hand, every time he made a comment he further alienated a society unable to tolerate such flagrant violations of its mores; but, on the other, his persistence in speaking out revealed his compulsive attention—despite his actions—to social sentiment. Had he been a complete iconoclast he would have said nothing at all, let alone make conciliatory gestures. But he had to make a living and to coexist with his neighbors; his new role as a critic of social customs and advocate of moral reform, while putting him on the defensive, also obliged him to speak his mind.

In the "Christmas message" Wright offered an interpretation of the events leading to his removal from Oak Park. He and Catherine had grown irreconcilably apart, primarily because she had devoted herself to the children while he became absorbed in his work—neither was particularly to blame. Far from harming his family by leaving it, he had actually acted in its best interests, he claimed. Not only had he left it financially secure, but the new arrangement would in the long run be beneficial: living with another woman would be an example of integrity to the children, whereas to have lived a lie in their presence would only warp their character. The basic conflict in his own life, he said, had been between professional and domestic obligations: he could not simultaneously be a father and an architect. There had come a point when giving "expression to certain ideals in architecture" became more important than fatherhood, and since he was essentially an artist, he had discovered that his buildings were his *real* children. More than anything else he had wanted to develop an organic architecture, "American in spirit. . . . I feel I have succeeded in that," he said, and if the world rejected his work because of recent events, "it will be a misfortune."

Wright disclosed what was really on his mind in the last section of his statement. He admitted violating social mores, but he claimed to have been loyal to a "higher law." Prohibitions and laws "are made for the average," he declared. "The ordinary man cannot live without rules to guide his conduct. It is infinitely more difficult to live without [them] but that is what a really honest, sincere, thinking man is compelled to do. And I think," said Wright, now speaking more autobiographically, "that when he has displayed some spiritual power, has given concrete evidence of his ability to see and to feel the higher and better things of life, we ought to go slow in deciding he has acted badly."[25] Since the artist contributed to the improvement of society, Wright was arguing, it ought to trust his judgment in moral matters and absolve him from its petty obligations.

Since neither Wright nor the reporters were satisfied with the Christmas statement, he decided to prepare another, but in the meantime issued several short comments critizing the institutions of marriage and family for their tendency to turn people into property. No person should be "owned" by another, he said, as wives and husbands now legally "own" each other. He also assured Spring Green that he was not interested in defying convention, but simply wanted to work. "The fact that I am here in the 'front yard' of my family is sufficient proof . . . I have come to mind my own business in my own way. . . ." On December 30, Wright released his "last word," accurate from his point of view, he insisted. Reading his statement in the third person, he referred only to "four people, a wife and a man and a husband and a woman." He described the affair as if it had happened to someone else, as if it were a hypothetical situation from which he was abstracting great lessons for society's instruction. He told how a man and a woman had fallen in love, how they had waited a year to be sure, and how they had gone to Europe with the knowledge of all concerned. The husband and the wife, of course, tried to separate the lovers without understanding that the bond that held them was far stronger than mere infatuation.

During the year they had remained with their families "to make certain that love was love," "all was wretched, all false, all wasted." But they learned they could live honestly and happily only with each other, regardless of the social consequences. To abide by society's dictates and to stay with their legal mates was a mockery, and by 1909 their lives had become a lie. By the time the man returned to his family after a year with the woman in Europe, he had concluded there was no recourse but to make the ultimate break. "Thus may be written the drama that is played now in countless cases behind the curtain," Wright remarked bluntly, "so that honest souls may profit. And most will call it the triumph of 'selfishness.' I cannot care. . . ." Perhaps the truth is but "the 'selfishness' of nature."[26] He had recounted his and Mamah's leap of faith, he implied, so that others might take courage and follow their example, for integrity and happiness were far more important than legality. Such sensational views, of course, were eagerly received by the press, but unfortunately not by Spring Green.

Speaking for the community, *The Weekly Home News* saw a dangerous threat in Wright's behavior. Holding fast to traditional and provincial values, editor W. R. Purdy believed that "no man and no woman can live in the relation which these two brazenly flaunt and explain it to law-abiding, God-fearing people" without perpetuating an "insult to decency." The couple was "a menace to the morals of a community and an insult to every family therein." Their former spouses were better off without them, Purdy contended, since Wright and his companion were "either insane or degenerate." Far from being Mrs. Cheney's "soul-mate," Wright was merely engaging in a publicity stunt designed to bring even "more advertising than his knee-panties, long hair and other funny ways. . . ." The most tragic aspect of this affair, Purdy thought, was undoubtedly its impact on the Lloyd Joneses. As teachers and ministers, doing "all in their power to discourage vice and immorality," they were "disgusted, humiliated, and chagrined" by Wright's actions. The architect replied to Purdy's blast shortly after the New Year. He denied any intention of dragging scandal to the community, and said his behavior was not prompted by immorality or bravado. Praising Spring Green's "consideration and courtesy," he expressed his "admiration for the dignity [it] has maintained in this onslaught of slanderous insult." Someday, he promised, he would be "valuable and helpful to the people here. . . ."[27]*

* Fifty years later, cultural historian Alan Gowans upbraided Wright in terms Purdy would have appreciated. Wright thought himself superior to the many architects around 1910 who were clearly his equals, Gowans contends. Having read Herbert Spencer, he appointed himself the harbinger of a new America; since his mission was to herald the coming of the superman, Wright could arrogantly disregard society's customs and morals. In an age of great national achievement, few men wanted to be around people like Wright and, gathering from his tone, neither would Gowans (*Images of American Living: Four Centuries of Architecture and Furniture as Cultural Expression* [Philadel-

In any small town the newspaper editor is one of the principal spokesmen and formulators of public opinion. Since Wright coveted acceptance by the community, he had no intention of antagonizing Purdy—and everybody else—by replying to him in kind. So he showed humility and respect: "Give me the benefit of the doubt," he asked. "I like you people, and want to stay here with you," he wrote during another crisis a few years later.[28] Although he needed Spring Green in 1912 much more than it needed him, he still put severe strains upon its generosity. Promising nothing more than to be good, and to be a positive force "someday," he asked his neighbors to ignore the past and present irregularities that offended them so deeply.

He made equally difficult demands of his predominantly urban clientele. In Oak Park he had been minutes away from the Chicago Loop, where he maintained a business office.[29] Now his remote location forced clients to write or to make an arduous excursion to Taliesin. Hiring Frank Lloyd Wright after he moved to Wisconsin involved a ritualistic demonstration of how much he was needed, which is exactly what he wanted to know.

phia: Lippincott, 1964], pp. 414–417). Most of Gowans' contentions are actually quite untenable.

5. SPIRITUAL HEGIRA, PROFESSIONAL HIATUS

[1910–1914]

During the period of his involvement with Mamah Borthwick, Frank Lloyd Wright produced three architectural landmarks and three influential essays. A successful exhibition in Chicago enhanced his national stature, and his German publications made him a Continental celebrity. Yet he seemed to be preoccupied and, despite his accomplishments, to be characteristically uninterested in his work. Many of his designs were mechanical adaptations of earlier prairie houses, uninspired replicas of aging ideas. Occasionally, as in the case of the Midway Gardens and the Imperial Hotel, his imagination was stimulated and he rose to the challenge, but his thoughts were often elsewhere. These were years of reflection and self-evaluation, of restructuring private and social relationships, and of working out his philosophy. These were the first of the "in-between" years, the beginning of a quarter-century hiatus separating periods of major achievement.

Frank Lloyd Wright received twenty-two commissions in 1911, three more than ever before, leading some observers to believe that he had weathered the storm of the previous year quite handily. But a broader perspective shows 1911 to have been an aberration, for outspokenness and scandal had indeed damaged his practice. His twenty-one executions out of fifty-three commissions from 1910 to 1914 were conspicuously fewer than the fifty-seven of eighty-four in the preceding half-decade. Wright built only thirteen of thirty-one designs during the four years he actually lived with Mamah Borthwick (1910, 1912–1914), and of that thirteen two were alterations to existing structures, one was an addition to the Avery Coonley Estate, and another was a replacement for Taliesin. The most graphic measure of Wright's plummeting fortunes, however, was that in 1912, 1913, and 1914 he executed a total of only six full-fledged buildings for paying customers. Several of his clients had known him before 1910, so it appears that his two highly publicized "spiritual hegiras" with Mamah—to Europe and to Wisconsin—kept almost everyone but a few old friends from making the pilgrimage to Spring Green.[1]

With his building opportunities considerably circumscribed, he devoted more attention to writing, in 1910 and 1912 publishing important essays that further illuminated his concept of "organic architecture." Together they constitute his most lucid and comprehensive philosophical statement before the 1930s, when, in a torrent of books, articles, and lectures, his innovative thinking reached its peak. In the first of the essays, the introduction to *Ausgeführte Bauten und Entwürfe von Frank Lloyd Wright* (1910), written in Italy during his elopement with Mamah Borthwick, Wright placed himself firmly in a specific architectural tradition. The second, the short incisive text of *The Japanese Print: An Interpretation* (1912), a highly autobiographical theory of the artist's methodology and social function, has generally been neglected, since it was not specifically concerned with buildings. Wright's third noteworthy essay of the period—"In the Cause of Architecture, II" (1914)—added little to his philosophy, but is important as a personal evaluation and a professional critique.

Wright opened his introduction to the 1910 German portfolio[2] by remarking that his recent tour of Italian buildings and art had verified two things he already knew: while the "false ideals" of the Renaissance stifled organic architecture, the "Gothic spirit" encouraged it. Like folklore and folk song, a truly organic building was indigenous—intimately interrelated with environment and with the habits of the people. Unlike other styles, Gothic architecture had responded to actual needs, had been built by methods and tools appropriate to its time and place, and had looked to "natural law" for its structural principles and expressive forms. Renaissance or "inorganic" architecture, on the other hand, had pasted imitations of old styles over outmoded construction techniques, had ignored nature to eulogize curiosities, had disregarded contemporary needs and living habits, and had failed to develop its own standard of beauty. By copying classical antiquity, Wright charged, the Renaissance had perpetuated tired concepts and dead forms and was, architecturally, the antithesis of creativity.

He was not advocating a Gothic revival—"the conditions and ideals that fixed the forms of the twelfth are not [those] that can truthfully fix the forms of the twentieth century"—simply a reinvigoration of the Gothic spirit. An interpretation of the best traditions using contemporary architectural language, the "spirit" of which, he wrote, was "not a stupid attempt to fasten [ancient] forms upon a life that has outgrown them." On the contrary, if modern architecture embraced the Gothic attitude it would necessarily acknowledge national aspirations—democratic institutions, personal liberty, and technological change. With machinery dictating its methods, and democratic individualism its organization and appearance, organic design would be an outgrowth of the conditions of life and work it arose to express. Anything else would deny the character of the twentieth century, and, like the inorganic creations of the Renaissance, would be absolutely removed from time, place, or people—"borrowed finery put on hastily," not developed "from within."

With the exception of Louis Sullivan's work, Wright claimed, his was the first consistent protest—in five hundred years, be it noted—against the "pitiful waste" of the Renaissance. It was a serious attempt to formulate industrial and aesthetic ideals—based on native tools and living conditions—for American residential design. Since the real national characteristics of broadmindedness, independent thought and judgment, and common sense were primarily western and midwestern, the Gothic spirit would most likely take root there. Although the fashion-setters still preferred outmoded Old World styles, Wright believed the public would eventually rebel against their artistic tyranny and heed the businessman—that repository of clear thinking—who rarely made a wrong choice in architectural matters. Standing ahead of public opinion, many no-nonsense, hardheaded, practical-minded business leaders—the best and most representative Americans, Wright thought—had already recognized the advantages (but not the cultural import) of his designs. They are "part and parcel and helpful in producing the organic thing. They can comprehend it. . . . It is thus the only form of art expression . . . for a democracy, and, I will go so far as to say, the truest of all forms."

The concept of organic architecture was based on several as yet unstated assumptions. Implicit was Wright's notion that truth and beauty were not relative but absolute, waiting for discovery and expression by the artist who probed the fundamental law and order inherent in every existing thing. Wright believed that everything—every tool, client, rock, building, or flower—had an essential truth about it, an unchanging and absolutely unique "nature." Once the nature of a problem, for example, was understood, its solution became obvious. Since any given building was nothing more than the solution to a specific human and architectural problem, an organic design would be the only, inevitable expression of the conditions that had called it into being, conditions the architect would discover, since his primary obligation was to explore the "nature" of everything he encountered. Hence, a man disciplined by a conception of the organic nature of his task, knowing his tools and his opportunity, "working out his problems with what sense of beauty the gods gave him," is governed by the very nature of his undertaking. Clients could trust him implicitly because, limited by organic law, he was "the only safe man."

The goal for which he searched, Wright stated, was unity. Every aspect of a building—the furniture, light fixtures, rugs, pictures, heating apparatus, and downspouts—should be harmonious. If the architect envisioned appurtenances as solutions to problems within an organic whole, each aspect of the project would assume its inevitable place and form, as leaves and branches took theirs on a tree. The same principle, he said, applied to buildings in relation to each other. Given similar tools and social conditions, and a proper regard for organic principle, Wright believed that architects would arrive at mutually harmonious conclusions. If all the organic buildings in the world—prairie and Gothic, tall and short, pointed and square, horizontal and vertical, in their "bewildering variety"—were put in one place, "harmony in the general ensemble [would] inevitably result; the common chord . . . being sufficient to bring them all unconsciously into harmonious relation." Far from contradicting each other, the combined efforts of all the American architects committed to organic principles would ultimately constitute an authentic native genre.

The self-consciously American architect closed his German essay by admitting his designs owed "their debt to Japanese ideals," his most explicit reference yet to that source of inspiration. It was appropriate, therefore, that his next important statement of aesthetic and philosophical principles was *The Japanese Print* (1912), a short but impressive book not directly concerned with architecture.[3] Several scholars trace Wright's interest in Japan to displays at the 1893 Columbian Exposition in Chicago.[4] However influential that event may have been, he made but one passing reference to Japan—in the 1901 Hull House lecture—before visiting it from February to April 1905, his first overseas excursion. He returned with enough prints and with sufficient expertise to stage an exhibition at the Chicago Art Institute in March 1906 and to publish *Hiroshige*, a descriptive essay in catalogue form. By 1912 he was a nationally known expert on Japanese painting, on his way to building "one of the most important collections . . . in the world," a fact not generally appreciated by Wright scholars.[5] Had he not succeeded at architecture, he might conceivably have fashioned a career out of the study of Oriental art.

In *The Japanese Print* Wright turned several of his 1910 assumptions into explicit statements. He took as his own the platonic notion that "the laws of the beautiful are like the laws of physics. . . . They pre-exist any perception of them." A thing was beautiful because its very essence was an embodiment and a significant expression of "that precious something in ourselves" we know to be life. Therefore a true work of art—an organic conception—derived its life from the absolute beauty of the creative effort, while its structure and form was a calculated organization of its parts into a larger unity—a vital whole—which must always persuade us of its reasonableness. The grammar of structure was geometry, and Wright believed that certain shapes were endowed with "spell power." The circle, for example, indicated infinity; the spire, aspiration; the spiral, organic process; the triangle, structural unity; and the square, integrity. The artist might express his idea of the beautiful and find the hidden core of reality by knowing the value-laden nature of these shapes, which were "fundamental verities of structure, pre-existing and surviving particular embodiments in [the] material world."

Of all artists, Wright averred, the Japanese print maker was best at giving form to Idea through geometry. After studying a pine tree, for example, he would attempt to express not its literal appearance but its very nature, those essentials that made it a pine and not an oak or a maple. If the species disappeared from the earth, he would be able to preserve it for all time with a few lines and simple shapes because he had mastered its specific and distinguishing characteristics—its nature. By "nature" Wright meant neither the great outdoors with its plants and animals, as he once had, nor "that outward aspect that strikes the eye as a visual image," but that "inner harmony which permeates the outward form . . . and is its determining character; that quality in the thing . . . that is its significance and it's [sic] Life for us,—what Plato called . . . the 'eternal Idea of the thing,' " knowable by patient, sympathetic study.

The central problem for the artist, therefore, was to put his Idea of the nature of something—for an architect, a building—into appropriate form. Since ideas existed only by virtue of their forms, which, in turn, could never be detached from ideas, Wright insisted in the best Socratic manner that there was inevitably but one way for a particular artist to express anything—flower, emotion, or dwelling place. And that expression, furthermore, should include only what was absolutely necessary to convey his meaning. The Japanese had perfected the technique of stringent simplification—"elimination of the insignificant and consequent emphasis on reality." By stripping away nonessentials they arrived at the nature of the object—its geometry, its pure form, its fundamental, irreducible substance. The trick, of course, was to know when to stop simplifying. While "more would have been profane," Wright explained, "less would have failed of the intended effect." Like Japanese prints, organic architecture occupied a tenuous position somewhere between profanity and failure.

To simplify, Wright continued, was in a sense to dramatize, and to dramatize was to conventionalize, a concept that seems to have dropped from the artistic vocabulary in subsequent years. Conventionalization was the process of capturing essence—of reducing a subject to its fundamentals—for the purpose of preserving it indefinitely. Western art was based on precisely the opposite instincts, Wright claimed, upon imitation, literal reproduction, and realism. It lived on surfaces, unconcerned with interpretation or with searching for the living conception that gave life to the artist's subjects. Ancient Egypt had understood conventionalization, and her art was everything Western art was not. Egypt knew the lotus, for example, "and translated the flower to the dignified stone forms of her architecture. Such was the lotus conventionalized. . . . If Egypt . . . had plucked the flowers as they grew, and given us a mere imitation of them in stone, the stone forms would have died with the original." But her artists passed the very principles of "lotusness" through a spiritual process whereby its nature was intensified and adapted to practical use. Thus the lotus gained everlasting life.

The process of conventionalization held crucial implications for mankind itself, as well as for organic architecture. The main problem in any society, Wright thought, was its continuing struggle to domesticate or civilize itself. In the search for the right ordering of human life, society—though well intentioned—usually institutionalized friction and discord. Real civilization, the true goal of social organization, would be

a right conventionalizing of our original state of nature, just such a conventionalizing as the true artist imposes on natural forms. The lawgiver and reformer of social customs must have, however, the artist's soul . . . if the light of the race is not to go out. So, art is not alone the expression, but in turn the great conservator and transmitter of the finer sensibilities of a people. More still, it is to show . . . just where and how we shall bring coercion to bear upon the majority of human conduct. So the indigenous art of a people is their only true prophecy and their school of anointed prophets and kings. Our own art is the only light by which . . . "civilization" may eventually make its institutions harmonious with the fairest conditions of our individual and social life.

So if civilization was obliged to fit the natural man into "this great piece of architecture we call the social state," it must rely on its artists—not its scientists, clergymen, or politicians—to reconcile society harmoniously with the life-principle of all men. Behind all social institutions, Wright insisted, was the artist's vision, for he alone could translate into structure and form the essence of what it meant to be human and to live happily with others.

Wright had stated these ideas more primitively at his Taliesin press conference, December 25, 1911. Then he had argued that society should recognize the artist's unique social functions, his special ability to understand human nature, and, because of his contribution to the general welfare, absolve him from tedious obligations and responsibilities. Having demonstrated his allegiance to a "higher law," he should be exempted from the rules and regulations governing "average" people. Now, less than a year later, Wright urged the artist to take an active leadership role, to bait the hook rather than get off it. Since society's peace required a harmonious interrelationship of parts similar to organic architecture, who better to give laws and administer state than the architect himself? Wright did not repeat these suggestions until the 1930s, when his Broadacre City plans featured the architect, with sweeping regulatory powers, as head of state. (Always a staunch opponent of political fascism and any kind of government centralization, Wright may not have detected the authoritarian implications of his own ideas.)

Nevertheless, *The Japanese Print* was an extended metaphor, if not for political, then certainly for architectural, considerations, for it was obvious that in analyzing print making Wright was actually describing the methods by which he worked and the objectives he himself sought. *The Japanese Print* revealed the many affinities between that art form and his architecture, not so much in the visual similarities of structure and expression, but in philosophy and technique. The book was one of Wright's most coherent statements of the function of art and of the principles upon which his own work was based. Unfortunately, it has been buried under the mountain of his later writings, its importance reduced by the imprecision of his later prose.

Wright's knowledge of Japanese art may have helped him land the commission for the massive Imperial Hotel in Tokyo. Since the emperor intended it to serve as a social center for Japan's growing number of North American and European visitors, he wanted a Western architect, and none was more sympathetic to the East than Wright. His version of how he received the commission, however, does not coincide with the facts of the matter. A delegation of prominent Japanese had been touring the world in search of just the right architect, Wright recalled in his autobiography, when they came upon several of his prairie buildings near Chicago. Impressed, they offered him the job after he drew a preliminary sketch during their week-long stay at Taliesin, sometime in early 1915. Actually, the circumstances were a bit different. It is now known that Wright secured the commission as well as approval for a detailed preliminary plan during his visit to Japan with Mamah Borthwick—at the invitation of the emperor—from January to May 1913. So if a delegation reached Taliesin it must have been in 1912, although there is no mention of it in the contemporary sources. For most of the year after his return to the United States, Wright labored over the working drawings, which were finally put off until 1916, interrupted among other things by his rush to complete the spectacular but short-lived Midway Gardens.[6]

The block-long pleasure palace on Chicago's Midway Plaissance at Cottage Grove Avenue was demolished in 1929, but for a year or two before Prohibition was a unique experiment in American entertainment. The idea was to create a Continental *garten* with facilities for opera, classical and popular music, indoor and outdoor dining, dancing, banquets, and liquid refreshment. Commissioned late in 1913 by Edward Waller, Jr., the son of one of Wright's first clients, and designed very rapidly, the $350,000 structure opened in August 1914 after frenzied construction. Despite initial fanfare, the owners soon went bankrupt, and in 1916 sold to the Edelweiss Brewing Company. The reasons for failure were not architectural, but can be traced to World War I's inhibiting impact on night life, to the Gardens' untimely association in the public mind with Germany, to Chicago's reluctance to experiment with unfamiliar styles of recreation, and to Midway's location in an ethnically changing residential neighborhood some distance from the Loop. Edelweiss turned the place into a grandiose tavern with a working-class clientele. After Prohibition it changed hands several times, serving as a garage and a car wash before its demolition—along with the stock market—in October 1929. Wright had virtually dissociated himself from Midway by this time, but derived a certain satisfaction when its sturdy construction drove razing costs high enough to put the contractor out of business.[7]

Despite its short life, the Gardens was a brilliant achievement, Wright's personal attempt to reestablish the pre-Renaissance situation when, he had claimed at Hull House, "all other arts simply obeyed and placed themselves under the discipline of architecture."[8] Midway was Wright's Gothic cathedral, in which music, painting, and sculpture were subordinate aspects of his master plan—"a synthesis of all the Arts," as he put it. Whether he actually solved the acoustical problems of the orchestra pit himself is unknown, but his work in the other arts was especially innovative. The murals, sculpture, painting, and windows, which reflected the overall themes of the structure, were mostly of his own making. "The remarkable thing," one scholar writes, is that although his nonobjective creations were entirely his own, they were "almost exactly contemporary parallels to the work of the

most advanced French and German painters and sculptors." Indeed, Midway's cubist, abstract, and semicubist adornments were as important—if not more prophetic—in the unfolding of the American modernist movement as the famous Armory Show of 1913.[9]

The Gardens itself was a massive, complicated brick and concrete edifice, with a myriad of individually articulated members—so visually stimulating they were almost distracting—yet somehow harmoniously resolved. At the same time playful and dignified, spacious and intimate, the Gardens' union of opposites and its orderly arrangement of disparate pieces gave functional coherence and a pleasing aspect to the ofttimes bewildering complexities of urban living. Its demolition after only two years of intended purpose and more than a decade of abuse was itself symbolic of urban unpredictability (some might say decay), and was a tragic loss to American architecture. For, as one happy Chicagoan remarked in

Midway Gardens, 1914, Chicago.
View across restaurant

1914, Midway Gardens was "the finest thing of the kind in the country . . . if not in Europe, to boot."[10]

The Gardens, Taliesin, and the preliminary plans for the Imperial Hotel were Wright's best designs during his years with Mamah. However, measured against the consistent quality of his Oak Park work, the period as a whole was comparatively undistinguished. The Herbert C. Angster House in Lake Bluff, Illinois, the A. M. Cutten and Edward Schroeder projects in Downer's Grove and Milwaukee (all in 1911), and the William B. Green House (1912) in Aurora, Illinois, are typical of Wright's generally unimaginative late prairie work. The house for Harry S. Adams (1912) in Oak Park bears a very close resemblance to that for Frank Thomas (1901) down the street, and the impressive "Northome" (1913) for Francis Little in Wayzata, Minnesota, which nevertheless failed to take full advantage of Lake Minnetonka, is sterile and impersonal in parts of the interior, and on the outside is redundant and uncertain, a missed opportunity on a

William B. Green House, 1912, Aurora, Illinois

gigantic scale. These and other buildings are the products of an uninterested architect who, unchallenged by his commissions and distracted by personal matters, mechanically reproduced ideas he had worked out before, tired variations on an old formula.

A smaller group of slab roof designs were also related to earlier experiments, though generally of higher quality than the more representative prairie house. The Carnegie Library project (1913) in Ottawa is quite similar to the unexecuted Yahara Boat Club (1902) in Madison, Wisconsin, and the design for a State Bank (1914) in Spring Green is a much-refined version of the Village Bank Wright had published in *The Brickbuilder* in 1901. The ancestry of others, however, is not so obvious. The O. B. Balch House (1911) in Oak Park is pleasing but uninspiring. Of the two homes he designed for himself but never built, the 1911 Goethe Street residence in Chicago—closely related to the Kehl Dance Academy project (1912) in Madison—was compact, elaborately trimmed, and vertically articulated, clearly superior to the horizontal, awkward, and rather dull studio-home (1910) for Fiesole, Italy. The best of the slab buildings was the kindergarten project (1911) for Avery Coonley in Riverside, Illinois, closely rivaled the same year by Coonley's Playhouse, which also acknowledged the Yahara Boat Club. With its abstract leaded windows, its balanced massing, and its shifting, interrelated planes and surfaces, the Playhouse led directly to Midway Gardens a year later, and in some respects to the Usonian homes of the 1930s.

The original version (1911) of the Sherman Booth House—one of Wright's finest designs during these years—illustrates other developments in his work. Like a number of its contemporaries (the Angster and Little houses, and Taliesin) the Booth project was obscured by trees in a distinctly nonurban setting, and, as Henry-Russell Hitchcock has noticed, its floor plan was more open and its exterior more massive than the typical prairie house of the preceding decade.[11] To reemphasize privacy, protectiveness, and interior mutuality was hardly a step forward for Wright, but perhaps they were the only devices available; certainly he dwelled on these themes even more strongly in the 1920s. Like the Cutten project, Taliesin, and even Northome, the original Booth plan sent horizontal wings—and a porte cochere, a bridge, and a pergola—spinning off in several directions from a central core. Its symmetry and system of ordering were even more abstract than the Robie or Coonley houses—indicating that Wright was still exploring the implications of "form follows function"—and like Taliesin it was excellently sited, in this case linking two ravines. When the Booth House was finally erected in 1915, without Wright's supervision, it was a pale imitation of the original, despite the success of its spacious living room.

Three nonresidential buildings also deserve brief attention. The hotel at Lake Geneva, Wisconsin, designed in the summer and fall of 1911, was a block-long, two-story rectangle, to have been intersected twice by cross axes of porches, public rooms, and patios. Its gently sloping site was intended to be a landscaped garden, culminating in a pavilion-boathouse at the lake shore. Most of this was never built, and the finished product looks a great deal like Wright's National Park recreation building (1912?) in Banff, Alberta. Both illustrate how closely his public and private structures resembled each other, and how easily he could adapt his architectural system to various kinds of problems. In this respect the unexecuted twenty-six-story tower for the San Francisco Call (1912) is also noteworthy. Its emphatic vertical articulation had its origin in the best work of Louis Sullivan, but its concrete-slab construction left a heavier, more textured surface than most skyscrapers. Its far-projecting roof ended in pergola slabs like the Coonley Playhouse, and its ornate lower facade—with recessed entry, greenery-dripping urns, spandrel-friezes, and elaborate trim —closely resembled the Goethe Street and Kehl Academy projects.

Wright's most successful buildings during his interlude with Mamah Borthwick were called up by special circumstances. Confronted with exceptionally difficult challenges, like the Midway Gardens and the Imperial Hotel, he produced exceptional designs. He performed equally well when he was personally involved: in the case of Taliesin, of course, for his attorney Sherman Booth, and for Avery Coonley, by this time a good friend. Wright also performed creditably in the concrete-slab genre, where he was no stranger and which he knew offered numerous possibilities, as the 1920s would demonstrate. With these exceptions, however, the majority of his commissions did not seem greatly to interest him; apparently neither the landscape nor Mamah Borthwick offered sufficient inspiration to make architecture live again.

He was certain, however, that his waning enthusiasm was not entirely his fault, but was partly due to professionalization. So repellent had the very notion become that in 1914 he severed his ties with friend and foe alike by publishing "In the Cause of Architecture, II" in the May *Architectural Record*. In a strongly worded attack on the Chicago School, he claimed sole responsibility for its every distinguishing characteristic, and insisted that he "alone, absolutely alone," had developed the prairie residence. The essay added almost nothing to his philosophy but it was nonetheless crucial, for it marked his sharp break with all professional groups and his assumption of a completely independent posture. It was also his first proclamation of the "persecuted genius" legend, the interpretation of his life as a continuous battle against overwhelming odds, as a struggle for principle despite social ostracism, professional ignorance, financial loss, ridicule, and rejection. Having hewn his personal independence and uncompromising architecture out of the rock of skepticism and conflict, so the story goes, he was proved correct over and over again. Begun by Wright in 1914, and perpetuated by his admirers until the present day, the "persecuted genius" legend later became a crucial aspect of his self-image.[12]

Twenty years before, in 1893, Wright contended in the *Record*, "I took my stand, alone in my field [when] the cause was unprofitable, seemingly impossible, almost unknown, or, . . . as a rule, unhonored and ridiculed." Distinguishing between the reception given to his work—which had more than its share of attention and had attracted to itself "abuses seldom described (never openly attacked)"—and that given to the "cause," Wright claimed that, while the *appearance* of his buildings had been widely copied, his fundamental objectives had received little or no attention. His purpose had never been novelty for its own sake, nor to achieve success in any commonly accepted sense, but to develop an organic architecture, whose principles "are common to all work that ever rang true in the architecture of the world." Thus "the cause" was the revitalization of the profession through the ideals and methods of organic design, and for its sake he "deliberately chose to break with traditions in order to be more true to tradition than current conventions . . . would permit." Since the first day of independent practice, he insisted, he had struggled for this end.

Although Wright did not specifically say so, organic architecture was as much a process as it was a finished product. How the architect arrived at his ideas and developed his plans was as important as the building itself, a factor lost on his many followers. Copying appearances only, he wrote, they had pretentiously put forward "half-baked, imitative designs (fictitious semblances) . . . in the name of a movement . . . , particularly while novelty is the chief popular standard." His buildings had opened a market for "something different" in a period clamoring for reform. The prairie architects who popped up in response, he believed, had advanced his ideas as their own, changing a detail here and adding a touch there. Abandoning original thinking and creative effort, and ignoring the *substance* of his work, they were the new eclectics, the direct descendents of the Victorians he had battled in the 1890s. Although he would be accused of unbecoming motives, he felt obliged for the sake of the cause, he said, to tell the truth: the "New School of the Middle West" had gone sour, "a promising garden seems to have been overcome with weeds." The "movement" had degenerated into just another style, offered for sale to the progressive socially conscious, like colonial, Tudor, and French provincial to the more conservative. In pursuit of the almighty dollar, architects had become "prostitutes," pandering anything— even his own unconventional ideas—as long as it sold.

"In the Cause of Architecture, II" was a literary counterpart of Wright's move to Taliesin. By dissociating himself from the very group of architects he had publicly embraced in 1908, he extended his iconoclasm into his professional life. The 1914 article marked the emergence of Wright's legendary irascibility, of his overblown ego, of his unwillingness to say anything good about his colleagues or their work. In his 1908 "In the Cause" essay, he had prophesied that the "New School of the Middle West" would someday be a significant force in American life, and he had affectionately noted his warm "comradeship" with Robert Spencer, Dwight Perkins, Myron Hunt, and other fellow pioneers on the architectural frontier. But in 1914 he suddenly implied that their only accomplishment had been to follow his lead, that they had no ideas of their own. His words recalled "The Architect" speech of 1900, except that the neophyte's courteous criticism of his elders had devolved into an elder's bitter attack on colleagues and friends. What irked his associates most was not Wright's claim to unrivaled greatness, or his assertion that plagiarizing him was an improvement over plagiarizing the Renaissance, but his suggestion that all their work was derivative, that no one else was any good at all.

There were several reasons for Wright's inflamed rhetoric and passionate accusations. One was certainly his belief, probably incorrect, that several of his commissions had been stolen during his year abroad in 1910. The promoters of Wright's City National Bank and Hotel (1909) in Mason City, Iowa, for example, had planned to finance two small residential communities—Rock Glen and Rock Crest—involving a number of private and public buildings. Wright expected to receive the commission that in 1910 went to Walter Burley Griffin, a former apprentice. Although Griffin's wife, Marion Mahoney, had been a trusted employee for eleven years in the Oak Park office, Wright accused them both of treachery, opening an "unalterable breach" that never healed.[13] Equally unfounded were his suspicions of Herman V. von Holst who, with Mahoney to assist him, had been left in charge of Wright's uncompleted buildings in September 1909. The difficulty here was that drawings of the D. M. Amberg House (1909) in Grand Rapids, considerably altered from Wright's preliminary sketches, were published under the names of von Holst and Marion M. Griffin, without acknowledging him, and also that the E. P. Irving House (1909) in Decatur, Illinois, had led to additional commissions, on the same street, which Wright apparently felt ought to have been his, not von Holst's. So when he charged in December 1911 that his work had been "unscrupulously taken" away, he undoubtedly believed that von Holst, Mahoney, and Griffin, who had landscaped the Decatur group, had capitalized on his absence to take credit for his commissions and to secure additional clients.[14]*

Equally infuriating to Wright were slights from his colleagues, many of which he imagined or exaggerated, although it is clear that by 1912 his ideas were so commonly accepted that his innovating role was being slighted. In that year, for example, Hugh M. Garden, once an occasional draftsman at the Oak Park studio, in an essay entitled "A Style for the Western Plains," described Wright as merely one of many prairie architects. The caption on the untitled illustration of the Coonley House—competing with photographs of several quite inferior buildings—read only, "a house at Riverside, Illinois, that is typical of the so-called 'Chicago School.'" To make matters worse, Garden implied that Louis Sullivan, not Wright, had founded the "western" style of domestic architecture. Another article the same year by Charles

* A complete list of Wright-designed buildings supervised by von Holst has never been assembled, but he certainly worked on the Mason City National Bank and Hotel, and on the homes for D. M. Amberg in Grand Rapids and E. P. Irving in Decatur. The two houses are usually attributed to 1910, but since Wright left preliminary drawings for von Holst to work with, they must have been designed in 1909. Von Holst was also the benefactor of Wright's negotiations regarding "Fairlane," Henry Ford's palatial estate in Dearborn, Michigan, but apparently was unable to hold Ford's interest, for the commission was given to the Pittsburgh architect, W. H. Van Tine. Although Wright never drew a line for Ford, he may have hoped to return to this project, and blamed von Holst for losing it.

White—his collaborator on the River Forest, Illinois, Tennis Club (1906)—extolled the virtues of casement windows, broad eaves, natural wood finish, and harmony between house and site but failed to mention their foremost advocate, demonstrating the extent to which the prairie house had become, as one historian writes, "a standard commodity."[15]

Additional developments in 1913 annoyed Wright even more. The photographs in feature-length articles by Griffin, and by William Purcell and George Elmslie—who received significant attention earlier in their careers than Wright—revealed how heavily their work depended on his, but the texts said nothing at all about his influence or their indebtedness.* The American Institute of Architects seems to have intentionally insulted Wright in 1913 when it chose George Maher, a sometime prairie school designer, and Dwight Perkins, Wright's early associate, to define and explain midwestern "progressive architecture." Their instructions were to analyze their own work, that of Sullivan who had "founded" the genre, of Irving Pond, and of others "whose names do not readily come to mind."[16] Wright was not mentioned; indeed, he appears to have been specifically unmentioned. Clearly, the factors that had encouraged him to close his practice in 1909 were still evident. There had been much "comment," he told

---

* Note the obviously derivative buildings by Purcell and Elmslie, "The Statics and Dynamics of Architecture," *The Western Architect* 19 (January 1913): 1–10 plus plates; and by Walter Burley Griffin, "Trier Center Neighborhood, Winnetka, Illinois," ibid. 20 (August 1913): 67–80 plus plates. Publication of unabashedly imitative work reached its peak in 1915 and 1916. The designs of Purcell and Elmslie extensively illustrated in the January 1915 *Western Architect*, of the Louis Guenzel–William Drummond partnership the next month, and of John S. Van Bergen in April, while skillful and inventive, were obviously dependent on Wright. Drummond's own home, next door to Wright's Isabel Roberts House in River Forest, Illinois, owed its total ambience to the master, while the C. B. Scholes House by Henry K. Holsman was similar enough to Wright's 1901 Arthur Davenport residence (both were also in River Forest) to suggest outright plagiarism. See Peter B. Wight, "Country House Architecture in the Middle West," *The Architectural Record* 40 (October 1916): 291–322.

Harriet Monroe, in reference to his 1914 Chicago Architectural Club exhibition, but "almost no criticism—in fact no criticism," except ad hominum.

By themselves, these incidents do not account for Wright's vehemence in 1914, let alone the forty-five-year antiprofessionalism crusade that followed. There must have been more fundamental impulses at work. Beyond his apparent belief in the existence of a conspiracy to exploit and discredit him, Wright may even have developed a mild paranoia. Certainly he displayed suspicious symptoms. In his essay, for example, he claimed that his buildings had frequently been attacked, but "never openly." Describing his violation of architectural tradition as a "dangerous" course full of "sacrifice" and "severe punishment," he expected it to be "fatal," since only one in a thousand dissenters survived. In private he confirmed his public stance: "I seem to be be-set on all sides," he wrote to Miss Monroe "with prejudiced and sometimes evil intent."[17] This was the language of suspicion and fear, buttressed by a mental set that transformed mundane affairs into cosmic events. Unable to distinguish between normal professional rivalry and ego-gratification, and premeditated attack, Wright interpreted imitation as robbery, ignorance as insult, and competition as open warfare. Expecting his colleagues to express their gratefulness, he did not understand that pirated ideas, pettiness, and envy were the inevitable concomitants of success. Having experienced social ostracism because he had broken society's rules, it was not difficult for Wright to imagine the profession mustering its forces for similar assaults.

But Wright's perceptions were often inaccurate. During his years with Mamah Borthwick, for instance, he continued to receive interested and objective coverage in the architectural press. The W. Scott Thurber Galleries in Chicago and the City National Bank in Mason City (both 1909) were given thorough analysis, though neither were major achievements.[18] Taliesin was lavishly praised several times in word and picture.[19] Montgomery Schuyler reviewed Wright's Wasmuth portfolio in 1912, pointing out the "real impressiveness of these designs." Like Schuyler, Harriet Monroe had reservations about Wright's work, but urged the public to attend his exhibition at the Chicago Architectural Club in April 1914. Even his unsparing "In the Cause" essay was praised for its frankness and courage by The Western Architect's editors, who admired Wright's philosophical integrity.[20] There were uncomplimentary remarks, of course, but a perusal of the professional literature indicates no significant change in the kinds and amount of coverage compared to the preceding decade.

In the daily press, Wright gradually moved from the headlines to the second section, and finally out of the news altogether. After his flamboyant remarks in December 1911, he and Mamah withdrew into a quiet, detached, almost remote existence, and, try as they might, the papers found very little to report. Safe within the walls of Taliesin, however, Wright made no compromise with the perquisites of the artist's life: he paid his bills reluctantly, with little regard for financial responsibility; he dressed individualistically, in Norfolk jacket, high laced boots, riding pants, and flowing tie; and with Mamah he continued to translate Goethe's poetry and the unpopular feminism of Ellen Key. One newspaper noted his "several mysterious trips" to Madison, where on one occasion he paced the streets for hours with a large bundle under his arm, finally meeting an unknown couple with whom he rushed to the railroad station. And, of course, his living arrangements and general life-style were by most standards "unconventional."[21]

Still, if Wright and Mamah kept to themselves, they did not shun contact with their neighbors, but tried to establish at least a modicum of friendly relations. The architect employed local craftsmen to build and maintain Taliesin, and purchased his supplies in town. He had, of course, taken care to explain himself to the community, and there is no indication that he replied in kind to hostility, like W. R. Purdy's editorial in December 1911. For her part, Mamah was gracious in her limited social contacts, a fact appreciated and remarked upon. She, too, shopped in Spring Green and, despite the heads that turned whenever she appeared

Frank Lloyd Wright around 1914

in public, never lost her poise. In 1913 and 1914 Wright helped organize the art exhibit at the intercounty affair, and his gracious loan of several valuable prints and pieces of pottery made the event a success. Aware of constant scrutiny, the couple kept a discreet distance, but they remained on their best behavior, never totally removed from the fringes of community participation.[22]

By the summer of 1914, the worst seemed to be over for Wright. A threatened police investigation of Taliesin and legal action against its inhabitants had never materialized. The hostile social climate had been considerably mitigated by Mamah's personality and Wright's gestures to the community. His successful exhibition at the Chicago Architectural Club indicated a continuing interest in his work, even if commissions did not immediately increase. Taliesin was finished and widely admired, by art critics and local farmers alike. In mid-August Wright was working strenuously to complete the massive Midway Gardens for a tidy fee and the promise of considerable publicity, with the knowledge that his next effort would be the even more spectacular Imperial Hotel in Tokyo. Having achieved a modus vivendi in his social relationships, and a happy home life with Mamah, Wright looked forward to an expanded market for his architecture.

Then came the most devastating blow of his life. At noontime on August 14, 1914, while Wright was in Chicago at the Midway site, Mamah was presiding at lunch with her two visiting children, three Taliesin employees, and a local craftsman's son. Surreptitiously, the recently hired chef, Julian Carlston, locked them in the dining room, set fires under the windows, and stationed himself at the single exit, killing with an axe those who tried to force their way out. Knowing only that Taliesin was in flames, Wright rushed back on the first train, arriving to find his worst fears confirmed, for, among the ashes of his home, Mamah and the other six lay dead. Emotionally shattered and physically sick, Wright was in part sustained by Mamah's former husband, Edwin Cheney, who had accompanied him to Spring Green, and by many of the very residents who had condemned him three years before.

Working through the night without sleep, they helped extinguish the blaze, salvage Wright's possessions, and search for the murderer, who was found the next morning, hiding in the furnace room rubble.

Carlston's foul deed has never been sufficiently explained. Wright and his son John believed simply that he had gone mad, an adequate interpretation at the time, perhaps, for the tortured architect. Carlston's own story—he was seeking revenge against a fellow employee who had insulted him, and who was dining with the others—does not account for the brutality of a multiple killing. And the rumor that the highly superstitious Barbadian émigré had taken it upon himself to punish Wright's "immorality," prodded by vindictive preaching at a local evangelical church, does not explain why he acted in the architect's absence. A few days after he was jailed Carlston committed suicide, and with him died his secret. After Mamah's simple funeral, on the verge of breakdown, Wright secluded himself in the remaining portion of Taliesin, while outside six armed guards fended off the "morbidly curious" who came to gather souvenirs.[23]

Still in seclusion a few days later, Wright's first action was to thank Spring Green through the pages of The Weekly Home News, the local paper.[24] "To you who have been so invariably kind to us all," he began his eulogy to Mamah, "I would say something to defend a brave and lovely woman" from those who attack her in death as viciously as they did in life. "I am thankful to all who showed her kindness. . . . No community anywhere could have received the trying circumstances of her life . . . in a more high-minded way." Spring Green had shown her sympathy and courtesy, he noted, and "this she won for herself by her innate dignity and gentleness of character." Although their life together had been misrepresented, and although Mamah was even now referred to as "another man's wife," she was a noble woman who valued her freedom more than motherhood, wifehood, or chastity, and who had the courage to live by her convictions.

"We lived frankly and sincerely," without secrecy or pretense,

Wright insisted, "and we have tried to help others live . . . according to their ideals." Mamah was not a slave to theory; her unorthodox existence was not intended as a demonstration of Ellen Key's principles, and had nothing to do with so-called free love. "The 'freedom' in which we joined," he maintained, "was infinitely more difficult than any conformity with customs. . . . Few will ever venture it." Lives like ours do not threaten society but "can only serve to ennoble it." There were lessons to be learned from Mamah's example, Wright informed his readers: "You wives with your certificates for loving—pray that you may love as much and be loved as well as was Mamah Borthwick! You mothers and fathers with daughters—be satisfied if what life you have invested in them works itself out upon as high a plane as it has done in the life of this lovely woman." There is no past, Wright claimed, and there is no future, so unless we realize that Now is Eternity—a thoroughly existentialist notion—"there will come a bitter time when the thought of how much more potent with love and affection that precious 'Present' might have been, will desolate our hearts."

"She is dead. I have buried her in the little Chapel burying ground of my people. . . . The place where she lived with me is a charred and blackened ruin . . . , [but] I shall replace it . . . as nearly as it may be done. I shall set it all up again for the spirit of the mortal that lived in it and loved it—will live in it still. My home will still be there."

Wright closed his eulogy by reproducing a section of Goethe's "Hymn to Nature," which he and Mamah had found in a Berlin bookshop and translated together. It had comforted him once. He hoped it would again.

6. A REGULAR LIFE
IS CUNNINGLY AMBUSHED

[1914–1932]

The affirmation of life in Frank Lloyd Wright's eulogy for Mamah Borthwick did not impress the gods governing his fate, for the next two decades were filled with personal disaster and architectural disappointment. The Imperial Hotel kept him occupied during World War I, but extensive marital and financial difficulties in the 1920s contributed to his own personal and architectural doldrums long before the stock market crash affected the rest of the nation. Just as he successfully resolved the problems that had denied him a share of the Great Prosperity, the depression interfered and he lost many opportunities to build impressive designs. With no work available, he turned to writing and oratory. Generally considered an elder statesman whose career had ended long before, Wright was known by 1932 as a cranky, unpredictable eccentric who criticized others vociferously but who produced little himself.

"Something in him died with her," John Lloyd Wright remembered sadly, "something loveable and gentle . . . in my father" that Mamah Borthwick had nurtured.[1] To escape his sorrow

Wright threw himself into his work, deriving from it more satisfaction—perhaps sustenance is more accurate—than he had for
several years. After seeing to details on the Midway Gardens in the
fall of 1914, he began to rebuild Taliesin (Taliesin II, he called
it), completing it about a year later. Shortly thereafter he published his first planned community—an outline for a suburban
quarter section—and made preparations for the commercial distribution of his "American System Ready-Cut" standardized houses,
a scheme for low-cost apartment units, some of which were erected
after 1916.[2] By that March his detailed drawings for the Imperial
Hotel were done, so late in December 1916, after a farewell
banquet given by Chicago friends, Wright sailed from Seattle to
Tokyo, where he would live for much of the next six years.[3] His
willingness to tackle ambitious projects was in large part prompted
by the necessity to regain control of himself, for, as his son John
recalled, "only architecturally was he able to hold his own."[4]

Wright leaned heavily, however, though at times uncertainly,
on a new source of inspiration, a woman who had entered his life
shortly after Mamah's death and who accompanied him to Japan
—Maud Miriam Noel. A forty-three-year-old divorcée, Miriam
Noel met Wright late in 1914 or early in 1915, when he invited
her to his Chicago office in response to her letter of consolation
following the Taliesin tragedy. The daughter of a Kentucky doc-
tor, she had had three children by Thomas Noel, scion of a
wealthy Tennessee family. After her divorce Miriam acquired
further sophistication and additional credentials among the Harry
Payne Whitneys and Whitelaw Reids in Paris, where she had
lived for several years prior to the outbreak of World War I.
Alimony enabled her to act and sculpt, to associate with artistic
and literary people even though her own talents were limited. She
was, one observer noted, "an extremely pretty woman. Her eyes
are dark and luminous and her face is singularly mobile, expressive." In the parlance of the day she was "distinctly spirituelle,"
and Wright, fascinated by her élan, moved her into Taliesin with
his mother shortly after they met.[5]

Miriam considered herself a liberated woman, and, much more than Mamah Borthwick, was self-consciously artistic, affecting a life-style and a public posture similar to her famous contemporary, Mabel Dodge Luhan. Mamah had been content to bask in Wright's glow, but Miriam competed for the limelight, which he found intriguing at first. In public statements in 1915 she outlined a social philosophy quite close to his own: Contrary to popular belief, she said, there existed an aristocracy composed of artists performing socially uplifting work who should not be impeded by customs and institutions that might inhibit free expression. Responsible to higher laws than those society created, the artist was nevertheless strictly disciplined. "Frank Lloyd Wright and I," she insisted at a press conference, "are as capable of making laws of our own as were the dead men who framed the laws by which they hoped to rule the generations that followed them." She and her lover were among the few who had achieved the true freedom possible "only through the illumination of the spiritual consciousness."[6] They lived, as she and many of her contemporaries liked to put it, only for art. Wright was undoubtedly attracted by a woman who articulated a philosophy to which he was already publicly committed.

Despite their similar beliefs, their relationship was tempestuous. Wright could not give Miriam the total allegiance she demanded, partly because of his continuing devotion to Mamah, and partly because she threatened to stifle his personal independence. A very demanding woman, Miriam resented her inability to penetrate Wright's innermost thoughts and feelings. She was unreasonably impatient on the subject of Mamah, "a dead woman whom you tortured as you have tortured me," she claimed in a moment of anger, "and to whose memory you have given no real loyalty— merely a sentimental attempt to soothe your own conscience."[7] There were those who thought Wright hypocritical for taking up with Miriam so soon after Mamah's death, especially when he had spoken so movingly of his love. The fact seems to be, however, that he could not function without "a sympathetic comrade," as he put it. Despite the contrary impression given by Miriam's presence, the irony was that Wright had *not* neglected Mamah. Forced to compete with her, Miriam probably sensed that the architect did not love her as strongly as he had loved her predecessor. As a result she was overly sensitive to his every attention. Her rage at Wright's flirtation with a young woman symbolized her own feelings of insecurity in the relationship as well as her threat to his personal freedom.

Difficulties like these—the clash of two strong and independent personalities—forced Miriam out of Taliesin around August 1915, after nine months with Wright. Their relationship was not discovered until November, when letters she wrote from 19 Cedar Street, Chicago—Wright's apartment to which she had moved—were stolen by Nellie Breen, a former housekeeper at Taliesin whom Wright had discharged because of her hostility to Miriam. Mrs. Breen published the letters, threatening a federal investigation for violation of the Mann Act, but the dubious nature of the allegations, together with the legal skill of Clarence Darrow, Wright's attorney, prevented prosecution. Compared to the "affinity tangles" of 1909 and 1911, this scandal received less attention outside Chicago, but, under mutual attack, Miriam and Wright resolved their differences and reunited, presenting a common front to the world.[8]

Although Miriam provided Wright with several thousand dollars to rebuild Taliesin, the enormity of the task and a lack of clients brought him close to bankruptcy in 1916. But the promise of a $300,000 fee for the Imperial Hotel undoubtedly sustained him until December 1916, when he left to begin the project. For the next seven years he and Miriam lived together in Tokyo, California, and Wisconsin, while Wright devoted most of his attention to the hotel and to a few other American and Japanese commissions. The story of the Imperial has been retold many times, making further repetition here unnecessary. Suffice it to say that a unique cantilevered construction, enabling the building to ride out the earthquake of September 1923, when much of the city was leveled, won Wright international plaudits. The hotel was a massive structure of brick and limestone, occupying an entire city block. Extravagant, ornate, intricately detailed, and exceedingly complicated, it combined Western construction techniques with Eastern aesthetics in a unified but excessively fussy manner. The Imperial, often cited as one of Wright's great achievements, was actually an aberration in his career, a tour de force contributing little to the overall development of his architecture, an isolated though monumental dead end, which distracted him during the First World War and mitigated personal anxiety.[9]

The Imperial was still unfinished when Wright left Japan for the last time in November 1922. During his six years there he had often been exhausted, sick, weakened by the climate, and quite lonely, despite Miriam's presence. He had also been disturbed by international developments, not so much American entrance into World War I as the growing enmity between this country and Japan. By 1922 he was quite happy to leave the disintegrating political climate for a long rest at Taliesin.[10] In November, as soon as he returned, he secured an uncontested divorce from Catherine Wright—thirteen years after their initial separation—on the grounds of voluntary estrangement for more than five years. He could have taken this step any time after 1916, and that he did not may indicate reluctance to wed Miriam. It was presumably at her insistence, therefore, that one year after his divorce, according to Wisconsin law, they were married in November 1923, in a midnight ceremony on a bridge over the Wisconsin River. After nine years of sharing him with the Imperial Hotel, with Mamah Borthwick, and with his mother, Anna—who had moved to Taliesin in 1914 and who, at the age of seventy-eight, had traveled to Japan in 1920 when he was dangerously ill—Miriam finally had Wright all to herself.[11] But, by the time of Anna's death in February 1923, it was too late. Their relationship, highly unstable from the very beginning, doomed the marriage before it began.

Not all the blame for their inability to coexist happily should be placed on Wright's preoccupation with other people and other things. As her published letters reveal, Miriam was a volatile, highly excitable, emotionally mercurial woman whose moods changed unpredictably and totally from day to day. She was given to exaggeration, indeed, to completely misrepresenting facts to make them conform to her preconceptions or her state of mind. Without offering any evidence, for example, she frequently alleged that Taliesin—with Anna Wright living there—was a den of orgies and debauchery, and claimed that Wright assaulted her repeatedly. After the marriage she became alarmingly erratic, completely eradicating what little was left of his initial fascination. He married her to calm her, he said, but their visit to a psychiatrist may have only unsettled her further.[12]

The truth was more nearly that he married her out of a sense of protectiveness and obligation, and because of a weird artistic symbiosis. Miriam had assisted him financially, after all, had seen him through an emotionally trying period, had committed herself to him and publicly supported his views at a time when he was a social and professional outcast. They had passed through a great deal together, a fact he fully appreciated. It is probably an intentional overstatement to say, as did his son, that Wright was "wooed, grabbed and bagged. . .'. dominated, seduced, coerced, chastised, conscripted, overridden, and beshawed" by Miriam, but it is undoubtedly true that his need for female companionship worked to her advantage. Nevertheless, theirs was not a marriage likely to last, and it was fortunate for both of them when Miriam left Wright in April 1924, five months after the wedding.[13]

During the next year or so, he seemed to mark time, casting about for new directions without any clear idea of what to do. Relaxing as frequently as possible at Taliesin, he published two articles in commemoration of Louis Sullivan, whose death that April saddened him considerably. He designed several concrete houses in California, but in November announced that after January 1, 1925, he would make his home in Chicago—where he was preparing an office at 19 Cedar Street to accommodate twelve draftsmen—and devote himself exclusively to commercial archi-

Miriam Noel Wright

tecture.[14] But neither his Cedar Street studio nor his commercial practice materialized, for after April 1925 a series of misfortunes foreshadowed further disasters. Defective telephone wiring started a fire at Taliesin in April that caused between a quarter and a half million dollars' damage. With only $30,000 insurance, Wright was forced to sell his old Oak Park home for $33,500.[15]

Then, in July, he filed for divorce on grounds of desertion but soon withdrew the suit when Miriam threatened to counter with a charge of physical cruelty. On Thanksgiving Day, 1925, Miriam announced to the press that she had opened her own divorce proceedings, accusing Wright of assault, specifically with beating her on two occasions. Eager to end the business, Wright immediately offered her a $10,000 lump-sum payment with an additional $250 a month for the rest of her life, but he refused to consider her demand for separate maintenance of his estate. Miriam's November press conference was the first revelation of their separation, or of their marriage, for that matter. So once again reporters in search of sensation flocked to Spring Green, to receive an unexpected scoop when they discovered that since the previous February, at least, Wright had been living with yet another woman, Montenegrin divorcée Olga Milanoff. At this disclosure Miriam rejected his financial offer and withdrew her suit, presumably to consider new tactics, beginning a complicated legal (and extralegal) battle that lasted until 1930. At the end of November Wright renewed his desertion charge against Miriam, who responded by lodging a misconduct complaint against Olgivanna (her nickname) with the Bureau of Immigration. At first Wright insisted that she was merely his hundred-dollar-a-month housekeeper, but when they were found registered in Chicago's Congress Hotel—in separate rooms, to be sure—he dropped all pretense.[16]

The granddaughter of a Montenegrin general and the daughter of a judge, Olgivanna was twenty-six and Wright fifty-seven when they met. She was born in Cetinje, Yugoslavia, educated privately in czarist Russia and in Turkey, and while still in her teens, married Vlademar Hinzenberg, an architect ten years her senior, by whom she gave birth to a daughter, Svetlana, in 1917. After the war she left her husband and moved to Paris, where she pursued a life of art and mysticism. She had come to Chicago only to confer with Hinzenberg on business, and was about to return to New York and Paris when she met Wright, more than likely at the Petrograd Ballet, November 30, 1924. Olgivanna was very beautiful—dark, aristocratic, and mysterious, according to Wright—and he was immediately captivated. Inviting her to Spring Green, and visiting her in New York, Wright wooed her vigorously until, in a matter of weeks, "Olgivanna was mine." She moved into Taliesin by February 1925, was granted a divorce two months later, and before the year was out gave birth to Wright's daughter, Iovanna.[17]

Younger when she met him than all his other women except Catherine Tobin, Olgivanna represented the culmination of a logical progression in Wright's love objects—from socially con-

Olgivanna, 1927

scious suburbanite to liberated feminist to expatriate artist to foreign-born mystic. As he removed himself further from professionalism, suburban mores, middle-class respectability, and conventional behavior, he attracted companions, each of whom more than her predecessor, was unwilling to accept the roles or perform the functions society had decreed for its women. In France Olgivanna had joined Georgi Gurdjieff's Institute for the Harmonious Development of Man, one of the "high thought colonies," in Sinclair Lewis's phrase, that grew up after World War I. Gurdjieff taught that civilization had corrupted the primordial harmony among man's intellectual, physical, and emotional faculties or "centers"; his followers tried to reunify themselves through work, contemplation, fasting, "self-observation," and other coordinated activities. Olgivanna, for example, spent her days at Fontainebleau in physical labor and her evenings studying Oriental-type dance.* Even more than her youthful beauty, Wright was taken by Olgivanna's quietly mysterious, even exotic, demeanor, as well as by her mystical notions. An aristocratic, foreign-born "artiste," she was even less committed to the American Way of Life than Wright's earlier women.

As late as June 1926, Miriam's strategy toward the architect and

* After Sinclair Lewis visited Gurdjieff's Institute in 1923, he described the "notorious establishment," to use Mark Schorer's label, in an acerbic but not altogether prejudiced manner: "We went to the dances of the Goudjieff [sic] colony, which happens to be about five minutes walk from my place. . . . The people do their own work—everything from cooking to digging rock— learn elaborate dances, and listen to 'esoteric lectures'. . . . some of the dances are imitations of Oriental sacred temple rights [sic], some of them stunts requiring a high degree of muscle control—doing quite different things with the two arms at the same time. But it must be a hell of a place to live—they sleep only four hours a night, and eat almost nothing, with occasional fasts of six or eight or ten days: The place itself is beautiful . . . with a sweep of gardens and tree alleys. Here they have built their own 'gymnasium,' as they call it, though essentially it's a kind of hall for dancing, so hung with Oriental carpets that it looks like a cross between a cabaret and a harem" (Letter to his father, n.d., quoted in Mark Schorer, *Sinclair Lewis: An American Life* [New York: McGraw-Hill, 1961], p. 378.) For another view see Olgivanna (Mrs. Frank Lloyd Wright), "The Last Days of Katherine Mansfield," *The Bookman* 73 (March 1931): 6–13.

his mistress was still ambiguous. Delays and postponements in Wright's divorce proceedings encouraged rumors that she would charge him with adultery or insist upon separate maintenance (partial control) of his estate. Using the press to dramatic advantage, she claimed to be penniless, sick, and alone, with no place to go. "I am still his wife and 'Taliesin' is still my home," Miriam lamented. "If I can have just a corner of the bungalow to myself I will be satisfied." It was more than a corner she wanted, however, for early in June she tried for three days to take Taliesin by force. Rebuffed by Wright's employees, she succeeded only in destroying two signs reading "No visitors allowed," in detaining Wright briefly on a peace warrant, and in forcing the frightened Olgivanna into hiding.

A few days earlier Wright had abandoned divorce proceedings for a second time. He now offered Miriam $125 a month if she would leave him alone, and, in view of her abortive siege of Taliesin, he decided to make a public explanation of his latest imbroglio.[18] In a letter "To the Countryside," published in the Spring Green *Weekly Home News*, June 10, 1926, Wright thanked the community for its patience, apologizing as he had in 1914 for causing scandal. He recognized that his home had been a storm center of conflict and that his "direct ways of meeting life" had embarrassed everyone. All he had ever wanted, he maintained, was a quiet hearth and a sympathetic comrade, but his best intentions had brought him odious notoriety and an intolerable domestic situation. The present conflict had developed, Wright explained, because he had really believed Miriam gone for good. Thinking "no difficulty could arise to prevent me from making my life 'regular' here at last," he invited Olgivanna to join him. But he had misjudged Miriam, and found himself in "an ambush laid with a good deal of cunning. . . .

"What I wanted to say to you," Wright emphasized, "was that I like you people. . . ." He noted that he was a third generation Lloyd Jones, that he had invested heavily in Taliesin, and that Spring Green was the one place in all the world where he was genu-

Frank Lloyd Wright at Taliesin East, 1924

inely happy. "I want to stay here with you, working until I die. I want to mind my own business and not be subject to public question if I can help it." He knew he had a difficult road to travel before that happened, and only hoped he would live long enough. He realized that many readers would not believe a word he said, but expected his subsequent behavior to reassure friends and convince skeptics. "I think the countryside deserves the best of me," he concluded, "and if you . . . give me the benefit of the doubt . . . for a year or two I will come through right side up and you may yet take pride in Taliesin. . . . Such as I am," he signed his letter, "with affection . . . your—Frank Lloyd Wright."

The expiation did not forestall further misfortune, but his two-year estimate proved to be remarkably accurate. The next few weeks were the quiet before a storm. Although Miriam had accepted Wright's voluntary monthly payments of $125 without question or acknowledgment, on August 30 she suddenly filed a $100,000 alienation of affection suit against Olgivanna, who had met Wright months after Miriam left. Events then broke swiftly. Wright disappeared the next day to join Olgivanna in hiding, saying only he was going abroad. Two days later, Vlademar Hinzenberg, her former husband, entered the proceedings by securing an injunction in Chicago that prevented her from taking Svetlana, their nine-year-old daughter, out of the country. Claiming that the birth of Wright's child, Iovanna, in December 1925, proved Olgivanna an unfit mother, Hinzenberg then obtained a writ of habeas corpus for the purpose of gaining Svetlana's custody, immediately following this with warrants for the arrest of the fugitives under the Mann Act.[19]

Adversity began to accumulate with the melodramatic rapidity of a Horatio Alger novel. While the sheriff of Sauk County, Wisconsin, broadcast pictures and descriptions of Wright, Olgivanna, Svetlana, and their infant daughter, Iovanna, Hinzenberg telegraphed Seattle to prevent the architect from sailing for Japan, where it was believed he had a standing invitation to practice. On September 6, 1926, the Bank of Wisconsin foreclosed on a $25,000 mortgage, and, holding an additional $18,000 in liens and claims against Taliesin, took possession of the estate with the intention of auctioning Wright's personal property. Miriam Noel won a court order granting her joint access, but before she could move in the bank secured an injunction preventing either Mr. or Mrs. Wright from entering the grounds lest they damage anything on which it held a chattel mortgage. Miriam initiated, then abandoned, an involuntary bankruptcy suit against Wright, and at the end of September Hinzenberg offered a $500 reward for his arrest. Meanwhile a Madison, Wisconsin, construction firm sued the architect for $4,000 still outstanding on repairs to Taliesin after the 1925 fire.[20]

Despite the persistent rumors that the Wright entourage had fled to Mexico, they were discovered on October 20 hiding in a cottage on Lake Minnetonka in Wildhurst, Minnesota, a few miles west of Minneapolis, where they had been since September 7. (At the moment of his arrest, Wright was dictating the concluding pages of Book One of his autobiography.) After a night in the Hennepin County jail, he and Olgivanna were released on $12,500 bonds for violating the Mann Act, but were immediately taken from the county to a municipal court where they posted another $3,000 to avoid detention on Hinzenberg's adultery warrant. Legal wranglings kept them in Minneapolis until the middle of November, when they were given permission to leave the state. Still barred from Taliesin, they traveled to California, where they hoped to enjoy a respite from a year of unsolicited publicity.[21]

By October 1926 it was obvious that Miriam was as interested in punishing Wright for his association with Olgivanna as she was in extracting his money. Insisting she would never grant a divorce, she instructed her attorney to threaten an investigation of the 1914 fire at Taliesin, and to inquire if Olgivanna had overstayed her American passport. As her behavior became more vitriolic, developments began to shift in Wright's favor. When Miriam claimed that the Bank of Wisconsin had conspired with him to deny her access to Taliesin, she was assessed fifty dollars in court costs, and her allegation expunged from the records. The architect's son John and his former wife Catherine announced they were prepared to give him whatever assistance they could. Several prominent persons—including the poet Carl Sandburg and New Republic editor Robert Morse Lovett—publicly urged the federal district attorney for Minnesota to drop the Mann Act indictments. Vlademar Hinzenberg withdrew his adultery charges after securing visitation rights with Svetlana.[22] Public opinion began to shift behind Wright when he and Olgivanna published articles in Madison's *Capital Times* describing Miriam's "tyrannies," including the story of how she had forced Olgivanna and her three-day-old baby out of a hospital into the Chicago streets. The Sauk County district attorney, denouncing Miriam's alienation of affection suit as a "black-mailing stunt," withdrew his office from the case, while her counsel, noting her repeated rejections of the architect's financial offers, resigned, remarking, "I wanted to be a lawyer and Mrs. Wright wanted me to be an avenging angel."[23]

The architect's fortunes improved considerably in 1927, even though the year opened unpromisingly. Miriam followed him to California, where she tried to have him arrested for abandonment. A third fire at Taliesin in February destroyed about $2,500 of books, blueprints, and architectural renderings. Wright's $100,000 Japanese print collection was auctioned for under $37,000, after a January and February exhibition at the Anderson Galleries in New York. At first, the proceeds were awarded to Miriam, who had secured a writ of attachment to regain the money she had spent to rebuild Taliesin in 1915, but ultimately they were granted to the gallery as payment for loans to Wright. In March the Minnesota authorities dropped the Mann Act indictment for lack of sufficient evidence, but a month later the Bank of Wisconsin sold the livestock at Taliesin, and renewed its efforts to take permanent title, which had been interrupted when the February fire raised questions about actual property value.[24]

When Wright returned to Madison in May 1927, he was hit with a summons from Miriam to show why he should not contribute to her financial support. (He had suspended the $125 voluntary payments after her alienation of affection suit the previous August.) Still refusing a divorce, she insisted on separate maintenance of his estate. Despite her challenge to its claim, the bank won two settlements against Wright totaling $43,000, and gave him until May 1928 to pay before taking title. With Miriam instructed to keep away from Taliesin while Wright used his studio to work off his debts, she realized by the summer of 1927 that she must come to terms or receive even less alimony than the original 1925 agreement. During June and July she pondered several offers, quibbling here with details, there with wording, until finally, after more than two years of unprofitable turmoil, she granted a divorce on August 25, 1927. In return she received $6,000 in cash and a $30,000 trust fund from which she might draw $250 a month for the rest of her life. Four days later several of the architect's friends organized "Wright, Incorporated," authorized to issue $75,000 in stock and to assume control of his estate and finances; with no money, Wright was forced to sell shares in himself against his future earning power.[25]

After the divorce Miriam's behavior became increasingly erratic. In September she divulged plans to begin screen tests for a Hollywood career, after which she would study sculpture and philosophy in Paris. In October she threatened to renew morals charges against Olgivanna, announced she was going to have her face lifted, and claimed to have given birth to a baby girl, the daughter of an heir to a European crown, who loved her and would marry her, she said. Wright had her arrested for sending him a letter he claimed was so obscene, lewd, and indecent it could not be admitted as evidence. After contracting to give a lecture in Milwaukee on "Morality and Art," she tried to convince the Immigration Bureau to deport Olgivanna. By the time she chased Wisconsin Governor Fred R. Zimmerman through the kitchen of a Chicago hotel trying to enlist him in her campaign to arrest Wright for violating his alleged divorce stipulation not to see Olgivanna for a year, and by the time she asked a United States senator to force the Justice Department to investigate why the Mann Act indictment had been dropped—very little remained of her credibility. Her reward in July 1928 for breaking into Wright's rented home in La Jolla, California, one night while he was away and smashing several hundred dollars' worth of furniture, was a thirty-day suspended sentence. This was her last contact with her former husband. Miriam Noel left his life as she had entered it—clandestinely.[26]

Unable to pay his $43,000 obligation to the Bank of Wisconsin by May 1928, Wright's personal effects, art pieces, and farm machinery were sold at public auction. In July, when the bank assumed title to Taliesin in satisfaction of $25,000, he still owed over $10,000 more. But the news was not entirely bad. On August 25, 1928, a year to the day after his divorce, and almost three years after Iovanna's birth, Wright married Olgivanna Milanoff in La Jolla, California. After an Arizona honeymoon, they returned to Wisconsin in October. Taliesin, meanwhile, had been redeemed and the remainder of the architect's debts paid by the stockholders of Wright, Incorporated, among whom were the critic Alexander Woollcott, the playwright Charles MacArthur, Mrs. Avery Coonley, and another early client, Darwin C. Martin of Buffalo, Wright's sister, Jane Porter, and his attorney, Philip La Follette, later governor of the state. Legally, Wright, Incorporated, owned Taliesin and everything in it. Its hopes for financial return were based on the architect's ability to design buildings for profit, something he had not been able to do for several years.[27]

After his successful work on the Imperial Hotel, Wright's difficulties with Miriam Noel brought his practice to a virtual standstill. From 1915 to 1932 he executed only thirty-four commissions —two a year—of which twenty-nine were erected before 1924, and only five thereafter, including two for himself and another for a relative.[28] Obviously World War I and his own absence from the country reduced his building opportunities, but not as much as his marital problems during the halcyon days of the Great Prosperity. Compared to the Oak Park years, and even to the troubled period at Taliesin with Mamah Borthwick, the 1920s were a disaster for Wright, who, long before the stock market crash, was quite familiar with unemployment. Blaming society for his architectural doldrums, and staunchly maintaining his innocence of any social irregularities—in the context of Miriam's antics, his behavior looked almost beatific—Wright felt even more harassed than in 1911 or 1915. The few designs he did execute from 1915 through the 1920s reflected the suspicion, frustration, and disappointments plaguing his private life. After 1914 he built no more prairie houses, and his residences of the next decade offered little in the way of an applicable theory of family organization. But they do provide important clues to his own emotional and intellectual condition.

With Taliesin in 1911 Wright had stated that his own purposes could best be served by close contact with nature in a home insuring privacy through controlled access, making gestures toward limited community contact. The majority of his residential designs after 1914 de-emphasized these themes in favor of a more socially conservative posture. Compared to the prairie house, the designs of 1915 and 1916 tended to be boxy, stolid, and self-contained, with inconspicuous entrances, smaller and fewer windows—sometimes only on the second level—and facades with greater areas of unbroken surface. In many cases, a severe slab roof replaced the gentle hip, sacrificing an easy horizontality for a cramped and nervous solidity. The Sherman Booth House (1915) in Glencoe, Illinois, and the Emil Bach House (1915) in Chicago, have particularly "semicubist" facades with flat roofs, numerous right angles and parallel lines, and emphatic contrasting trim, resembling Piet Mondriaan's paintings more than any of Wright's earlier buildings. In the F. C. Bogk House (1916) in Milwaukee, the windows are vertical slits or are tucked behind terrace walls, and the main door, on a side drive, is removed from passers-by, while in the project for an urban house (1916) the entrance is hidden altogether and the structure itself is a simple cube with exceptionally modest fenestration. Many of these features, of course, had appeared in Wright's previous work, but never so prominently. The new buildings were tightly organized, severely delimited bulwarks—with conspicuous trim effectively defining their psychological as well as their physical boundaries—against a dialogue between inside and out. Not tentative like the early prairie houses, they made no apology for their declaration of privacy, inwardness, and retreat from the community.

Seven of the nine buildings Wright executed in the United

Emil Bach House, 1915, Chicago

States from 1920 to 1924 were concrete California houses that carried the 1915–1916 tendencies much further. At least four utilized the "textile-block" system he developed in 1923 for Mrs. George Millard's "La Miniatura" in Pasadena—precast blocks with geometric patterns on the exposed sides, bound together at the site with steel tie rods and poured concrete. The material was appropriate for the climate because of its ability to repel heat in summer and retain it in winter, but these homes, particularly in block form, have metaphorical as well as technological significance. Most of their relatively few windows pierce the upper stories, usually facing the rear of the lot. With entrances turned from the street, and with real and symbolic barriers discouraging contact between inside and outdoors, the houses became secluded sanctuaries. Those for John Storer (1923) and for Charles Ennis and

Samuel Freeman (both 1924)—suspended from Los Angeles hills, and facing away from the street (unlike the prairie house) to take advantage of spectacular views—were literally almost impenetrable; arranged in separately articulated units according to function, they were extensions and symbolic representations of the rugged hillsides. Wright achieved a relationship between structure and site in this way, but one that dramatized topography at the expense of a dialogue with nature.

With little to offer in the way of a theory of family organization, several of the concrete residences, moreover, were hardly homes at all. Significantly, the only California buildings he discussed (at great length!) in his autobiography were for two middle-aged women—Miss Aline Barnsdall and the widowed Mrs. George Millard—who did not have families and who, like their architect (in his "Miriam years") were socially vulnerable and personally "unfulfilled." The Mayan "Hollyhock House" (1916–1920) in Los Angeles—a massive complex of individual units, courtyards, gardens, pergolas, bridges, hidden recesses, shadowed corners, and relatively few windows overwhelmed by masses of poured concrete—was a thoroughly confusing maze, protection against those who harassed her for her Bolshevik soirées, but perfect for Miss Barnsdall, who lived there, according to Wright, "like a princess in aristocratic seclusion." Mrs. Millard's La Miniatura, intended primarily as a library for her book collection and a gallery for her art, was a fireproof vault in which casual movement and human clutter seem disrespectful. And the intricately patterned, textile-block exteriors of the Ennis, Storer, and Freeman houses—their courtyards sun-baked plazas by day but ominous enclosures at night—were playgrounds for the imagination, which might easily envision their interiors as silent mausoleums or eerie covens. One Hollywood director showed a certain perspicacity when he used the Freeman House as the locale for a horror movie starring Vincent Price. It was obviously a monumental structure, as Henry-Russell Hitchcock has understated it, but "rather undomestic."[29]

Although the forms of Wright's work in the 1920s drew on

The Charles Ennis House, 1924, Los Angeles, California

architecture as disparate as International Style, Mayan revival, and, as Vincent Scully has suggested, Southwest American Indian, their overriding ambiance and expressiveness had a peculiar relevance to his private life. The 1914 tragedy had made it painfully clear that removal to a rural setting had not enhanced personal security. Whereas the 1915–1916 houses were hasty, sometimes unsupervised, reflex responses to that event—hinting at increased privacy and retreat from social contact—the concrete homes of the 1920s, expanding privacy into seclusion and retreat into escape, were carefully planned, meticulously executed essays in solitude and isolation. Building with textile blocks, furthermore, was a weaving together of myriads of lines, designs, and individual pieces—the solving of a complicated puzzle. The emphasis was on parts and detail, on process, rather than on total conception: putting and keeping something together was as crucial as what was kept together. Expanding on the fortresslike, not the environment-embracing, qualities of Taliesin, the concrete-block homes were less places to live than impregnable retreats from a hostile world, precisely constructed defense mechanisms suitable for a precarious existence with an erratic woman. The California houses—monuments to Wright's skill in architectural composition—were created when the fabric of his life was in greatest danger, when the dynamics of interpersonal relationships were of utmost importance.

His preoccupation with architectural technique—heightened by work on the Imperial Hotel but almost myopic under Miriam Noel's destructive influence later—was also reflected in his publications during the 1920s. Shortly after his final return from Japan, his article on the Imperial in *The Western Architect* described its design and execution in greater detail than was usual for Wright. After the temblor of September 1923 he wrote an additional two-part essay for the same journal—also under the heading "In the Cause of Architecture"—subtitled "In the Wake of the Quake." Denying the accusation that the hotel was a reactionary, "inorganic" building, which violated his principles by ignoring Western technological innovations and his own previous aesthetics, he admitted modestly that his intention had been "to assist Japan to her own architectural feet." Having therefore to remain within her traditions and to rely upon her construction methods, he said, he had confronted innumerable unforeseen obstacles, described in the second article—his most technical yet—as "statement of the problem," "working out the plans," "the execution of the work," and "changes as the work proceeded."

Most of his other writings in the 1920s dealt with similar issues. In 1927 and 1928 he published two series of essays for *The Architectural Record* (inevitably) entitled "In the Cause of Architecture," for which he received a total fee of $7,500, even though he never produced the fifteenth and final installment. The first group of five treated such topics as machinery, standardization, steel, and prefabrication, while five of the second nine, subtitled "The Meaning of Materials," analyzed the characteristics and proper use of stone, glass, concrete, sheet metal, and terra cotta.[30] Never before had Wright written so exclusively about architectural *process*, minimizing theory, objectives, and polemics. The spate of publications on method and technique coincided almost exactly (1923–1928) with the nadir of his association with Miriam Noel, a time when he was concentrating on restructuring his own life and on building a viable relationship with Olgivanna. It might have been predicted, furthermore, that as soon as he married Olgivanna, and his life resumed a more normal course, his attention would return to broader concepts. After 1928, until his death over thirty years later, his voluminous writings were by and large general, abstract, and theoretical, with very little of a technical or methodological nature.

The *Record* series may have encouraged Wright to supplement his income with the pen, which, during the years of scarce clients, was mightier than the pencil. Whatever the motivation, these essays opened the floodgates of a speaking and writing deluge. From 1929 to 1932 he published at least twenty speeches, articles, and reviews, and he was frequently interviewed in the mass and professional press. His 1930 lectures at Princeton University and at the Chicago Art Institute were released the next year as *Modern Architecture* and *Two Lectures on Architecture*. He received widespread coverage when, in his September 1931 informal talks at New York's New School for Social Research, he called for improved skyscrapers, attacked urban planning, praised industrial architecture, and criticized the International Style.[31] The public was somewhat prepared, therefore, for The Disappearing City (1932), an analysis of urbanization and geographical centralization, and An Autobiography (1932), a difficult, revealing, inaccurate, but compelling book, which also focused on these topics. His steady stream of publications and speaking engagements—in which he usually denounced conformity in American life and art— gave him an enormous amount of exposure, which he undoubtedly enjoyed. For the rest of his life he was often in the news, popping off on one or another issue, whether or not he knew anything about it. Since many people thought his practicing days over, they consigned him to the role of elder statesman, one he relished, but not as a companion to retirement.

Nevertheless, his loss of several large and impressive commissions during the 1920s confirmed the general impression that he was destined to build no more. Hopes for Edward Doheny's enormous ranch complex (1921)—a multilevel, concrete-block network of terraces, arches, buildings, roadways, and forests, resembling a surreal set of the futuristic Things To Come, built up, into, and around the Los Angeles Sierra Madre Mountains—were dashed when the Harding scandals dried up a source of funds that the president of the Pan-American Oil Company might otherwise have invested in architecture. A summer colony for Lake Tahoe (1922–1923) with wooden buildings and houseboats of leaf and tepee motif (happily) never left the drawing boards. A thirty-two-story skyscraper (1924–1925) for the National Life Insurance Company in Chicago—four intricately detailed units set back against a main tower-spine with floors cantilevered from the center and copper- and glass-hung walls—remained a vision when its unconventional aspects frightened away its patron. There was also a planetarium (1925) with a spiral automobile ramp forming the exterior for Sugar Loaf Mountain, Maryland, and a fantastic steel cathedral (1926) with chapels for all denominations that would have accommodated a million New Yorkers in the tallest building in the world. All these highly detailed projects involved the blending together of innumerable pieces and segments. Like the "textile-block" houses in California, they emphasized method and process every bit as much as the finished product, for their intricacies were clearly their dominant visual characteristic.

Wright lost several more opportunities after the 1929 stock market crash ended the speculative spirit. Plans for the San-Marcos-in-the-Desert winter resort—another massive concrete block design—were first conceived in 1927 and completed in 1928, but never executed. One of his most interesting commissions, an adaptation of which was built in 1952, was a skyscraper apartment block (1929) for William Norman Gutherie's Saint Mark's in the Bowery Church in New York, three octagonal towers alternating vertical and horizontal facades, with cantilevered floors and hung exteriors of copper and glass. Construction scheduled for 1930 was abandoned, as were the grouped apartment towers (1930) in Chicago, based on the Saint Mark's idea. Another unfortunate loss was the Elizabeth Noble apartment house (1930) in Los Angeles, a small, horizontally oriented structure of glass and concrete with wood-sheathed cantilevered balconies, very much in the International style. Although Wright secured fewer commissions in the 1920s than ever before, several of them would have brought large fees and considerable acclaim. The apartment buildings were particularly fresh, and their loss was felt by American architecture in general. But those who knew about them understood that Wright's creativity had not yet run out.

Precisely when his fortunes were lowest, Wright began to receive honors and accolades, almost in inverse proportion to commissions. The Dutch architect H. Th. Widjeveld released *The Life-Work of the American Architect, Frank Lloyd Wright* in 1925, thereafter considered by him to be the best compilation of his designs. In 1927 he was elected to the Royal Academy of Fine Arts in Belgium, and five years later to similar institutions in Brazil and Berlin. While an exhibition of his work was touring the world in 1931, he was invited to Rio de Janeiro as the guest of the Pan

American Union to judge competitive entries for a Christopher Columbus Memorial.[32] Two years after he held his first showing in New York City, under auspices of the Architectural League of America, he was included in the now famous International Style exhibition of 1932, organized by Philip Johnson and Henry-Russell Hitchcock at the Museum of Modern Art. Balanced against Walter Gropius, Ludwig Mies van der Rohe, J. J. P. Oud, Le Corbusier, and other Americans and Europeans, Wright was the only non-Internationalist invited. Whether he appreciated the distinction is uncertain—he said he did not, but it may have been a case of protesting too much—for he was already on record as a staunch opponent of the new European architecture.[33]

Published in an obscure journal, World Unity, Wright's first important critique of the International Style has been overlooked by historians. Commenting on Le Corbusier's Towards a New Architecture (1923; trans. 1927) in the September 1928 issue,[34] he used the occasion to range far beyond the confines of a book review. In later years Wright was friendly to Mies van der Rohe and jovially patronizing to "Little Philip" Johnson, but he was unnecessarily caustic toward Le Corbusier, who became his greatest rival for international acclaim, was a tenacious defender of his own ideas, and a supreme egotist as well. Everything good in Le Corbusier's buildings, the reviewer insisted with characteristic modesty, had been developed twenty-five years before either by Louis Sullivan or Frank Lloyd Wright. Inspired by the look of machinery and its products, the Swiss's architecture was "as stark as one of his gas-pipe railings"—entirely without ornament, usually mono-material, with an exaggerated emphasis on surface appearance. All this was a necessary "dressing down" to Beaux Arts, classical, and Victorian practitioners, and an improvement on things in general, Wright declared, but it still had momentous shortcomings.

Although Le Corbusier had been quite right to eliminate "ornamentia," he had achieved only the "semblance of simplicity." By stressing surface and mass, his severely plain "picture-buildings" ignored the "third dimension"—depth—the external manifestation of the space within, which was the life of any edifice. Surface, mass, and appearance were not the reality of architecture, simply the expression of interior events, an idea about the organization of space. Le Corbusier conceived of buildings as pictures, Wright maintained, and designed them from the outside in; that is, he thought first of how they should look, then fit interiors to match. Since architecture was primarily the organization of human living space, the proper method of design was Wright's own—from inside out. The International Style was another kind of imitation, not of the ancient forms that the Victorians had copied, to be sure, but of modern machinery. It was a "new eclecticism"—a cold, sterile eulogy to the latest technology. Whereas Wright harnessed machinery for human pleasure, Le Corbusier reproduced it to human detriment, calling his houses "machines for living." Despite its pointedness and arrogance, Wright's review was a relatively calm, intelligent, and dispassionate critique of Internationalism. Later on, when his reasonableness on the subject took wings, he contributed little to what began as a promising dialogue.

Wright's reluctance to compliment anything was rivaled only by his facility for unending criticism, one reason he was omitted from the planning committee of the 1933 Chicago World's Fair. At a protest meeting organized by New York's Town Hall Club in February 1931, Wright expressed a lack of concern—compromised somewhat by his presence there—but feared, he said, that the nation would embrace the "new eclecticism" of the fair's format as it had the classical revival of the 1893 Columbian Exposition, and thus retard the development of an American organic architecture for another two generations.[35] The editors of *Outlook and Independent*, approving his exclusion, correctly supposed that Wright's well-known irascibility would reduce to shambles any committee on which he served, but they suggested he design the next fair all by himself. Douglas Haskell in *The Nation* argued that without Wright the event would be akin to a history of American letters without Ralph Waldo Emerson. Reporting from the Continent to *The New Republic*, Catherine K. Bauer agreed with Haskell that Wright was the only American artist respected in Europe. He had been responsible for its present architectural hegemony, and, if Europe had moved beyond him lately, it was only because he had had so few building opportunities. "It was very difficult to break away from Wright," Bauer quoted a Dutch architect as saying. "For a while it looked as if the whole country were going American." Despite these testimonials, and his suggestion of a fairgrounds floating in Lake Michigan, he remained on the sidelines.[36]

Wright generated public discussion in several other ways, though usually not as a cause célèbre. He acquired a reputation, which he did nothing to discourage, for visiting a city and ridiculing its architecture. He narrowly missed being subpoenaed by a local governmental agency in November 1930, after he called Milwaukee's new $10,000,000 County Building, of which the city fathers were unduly proud, a "pseudo-classic horror." On another occasion he told a *New York Times* reporter that there was no excuse whatever for the projected Radio City; better to clear the space for a park than build that "crime of crimes," he said. His image as a cranky iconoclast was considerably enhanced in 1932 after a street fight in Madison, in which he received a broken nose, prompting five of his apprentices to bullwhip his combatant. A kidnap threat from an organization calling itself the Vigilantes of America caused national press comment when he rather dramatically hired a bodyguard rather than pay protection money for his freedom.[37]

By 1932 Wright was shrouded in a mantle of unpredictability. At sixty-five he was considered even by many of his admirers as an eccentric, opinionated, flamboyant, arrogant, slightly screwy old man with strange ideas who talked too much. His imbroglio with Miriam Noel, while dispiriting and humiliating, had not disabled him, and although it ruined the market for his work, it may also have created a sympathetic public, willing to tolerate his verbal excesses. To those who considered him a master of modern design, others pointed out that he had built nothing significant for ten years. Henry-Russell Hitchcock and Philip Johnson listed him "among the architects of the older generation," discussing his work in the past tense as if there would be no more of it. "I have been reading my obituaries . . . the past year or two," he chided Fiske Kimball, one of several critics who had proclaimed Wright's architectural eclipse, but think, with Mark Twain, "the reports of my death greatly exaggerated."[38] As it turned out, he was very much alive, and in short order confounded layman and expert alike with a flood of ideas and buildings that rivaled his achievement of the momentous prairie years.

7. LITTLE EXPERIMENT STATIONS IN OUT OF THE WAY PLACES

[1932–1938]

The first order of business, however, was not new houses. Although Frank Lloyd Wright is usually remembered as a residential architect, he also devoted enormous energies to community planning. Indeed, the very year he announced the prairie house, he proposed a communal living arrangement that later served as the basis for his 1913 suburban development project. His ideas were given their fullest expression in his scale model of Broadacre City, a scheme for a decentralized America, which he advocated incessantly after 1935. The model was executed by the Taliesin Fellowship, a resident group of student-apprentices Wright established in 1932, who were soon constructing Taliesin West, his new winter headquarters. At Wright's disposal in its two isolated homes, the Fellowship was his only planned community ever actually to materialize.

The Taliesin Fellowship was an idea whose time finally came. Always on guard against European cultural imperialism, Frank Lloyd Wright in his 1930 Princeton University lectures proposed corporation-subsidized "industrial style centers" to develop America's creative energies. Under the direction of master craftsmen, the forty students at each center would, for seven hours a day, study glassmaking, pottery, textiles, sheet metals, woodworking, landscaping, dance, music, or any of a host of other arts, aided by the very latest techniques and the most modern machinery. For another three hours they would till the soil, learning to be self-sufficient in their "little experiment stations in out of the way places" where, with the best teachers and machinery available, they would be completely free to express themselves and to explore the possibilities of their crafts. Encouraged to write and to publish their ideas, they would also advertise and market their products when sufficiently skilled, dividing profits with the sponsoring companies. There would be no examinations and no graduation, but, when the students were deemed ready, they would become university instructors or high-level employees in the endowing corporations, which would have first claim on their talents. The primary function of the centers would be to develop an indigenous cultural expression from a synthesis of artistic creativity and modern technology, beneficial to the individual, to industry, and to the nation.[1]

Wright moved to implement his idea the following summer by announcing that in the fall of 1932 he would open a School of Allied Arts in a refurbished and expanded Hillside Home School at Spring Green. For $650 each, seventy students could study a variety of subjects under the tutelage of seven senior apprentices, three technical advisers, three resident associates, and the Master himself. Actually, Wright did not envision a school at all: instead of teachers, students, and pedagogy, there would be skilled craftsmen, apprentices, and physical labor. For three hours a day the young people would work in the fields, on Taliesin construction projects, in the kitchen, the laundry, or the barns, making the place as self-sufficient as possible. For another five hours they would study "organic" design and some related skill; everyone was expected to master Wright's teachings and also to specialize in molding and casting, pottery, weaving, sculpture, painting, drama and rhythm, "reproductive processes," or, of course, architecture. Finished products would be placed on sale as missionaries of modern art, to help finance the operation.[2] His purpose, he said, was "to make complete, well-rounded men, proficient in some special art or craft, and versed in all of them."

Critics speculated that Wright, short of capital for several years and in 1932 still without commissions, was assembling young people gullible enough to pay for the privilege of growing his food and keeping his estate in repair. However truthful the allegation, it did not impede the growth of the Taliesin Fellowship, as it was called when it opened in October 1932. Although tuition was immediately raised to $1,100 and enrollment lowered to thirty, Wright was forced to turn away nine Vassar coeds for lack of space, and before the year was out had a waiting list of twenty-seven. At first everyone lived in Taliesin proper, three-quarters of a mile away from the Hillside Home School where repairs, begun during the summer by local hired help, were taken over by the apprentices. The old gymnasium was remodeled into a playhouse and opened in November 1933, followed by a large drafting room-dormitory combination in late 1934, and by additional sleeping quarters, a dining room, a kitchen, and galleries, until the entire complex was finished in 1939. Wright supplemented tuition by opening the playhouse to the general public as soon as it was completed. On Sunday afternoons for fifty cents, guests could watch a foreign film, share doughnuts and a cup of tea with Olgivanna Wright, and chat with the man himself. After 1934 casual visitors were charged fifty cents for an apprentice-conducted tour of Taliesin and Hillside. Wright also solicited contributions from friends, former clients, and patrons of the arts.[3] He may have been exploiting all possible sources of income, but he was hardly turning a large profit, even if he did live in the grand manner.

Although Walter Gropius and Ludwig Mies van der Rohe were financial contributors,[4] the Taliesin Fellowship was quite different from the famous Bauhaus at Dessau, Germany. Before its closing

Aerial view of Taliesin Estate, Spring Green, Wisconsin, showing Taliesin (right center), Midway Farm Buildings *(left center), and Hillside Home School (top left)*

in 1933, the Bauhaus was very nearly a fellowship among equals, whereas Taliesin was not really a fellowship at all in this sense; for example, the reputations of several Bauhaus teachers—Lyonel Feininger, Paul Klee, Wassily Kandinsky, and Marcel Brever among them—rivaled those of directors Gropius and Mies van der Rohe, while at Taliesin no one, including the instructors, dared to compete with Frank Lloyd Wright. Both institutions attempted to relate art to technology, but as time passed the Fellowship veered off into handicrafts, music, dance, even spiritualism;* in Germany,

---

* A former apprentice of my acquaintance has testified to seances at Taliesin, after Wright's death. In an early publication Olgivanna alluded to the pos-

on the other hand, the teachers and students made significant innovations in machine-age aesthetics and lasting contributions to painting, sculpture, furniture design, and ceramics, as well as architecture. The Bauhaus curriculum was more formal and, as an urban institution, it remained in contact with cultural and political developments; at Spring Green the students became ingrown, isolated, and provincial, neither criticizing their Master nor equalling his achievements.[5]

Nor did the Fellowship closely resemble the old Oak Park studio, which in many ways was more like the Bauhaus. Wright had been the dominant force in Oak Park, of course, but he made excellent use of his talented assistants, drawing on them for inspiration, ideas, and advice. As paid draftsmen—not paying apprentices—they assumed active roles in the studio's life, handling plan revisions, dealing with client objections, and improving Wright's sometimes hasty renderings. He delegated enormous responsibility to Isabel Roberts, his business manager, and to Marion Mahoney, who designed interior decorations and prepared the drawings for final presentation. Others, like Walter Burley Griffin, Barry Byrne, and William Drummond, later achieved considerable prominence in their own right.[6] At Taliesin, by contrast, most apprentices were given no significant responsibilities. Olgivanna, her son-in-law William Wesley Peters (one of the original students), and a few select youngsters assisted Wright with business matters and design preparations, leaving the rest to compete for access to the inner circle. Uncritical acceptance became the best route to favor and success, while architectural or personal independence was not tolerated for long. As a result, Taliesin apprentices and "graduates" in good standing have not as a group equalled the achievements of their Oak Park predecessors. Wesley Peters, Edgar Tafel, and a few others are prominent pro-

---

sibility of achieving personal immortality through mental improvement ("The Last Days of Katherine Mansfield," *The Bookman* 78 [March 1931]: 6.)

fessionally but it is unlikely they will match Griffin's, Byrne's, or Drummond's impact on architectural history. Another handful, including John deKoven Hill, Robert Mosher, and Edgar Kaufmann, Jr., are best known as critics, editors, and authors, not as architects. Truly independent spirits like Bruce Goff or Paolo Soleri who occasionally surpassed even Wright in their genius did not find Taliesin to their liking. In less than half the time, the Oak Park studio compiled a record, the beginning of a legacy, that the Fellowship, now over forty years old, can only envy.

A more singular influence on the Fellowship than either the Bauhaus or the Oak Park studio was Georgi Gurdjieff's Institute for the Harmonious Development of Man at Fountainebleau, France. Having resided there and at its other locations for at least four years, it was undoubtedly Olgivanna who introduced Gurdjieff's teachings to her husband, who, whatever the initial source of contact, praised the Russian mystic in 1934 as "an organic man."[7] The similarities between the two institutions were considerable. Neither relied on formal instruction; indeed, some observers felt they gave no instruction at all. Both Masters (as they were called) emphasized the value of physical labor as a necessary prerequisite to self-knowledge and inner peace; both taught the importance of close contact with nature, and of music and dance as vehicles for achieving harmony of Being. The young people grew their own food, maintained the estates, and were expected to be completely loyal; they were isolated from, and considered themselves superior to, the outside world. Gathering en masse at least once a week at the Master's feet for an esoteric talk and a musicale, none of them could undertake any activity without specific permission or instruction.[8]

The Wrights departed from Gurdjieff by strictly regulating the personal habits, and attempting to control the thought processes, of the apprentices. Smoking, drinking, late hours, sloppy posture, and untidy clothes were all taboo. Wright laid down many of the rules, but Olgivanna enforced them relentlessly. In 1934, when a number of beards suddenly sprouted, she was tolerant for a while but finally banned them as an "unpleasant idiosyncrasy, a harmful whim." As the years passed, she recalled, discipline grew stronger: "We had to show them the delicate line . . . between self-expression and self-indulgence." When one apprentice told her that the young should seek a wide variety of experiences as the basis for self-discovery, she replied: "You are preaching dangerous doctrine." During the early years at Taliesin, Olgivanna later wrote, "I took it upon myself to exercise the utmost vigilance in order to preserve the cleanliness of spirit and the ideal we were serving." This apparently explains her prompt action in defense of the Fellowship when a young man wore rough, unlaced boots to a formal dinner; "You dare to come into our presence . . . in such deplorable attire," she demanded. "What right do you claim for such insolence in our house? Kindly leave this room."[9]

The Fellowship was a rigidly structured, hierarchical enterprise where individualism was reserved for the Master and social equality for the apprentices. Tentatively accepted applicants were screened during their first thirty days, with the architect reserving the right to dismiss them without explanation at any time, even after final admission. "The Fellowship . . . is not on trial," he explained, "the apprentice is." Therefore, "especial predelictions or idiosyncrasies, although respected, will not be encouraged." There were fixed hours for work, recreation, and sleep, and since the countryside was an unparalleled source of inspiration, "daily life will be planned to benefit by its beauty." Although Wright once compared the Fellowship to "Robin Hood and his medieval band of freebooters," he knew the analogy was inaccurate, since the Sherwood Forest crowd was insufficiently stratified. So on another occasion he told a newspaper reporter that his apprentices cooperated with each other "like fingers on my hand. They are the fingers of the hands of Frank Lloyd Wright, and will carry on the principles I have enunciated." Apprenticeship, he continued, as if there were any doubt, is "much like it was in feudal times . . . :

an apprentice then was his master's slave; at Taliesin he is his master's comrade"—"to the extent he qualifies himself. . . ." Not surprisingly, as one reporter observed, Wright "dominated every minute of every apprentice's day."[10] Ironically, it was the architect and not the students who first expressed dissatisfaction with this "pre-modern" relationship when he revealed in his autobiography that the Fellowship's performance during its first decade was disappointing: "I had hoped that the apprentices . . . would increase not only my interest and enthusiasm for my work . . . , but would also widen my capacity to apply it. The first came true. But the second," he admitted, is "temporarily frustrated. . . ."[11]

In keeping with Wright's proposals in his Princeton lectures, the Fellowship expanded its activities in 1934 to include publishing. The first issue of *Taliesin*, a glossy, twenty-eight-page magazine without advertising, rolled off the presses in December. Edited by Wright, with articles by students and friends, it was scheduled to appear nine times a year, but met the same fate as the Taliesin "quarterly" of 1940, which folded after two issues. Another publishing venture, however, was longer-lived. Beneath a masthead sketch of Wright's home, a column called "At Taliesin" appeared in both Madison newspapers, *The Capital Times* and the *Wisconsin State Journal*, beginning in February 1934, and later in two rural weeklies. Written to increase "understanding and appreciation of his work," and to give the apprentices experience in "articulation," Wright contributed occasionally, but generally left it to underlings.[12] Ostensibly it was a weekly column, but it ran intermittently, often failing to meet its Friday deadline, sometimes not appearing for weeks at a time. Announcements of films at the playhouse, summaries of Wright's Sunday talks at Unity Chapel, and paeans of praise for "organic" living were its regular fare.

"At Taliesin" was intended to develop self-expression and literary talent among the apprentices, but it appears to have become a device for currying Wright's favor. Virtually every writer extolled the glories of his philosophy and the benefits of his life-style. We should be "forever grateful to Mr. Wright for the privilege of belonging to the Fellowship," Marybud Lautner wrote. She was happy to return from visiting her family because "life at Taliesin is really life." "We bring the outside world to us," another explained, "only when and where we need it." "Sunday evenings are always interesting," Bob Mosher remarked imperiously, "because we come in contact with the outside world and the degenerate city through the medium of the various guests that Taliesin attracts."[13] Whether the "various guests"—among them their *Capital Times* publisher—repented their degeneracy is unrecorded, but it mattered little to the young authors, who, oblivious to public sentiment and to their own pretentiousness, somehow felt qualified after a few brief weeks with Wright to pontificate on art, culture, and life.

Having learned his jargon and his language patterns, each pint-sized Frank Lloyd Wright was able to bandy about the Master's ideas in no time without, however, having digested them. One anonymously written column exemplified the typical practice of enlarging upon a cryptic passage from the architect's writing: "I sing an ode to manure," this one opened joyously. Once, like you city folks, I held my nose at "the odious cow-flop . . . but now I proudly stand on a six foot pile of it," realizing that "manure is an essential link in the great cycle of life." All civilizations have been based upon it, and "when manure shall have vanished from . . . the earth you can be sure that the end of man's existence is not far behind," the author prophesied, one hopes with pun intended.[14] Presumably not a scatologist, he had undoubtedly been impressed by page 24 of Wright's autobiography, where "dung" is described as the "indispensable wealth that goes to bring back the jaded soil to a greenness of the hills, bring fertility to life itself—for man!" It is difficult to imagine such lyrical prose at the Bauhaus or the Oak Park studio, and it was a sad moment indeed for letters when the rebirth of Wright's practice put an end to the column in October 1937.

In 1936 the Fellowship organized its own drama group, the

Taliesin Players, followed two years later by the String Quartet, which gave summer concert series over Madison radio. A male chorus, a mixed choir, a recorder chorus, and a string ensemble began in 1940 and 1941; and in the 1950s, a full orchestra and a dance company whose Gurdjieff-inspired works were choreographed by Olgivanna and Iovanna.[15] In the last decade of his life, when Wright's practice increased astronomically and when he assumed enormous speaking and writing obligations, the Fellowship took over more of the secretarial, organizational, and drafting responsibilities. A handful of apprentices designed accessories in some of his buildings, and by the mid-fifties, when he was able to do very little drawing, he relied on one or two trusted assistants to work out his ideas on paper.[16] One of the most important projects the Fellowship executed under his direction was the twelve-by-twelve-foot model of Broadacre City, Wright's scheme for a decentralized America. Completed in March 1935, it was first shown the next month at the Industrial Arts Exposition in New York's Rockefeller Center.

The Fellowship worked on the model literally day and night from January until two weeks before the Exposition opened. Assembly took place in the Arizona desert near Chandler, at La Hacienda, a tourist hotel Wright rented each year from 1935 until 1938, when construction on his winter home, Taliesin West, was advanced sufficiently to permit habitation. Excluding his honeymoon the previous year, Wright's first venture to Arizona had been in January 1929, when he built a canvas-roofed "Ocatillo Camp" to accommodate the draftsmen he employed on the unrealized "San-Marcos-in-the-Desert" project, and on the Phoenix Biltmore Hotel, the commission of a former pupil, Albert McArthur, who asked Wright to advise him on the use of textile blocks. Near Ocatillo was an eight-mile-square ranch with a field of alfalfa running its entire length along one side—"a beautiful scene from the mountain top," one of Wright's employees wrote—named "Broad Acre."[17]

Since the late 1920s Wright had been arguing that the modern

American city was no longer habitable. Believing it too large, congested, frenetic, and unhealthy—physically and mentally—to support life, he thought it should be continued only as a commercial and travel center, while the people resettled the countryside. Broadacre City, Wright's confrontation with urban problems, was first systematically outlined in 1932 in his book *The Disappearing City*, in an article for *The New York Times*, and in several speeches.[18] He had been concerned with urban relationships, however, since 1901 when, along with the prairie house, he published his first community project, the beginning of a life-long preoccupation. Despite his insistence that no two buildings could be alike because no two people were, his interest in community organization was as intense as his devotion to residential architecture. And, despite his eccentricities and the emphasis he placed on personal independence, he was absorbed with the problems of group harmony. After half a century of struggle, Wright never satisfactorily resolved the classic dichotomy between individualism and social order; his own life-style extolled the one, his intellectual constructs the other.

Actually, Broadacre City was not a city at all, but a typical section of a decentralized and reintegrated America, four square miles of which Wright depicted in his model. Vast improvements in transportation and communication had conquered the time barrier, making decentralization possible, even desirable, as population grew. No longer an obstacle to organized social life, geographical dispersion would render municipal government obsolete, so Wright adopted the county as his basic administrative, economic, and social unit. Linked directly to the national government —which would perform only diplomatic, military, and overseas commercial duties—the county was large enough to be effective but small enough to permit meaningful citizen participation, thereby eliminating states and towns. All necessary services— schools, highways, commerce, recreation, police, and the judiciary—would be operated from the county level, where the highest authority—the architect—would see that all buildings were harmonious with each other and with their purposes, and that everything affecting the public was effectively and humanely administered.

Broadacre City, Wright emphasized, was to be integrated as well as decentralized; people might spread out to live, but the various ingredients of modern civilization should constitute a "diversity in unity," as he called it. A factory, for example, ought to be located near its sources of supply or its principal market, and, if its architecture and pollutants were carefully regulated, need not be banished from the rest of society. Under the supervision of the county architect, Wright believed, all services and facilities—business, industry, recreation—could coexist harmoniously, scattered in clusters over the land where they were most needed, side by side with farm and home. Each individual would have one acre of land as long as he used it; a family of six, therefore would have six acres, with its garden and its organic house complementing the abundant greenery. Although it bore similarities to back-to-the-farm movements and to other planned communities during the depression, Broadacre City was also the culmination of thirty years' evolution in Wright's thinking.

His first proposal for communal planning had appeared in "A Home in a Prairie Town," the 1901 *Ladies' Home Journal* article that had announced his new residence. The "quadruple block plan"—four suburban homes linked on a four-hundred-foot-square block by low walls enclosing a common landscaped area in the center—looked enticing, but was quite unrealistic. Its half acre per house found few advocates among real estate agents, eager to reduce lot size in desirable, high-priced suburbs. The upper middle class that could afford the idea, furthermore, valued privacy and architectural individuality above all; sharing acreage with distinctly similar houses was simply unheard of. Norris Kelly Smith's observation that only those with strong kinship or business ties would even consider such an arrangement is quite perceptive,[19] for the closest Wright came to executing a quadruple block was the George Barton–Darwin D. Martin complex (1903–1904) in

Buffalo, where Barton's wife was Martin's daughter. But the implication of Wright's plan was sweeping: if the beauty of a home partially depended on its surroundings, the only way to guarantee success was to design the entire neighborhood. Although the idea had little chance of implementation, he continued to publish it for several years.

His next excursion into community planning was the partly executed Como Orchards Summer Colony (1909–1910) at Darby, Montana, a scheme that depended upon, and provided for, closely linked interests among participants. Conceived by a group of University of Chicago professors as a vacation retreat and a rental property, Como Orchards consisted of fifty-three individual dwellings positioned around a recreation-dining hall. All the houses, variations on the same theme, were grouped in clusters of two to six, themselves parts of larger clusters. Wright made no attempt to scatter them in casual fashion, as vacation informality might suggest, or to take advantage of the rugged terrain, so conducive to architectural diversity. Consequently, Como Orchards is particularly inappropriate for its purpose, unless redefined by Wright from summer recreation to communal living, but even so he designed with a heavy hand. The dining hall—where all the families would eat together as if in a single household—governed the location of the dwellings, which were lined up like so many wooden soldiers on crossed and diagonal axes. The dominant symbols, the way they were expressed, and the atmosphere of the project emphasized the group, but in his attempt to indicate purposeful unity, Wright undermined individuality. Overall, the plan is stiff and lifeless, and, with its serf's cottages in the shadow of the manor house, it fixed one's place and prescribed one's movements. Much more than the quadruple block, Como Orchards harmonized group interests by imposing a rigid conformity on its members.

Wright's 1901 proposal for the suburbs surfaced again in 1913 as part of a "non-competitive plan" submitted to the National Conference on City Planning's contest for the development of a quarter section on the urban periphery. Wright must have believed strongly in the merits of his ideas, for not only did he spurn the prize, but he also published his plan in 1917, even though the Conference had included it among all the entries in a book the preceding year. His scheme incorporated three variations of the quadruple block, which, in the form of "seven and eight room houses, better class," and two-flat buildings, accounted for two-thirds of the land and nine-tenths of the residential units, but less than half the people. All the other housing—flats and apartments for working families and single men and women—was scattered around the perimeter in less desirable locations, a revelation of Wright's awareness and acceptance of class and sex distinctions.

The "non-competitive plan" was a tribute to Wright's inventiveness in landscape and public architecture, but it also revealed quite conventional notions of class structure and social organization. The six apartment buildings, at the corner extremities, were as far removed as possible from upper-income families. Two-family homes and "workmen's house groups" ran along the extreme southern row of eight blocks, separated from the "better class" by a park, a lagoon, and "two-flat" buildings. "Workmen's semi-detached" row houses, adjacent to the apartments near the northeast corner, looked across a narrow court to the produce market. The clusters of two- and three-room apartments for single men and women were conspicuously separated according to sex by the "better class" families, who, Wright seems to have been saying, led exemplary lives. Homes for the upper-middle, middle, and clerical classes dominated the choice locations near the parks and social services, while the workers lived on the fringes, poorly integrated into the whole. Indeed, they seemed almost an afterthought, farmed out to the periphery and grouped by themselves. Each class had its place, and they did not mix.

After the "better class" dwellings, the most desirable areas in the quarter section were allotted to parks and recreation, including two lagoons, zoological gardens, a bandstand, refectory, movie house, theater, gymnasium, natatorium, and an athletic field. There were also a few necessary social and cultural services: a kindergarten, school, "domestic science group," art galleries, library, museum, commercial arcade, power plant, garbage reduction plant, and fire department. No provision was made for industry, professional and health facilities, a public meeting hall, government buildings, or a police department. Housing and outdoor activities dominated the scheme, while regulatory state agencies were altogether absent. Wright may have assumed the city's proximity, but he also seemed to believe that people could live together harmoniously, without coercion, a notion implicit in his handling of religion. Society had hardly been clamoring for a nonsectarian "universal temple of worship," and by including it Wright was suggesting that the classes he had separated residentially would want to unite for worship. The religious facility, particularly, presupposed a community bound up by any number of common interests. Nurtured by an indefinable understanding of what was good and proper, by religion, recreation, and freedom from coercion, the quarter section was cemented by spiritual bonds that guaranteed social harmony and kept men in their place.

By the time Wright developed Broadacre City in the 1930s, his thinking on community structure had evolved considerably, but not at the expense of social unity. Although it retained the gridiron motif, Broadacres included enough winding streams and thoroughfares, enough circular buildings, pools, and lakes, and enough dead-end and nonthrough streets to modify the traditional rectilinear pattern of urban organization. All the unsightly aspects of modern life, which in Wright's plan would not be unsightly anyway—the railroad and the airport, factories and the power plant—were pushed to the periphery, along with many services: government and administration, recreational and tourist facilities, and the larger professional and commercial buildings. The parks and "better class" homes, which had dominated the most desirable center portion of the 1913 scheme, were supplanted in Broadacres by small houses, schools, neighborhood garages, stores, and professional services. Wright still recognized class distinctions, but he integrated the various income levels more thoroughly than he had before. Bathhouses and small farms were the nearest neighbors of the most luxurious residence, for example, while apartment towers, grammar schools, and forest cabins were placed close to the "commodious" homes. Earlier sex distinctions were abolished, and the fixed class structure weakened, at least residentially.

Broadacres was less notably suburban—more generalized in class and function—than the 1913 quarter section. Deriving much of its character from the small farms at its center, it was based on the concept of a sturdy yeomanry living close to the soil. By the 1930s Wright had also woven industry and government into the fabric of society, with pollutionless factories scattered about the countryside, and public buildings, without the usual symbols of authority, off in one corner. His provision for religion indicated increased awareness of social diversity. The "universal worship" center reappeared from 1913, perpetuating the notion of a single specified place for the utterance of commonly held beliefs, but around it were grouped nine sectarian temples, allowing variety in modes of expression. Education was paramount in Broadacre City. In 1913 the worship center had rivaled the schools in size, but it was now overshadowed, indeed humbled, by the contiguous educational complex, supplemented by small schools everywhere. Utilities and consumer-oriented industries were to be state owned, although the small business and professional clusters scattered casually about would remain in private hands. To do away with the "triple rent"—interest, speculation in real estate, and patent monopoly—which Wright felt to be the basis of modern economic exploitation, he replaced money in Broadacre City with a kind of social credit.

There were also significant omissions in Wright's planned community. Evidence of authority, for example, was almost entirely absent. The county seat and the administration building, tucked in an inconspicuous corner amidst recreational facilities and a few small factories, presumably housed the regulatory agencies, since there was no separate provision for police and courts, no jail, and no hint of uniformed personnel. Like the quarter section, Broadacres was based on the assumption that in healthful and beautiful surroundings man could live peacefully without coercion, environmentalism at its most optimistic. If anything stood out on the Broadacre model, over which Wright had labored so carefully, it was two large educational complexes, a meandering lake and stream, and something called a circus—with "a totem [pole] and beacon to the lost tribes of a continent"— resembling a forum for pagan rites. Broadacres prophesied a nonexclusive new America, and although the totem implied a "we" and a "they," it was probably intended as a beckoning call to skeptical observers. Like all its predecessors, Wright's scheme assumed a close-knit community with common interests and assumptions, undivided by racial, economic, political, or other problems—a most naïve, romantic view of modern America.

Broadacre City was certainly impossible of achievement, and Wright was almost deliberately vague on the details of its economic and political organization. He had no practical suggestions for implementation, no hints on how people would acquire their homes and their land, how the population relocation would be carried out, or how industry would become socially conscious. He foresaw an end to poverty, ignorance, crime, and illness in an aesthetically and socially beneficial environment, but he was exceedingly unenlightening on the specifics of reform. Such mundane matters did not concern the idealist. Consequently, the model—worked out in painstaking detail, an enormous investment of thought and energy—was virtually useless. But Wright may never have expected otherwise. Fundamentally, Broadacre City was a platform for criticism and a standard against which to measure prevailing conditions. It was a suggestion, not a solution, and Wright did not anticipate the details, or even the essentials for that matter, to be adopted. Broadacres identified urban problems and pointed a direction for the future; it was a strategy rather than a program, a theory rather than a definition. Most of all,

Wright was concerned with architectural harmony, with decentralization, and with the interrelationship of those parts of society included in his model. Measured against such standards, history has more than once proven him correct.

If Wright did not concern himself with implementing Broadacre City, he nevertheless offered many hardheaded proposals, some of which were later utilized, others of which seem relevant to problems more recently unearthed. Certainly, Broadacres anticipated by thirty years many of the criticisms leveled at the city in the 1960s and 1970s. Removing main arteries to the less populated outskirts, for example, would have benefited automobile-choked central cities fighting last-ditch battles against expressway bulldozers. Decentralization of services antedated suburban shopping and professional centers, while pollution-free factories in residential areas anticipated "clean" industrial zones, like Boston's Route 128 belt, and would have made unnecessary much subsequent environmentalist activity. Apartment towers amidst single family dwellings have become an accepted feature of suburban life, while challenges to zoning laws by lower income groups seem destined to threaten upper income monopoly on choice residential locales. Before most Americans, Wright understood the urban and human need for space, light, and air, as well as the psychic disruptions caused by excessive noise and limited vista.

Broadacre City was not a back-to-nature crusade, for it suggested a more equitable distribution of the amenities produced by modern technology. It was farther-reaching than the New Deal's Greenbelt towns, for example, which posited the continuation of the central city, of land-tenure systems, of restrictive zoning, and of traditional patterns of social organization. Broadacres assumed a completely new social fabric, a radical reordering of life-styles and priorities based on a rural-urban synthesis following a massive national retreat from the city. It also assumed that men could live together without coercion, that Art would improve Life through Architecture, that a benign environment would reduce poverty, ignorance, crime, and suffering—a noble sentiment, as yet untested in America. Broadacre City was undoubtedly utopian, visionary, and humanely motivated, a great deal more than can be said for the current urban situation.

Like the Taliesin Fellowship, however, Broadacre City illustrates a crucial flaw in Wright's concept of community. Based on the assumption that the architect knows what is best for the people, Wright's projects did not involve consultation with those primarily affected. Activities at the Fellowship were determined from on high, and no matter how Wright disguised the fact with democratic rhetoric, the county architect of Broadacre City would have had virtually unchecked power to organize life there—all in the name of "organic" living. In this respect Wright was not unlike many American planners whose disregard for the people they "serve" has often flawed their work. It has been much easier for architects to ignore the anonymous lower-class members of a large unorganized group than the individual upper-middle-class clients who pay dearly for private dwellings. And few would argue that Frank Lloyd Wright was anything but an elitist.

Less than three years after completion of the Broadacre model, the Taliesin Fellowship was hard at work on another important project. After a bout with pneumonia in 1937, Wright was told to find a warmer winter climate. Having fallen in love with Arizona during his excursions there since 1928, he purchased eight-hundred acres of government land in the Paradise Valley near Phoenix, and within a year he had designed, and the Fellowship was constructing, Taliesin West, a second home. Its first executed unit was the desert-stone, redwood-beam drafting room, with a white canvas roof providing a soft diffused light and, with the aid of side flaps open to the breezes, repelling the intense heat. Composed of emphatic triangles and diagonals, Taliesin West faced the looming Superstition Mountain on cross axis, taking an ancient symbol of stability as a reference point in the desert's shifting sands. Multicolored stone and huge redwood trusses, later enhanced by green irrigated gardens and deep blue pools, all provided an unexpected variety of color, subtly augmented when shadows cast by stone and beam played gaily with the sun. This oasis of beauty once again demonstrated Wright's unparalleled versatility.[20]

Assuming that an architect will design the optimum house for himself, and that it will be more revealing of his ideas on domesticity and social relations than client projects, it is useful to compare Wright's two Taliesins. Since both were altered over the years, they stand significantly different from their original plans, drawn in 1911 and 1938, but even as first conceived and published they chronicle change and continuity in Wright's thinking. Like its predecessor, Taliesin West takes its cues from the surroundings. Built from native materials and landscaped with local vegetation, its canvas and stone were appropriate in the hot climate. It skillfully integrated architecture and nature by nestling close to the ground (closer, in fact, than anything Wright had built before), by opening immediately to the outside, and by incorporating pools, gardens, and plant life within its perimeter. Its materials, far-flung terraces, open courts, and the edifice itself blended into the desert. Taliesin East (as it was now sometimes called) had merged into its hilltop so subtly at points that building and site were almost indistinguishable, and the same was true in Arizona.

This close interrelationship had contributed to a fortresslike atmosphere at Spring Green, but in the desert worked in completely different ways. Alone with his mistress in 1911, Wright had valued privacy, protection from hostile outsiders, and a sense of shelter above all. Happily married for a decade by 1938, with commissions coming and new ideas developing rapidly, he now faced the world confidently, without fear. Taliesin East achieved its security and its architectural success from its commanding hilltop position, overlooking the valley and controlling its own access routes like the castle of a feudal baron. Taliesin West, on the other hand, sits alone and unprotected on the desert floor, dominated by the mountains to which it pays tribute, exposed on all sides like the lonely home of a pioneer. Like the Okies and Arkies who took their tents to California in search of fortune, Wright's own canvas-roofed dwelling was an optimistic investment in the

Aerial view of Taliesin West, 1938 and after, near Scottsdale, Arizona. The architect's study stands free at the left. The drawing room (pitched beamed roof) begins the main axis, followed by service facilities (dark roof), leading into the residential compound with the architect's quarters on the right (just beyond tower), and apprentice rooms to the left across the courtyard. The semidetached unit with the pitched roof, behind Wright's quarters at the upper end of the triangular garden, is the lounge

growth of the Southwest.[21] In 1911 he had been a wounded warrior within enemy territory, licking his wounds in a stone retreat; twenty-seven years later, in Arizona, he used his solitude to map strategies for future campaigns, confident of ultimate victory. But the sand and the canvas and the water suggested a certain impermanence, as if Wright had learned that the strongest fortress guaranteed nothing. Only the looming mountain was certain of immortality.

There were also important internal differences between the two homes. In the 1911 Taliesin a central complex of courts, gardens, and terraces was ringed by the living, working, and service facilities. Clockwise around the periphery ran the draftsmen's and gardener's quarters, the stables, assistants' rooms, Wright's own suite, the guest wing, and outstretching walls and gardens. Wright separated himself from his draftsmen on the longest possible diagonal through the building, in rooms pulling away from the house over the hill's slope. Flanking himself on one side with guests and on the other with his private studio, he brought closest to him the things he trusted most. Taliesin East was anything but gloomy, yet it insisted upon reserved, orderly, and dignified behavior. Its inhabitants worked together but lived separate social lives. Its architectural unity left sufficient room for personal withdrawal.

The center of Taliesin West was devoted to living space, bringing residents together, not keeping them apart. In addition to the courts, gardens, and terraces at its core, there were also cooking, dining, and entertaining facilities, and the main drafting room, all of which had been left to the perimeter at Spring Green. Wright's quarters in an L at one end were separated from apprentice rooms only by a common court, indicating a quasi-family relationship. Taliesin West is more tightly organized and internally compact than Taliesin East. Reflecting the conservation of space and materials required by modern conditions, it also affirms close ties among inhabitants. Although many apprentices lived in tents and huts scattered over the desert, Taliesin West was built for a mutually interdependent group, subservient to a higher authority. With bright colors, dancing sunlit surfaces, breezy openings and passageways, and light textiles, it acknowledges the spirit of youth and the exuberance of life itself, intangibles more characteristic of the Master, ironically, than of those he controlled so thoroughly.

Although he continued to advocate Broadacre City for the rest of his life—in 1958 his last book was devoted to it—Wright made his final reputation from individual buildings, not from community projects. Taliesin West was one of many impressive new designs after 1936 that catapulted Wright back to the forefront of his profession, but his renaissance might not have occurred had not the Fellowship freed him from mundane considerations, had not the completion of the Broadacre model removed that burden from his mind, and had not his home life finally settled into a placid routine. Without the old burdens and with a sympathetic comrade, he achieved an emotional equilibrium conducive to intellectual accomplishment. The next few years more than compensated for the tribulations of the past.

8. BACK ON TOP

[1936–1945]

From 1936 until the Second World War intruded, Frank Lloyd Wright underwent an architectural renaissance. With a devoted wife and a corps of faithful apprentices to carry out his wishes, he was freed from the numerous burdens that for so long had destroyed his concentration and intimidated potential clients. His designs for a new kind of residence proved to be as popular as the prairie house and, with two particularly ambitious commissions that received critical acclaim, forced professional and layman alike to admit that Wright was as vital as thirty years before. His surge of creativity after two decades of frustration was one of the most dramatic resuscitations in American art history, made more impressive by the fact that Wright was seventy years old in 1937. He often made himself insufferable by demanding public adulation and by his constant criticism of established institutions, but many people who despised his irreverence also reluctantly acknowledged that he really was a living legend.

Frank Lloyd Wright's two periods of great achievement coincided with the Progressive Era and the New Deal, years of national introspection and reform. Perhaps intellectual and political ferment encouraged him to redefine the social purposes of his buildings, or perhaps the prevailing mood was unusually receptive to new ideas. Wright's architecture was popular because it satisfied genuine needs, and seemed even more responsive to the Great Depression than to the prosperity thirty years before. In 1936 and 1937 Wright produced designs that spoke directly to three current issues: working conditions, accumulated wealth, and housing. "Fallingwater," the 1936 weekend retreat at Bear Run, Pennsylvania, for a millionaire department store magnate, was by no means a social frivolity. The Administration Building (1936) for the Johnson Wax Company in Racine, Wisconsin, offered humane though antiquated theories of labor-management relations and working-class organization. And the Herbert Jacobs residence (1937) in Madison, Wisconsin, was an attempt to build inexpensive housing for a middle-income family. Wright's exotic departures in the 1920s had been of limited theoretical and practical value, but his simultaneous interest in the three major economic classes during the depression coincided with the mainstream of popular concern.

The Herbert Jacobs House was the first Usonian home Wright executed, though not the first he designed. Taking its name from Samuel Butler's term for the United States in *Erewhon* (1917), a utopian novel, Wright's new residential concept was intended to provide for the average modern family at low cost. Built during 1937 for $5,500 (about the price of a good-size prairie house), including $450 architect's fee, it utilized many technological economies. Its concrete slab "foundation," for example, "floated" on a drained bed of cinders and sand, in which hot water pipes produced "gravity" or radiant heat, which rose through the floor, eliminating ducts and radiators. The slab roof was insulated and contained the ventilation system, and its long overhangs protected the exterior. The "ready-made" walls were three layers of boards and two thicknesses of heavy duty tarpaper sandwiched together, raised in horizontal panels assembled at the site. According to the University of Wisconsin's Forest Products Laboratory, which followed construction closely, the assembly and insulation were cheaper and more efficient than conventional methods.[1]

The organization of the Jacobs House was as imaginative as its technology. The dining room was abolished in favor of a table alcove connecting the kitchen and the living area, which were further screened from each other by a large fireplace, the effect being to merge the three rooms into one. Wright raised the kitchen ceiling above the dominant roof line as a ventilation stack for the entire building. For privacy, the house was turned from the street, its only visible windows being a series of small openings running its length underneath the overhanging roof. Facing the interior of the lot, however, the eighteen-by-thirty-foot living room was lined with over twenty feet of floor-to-ceiling windows and doors leading out to the terrace extension of the foundation slab. The glass was wrapped around the corner of an L as the inside wall of a bedroom wing, which carried the overhead fenestration from the front of the house along its exterior. During the winter the sun passing across the expanse of glass provided enough light and heat to reduce utility costs significantly. In the summer, on the other

The Herbert Jacobs House, 1937, Westmoreland (now Madison), Wisconsin, the first executed Usonian house

hand, the sun crossed overhead without shining directly in, and the small windows under the roof line captured enough light in the late afternoon to prolong the day.

There were other ingenious innovations and economies in the Usonian house. The glass, stained wood, and brick walls made paint, varnish, plaster, and wallpaper obsolete. In place of a cellar, Wright tripled storage space, principally with a row of closets the length of the outside wall of the bedroom corridor. Holes cut through the roof overhangs conducted rainwater into drains in the foundation slab, eliminating gutters and downspouts. Believing that modern automobiles could withstand inclement weather, Wright replaced the garage with a carport walled by the house on two sides and connected to the front entry, hidden in a corner under the eaves. He removed the doors from kitchen cabinets, abolished light fixtures and radiators, and built in much of the furniture. Based on a careful study of spatial arrangements, the Jacobs House improved the efficiency and reduced the maintenance of the modern residence. Wright cut costs with technological shortcuts, but did not sacrifice a feeling of luxury.

Herbert Jacobs was immensely satisfied; not only did he publicly defend his home from skeptics,[2] but he also hired Wright to design another when his family outgrew its quarters a few years later. Although no cheaper than those nearby of comparable size, the house was more practical and attractive, better organized, had more usable space, needed less maintenance, and was therefore economical. It was also a boon for Wright, whose professional resurgence depended on the many clients who asked for similar designs. But of more profound importance, the Usonian house became a prototype of the modern American ranch home, with one floor, bedroom wing, glass-faced patio, carport, open plan, and ample window space. Wright scorned the jerry-built tracts that later characterized the national suburban landscape, but he was nonetheless instrumental in developing the typical residence of the mid-century American middle class. After the Second World War his designs were priced out of reach of all but a few, and he never fulfilled his ambition of providing inexpensive housing for average income families. But until the habits of the middle class change significantly, it is unlikely that the typical private home will evolve much beyond the many Usonian derivatives.

Wright's new residence was not without precedent. Evolving from his own few designs between 1929 and 1936, and influenced by characteristics of the International Style, it nonetheless owed its greatest debt to the prairie house, which in many ways it updated. The most obvious of the many similarities between them, of course, was the open plan, which Wright developed further in the 1930s by literally turning the main body of the house into a single large space. Like his earlier designs, the Usonian home stressed its close relationship to nature with increased fenestration, and by facilitating real and apparent contact between inside and out. It was uncompromisingly horizontal, rested on a cellarless slab, used casement windows only and regional materials frequently. Both houses had split-level roofs, modular unit construction systems, recessed entries, low ceilings, and fireplace cores from which they seemed to radiate. Furniture and accessories were often built in, along with the flower boxes that in the Usonian house replaced the inevitable concrete urn. There had been several slab roof designs during the prairie years, and even a few on one floor.

But new technology changed many standard prairie house features. The porte cochere, for instance, evolved into a carport. Improvements in the manufacture of plate glass appreciably increased window space, and with it sunlight, vista, and association with the outdoors. Dead air space under a sloping roof was now unnecessary for insulation, while new methods of waterproofing and surfacing made slab roofs practical. Changing social habits accounted for additional refinements. Porches were no longer as fashionable as patios, and servant quarters became totally irrelevant. Formal dining had lost its social prominence, and so a table in the living room corner next to the kitchen was more convenient than a separate room. Intricate stained and leaded glass was out of style and too expensive for the 1930s, and a second floor was impractical, so Wright reduced the levels from three or two to one.

The Usonian homes were lower and seemed longer than most prairie houses. With their overhanging eaves they had little need for string courses or contrasting trim to accentuate their close relation to the land. They were generally built of brick or horizontally lapped wood, but never the stucco and masonry of their predecessors. Some, like the Goetsch-Winkler House (1939) in Okemos, Michigan, integrated the bedrooms into its main body, but others, like the Jacobs House, were L-shaped, with a separate wing extending toward the rear. Unlike the suburban prairie houses, they were often in the country, on the edge of small cities, or in large wooded lots, taking advantage of irregular and spectacular sites—hillsides, inclines, or lake shores—more often. Partly because Wright's reputation was now national, and partly because he encouraged nonurban clients, his new buildings were much less regional than thirty years before; they were, in the words of architectural historian Peter Blake, "realistic and beautiful solutions to living in America."[3]

More than likely influenced by the International Style, Wright made the Usonian house "look more modern as well." Taking the appearance and the workings of machinery as their models, young architects from several European nations had made significant innovations in residential design since the First World War. Although there are many surface similarities between his work and theirs, it is impossible to "prove" conclusively that Wright borrowed from his younger colleagues. His constant and spirited denunciation of them, however, could easily have functioned to disguise his own indebtedness (even from himself). And the fact remains that the Usonian house particularly resembles some of the work by Ludwig Mies van der Rohe, whose project for a country home (1923), German Pavilion at the Barcelona Exposition in 1929, and Berlin Building Exposition House (1931), with their open plans, their glass surfaces, and their one level (or mostly one level) arrangements foreshadowed Wright. Superficially at least, a scattering of homes by others followed Mies's lead, among them Lois Welzenbacher's Schulz House (1928) at Westphalia, Germany, Karl Schneider's Werner House (1930) in Hamburg, and Hans Schmidt's Waldner House (1931) in Basle, Switzerland. And designs by Le Corbusier and Pierre Jeanneret, Otto Eisler, Walter Gropius, and J. J. P. Oud, if not as obviously related to Wright's, nevertheless compelled his attention.

He had ample opportunity to observe this work closely during the 1932 International Style Exhibition at the Museum of Modern Art in New York, in which he himself participated as a foil to the others. The problem of the relationship between his work and the Europeans' is a complicated one. There is little doubt they had been profoundly influenced by the prairie buildings depicted in Wright's 1910 and 1911 Wasmuth publications, and it seems likely they also admired certain designs in the 1925 Dutch Wendingen edition. His 1922 project for G. P. Lowes at Eagle Rock, California, for example, and his 1923 La Miniatura for Mrs. George Millard at Pasadena, were not unlike several Le Corbusier residences of the late 1920s and early 1930s. La Miniatura also bears striking similarities to Gerrit Rietveld's Shroder House (1925) in Utrecht, Netherlands, which is more closely related, however, to Le Corbusier's 1922 Citrohan project, which may in fact have influenced both Rietveld and Wright. And therein lies the confusion. Although the Millard house seems derivative, Wright would never admit leaning on another architect, particularly a younger and equally arrogant Le Corbusier. The Europeans freely acknowledged their indebtedness to him, but never he to them. Even without Wright's polemics, the architectural causality is difficult to determine.

In several fundamental respects, however, the Usonian house departed significantly from the International Style. The Europeans, first of all, pointedly embraced and attempted to increase the separation of nature from art and architecture. While Wright aimed to minimize the distinctions between building and site—between indoors and out—the Internationalists enlarged upon them, for to them the measure of a man was his distance from the primitive. Many of their buildings were poured concrete painted white, unsoftened by wood, trim, or contrasting color. Regardless of nationality or environment, their work was pictorially similar—sometimes virtually interchangeable—making no brief for regional, social, or cultural diversity. Their houses, which were often called "machines for living," were rational, logical, precise, and efficient, to be sure, the epitome of functionalism, in a very mechanistic way. But they were often cold, sterile, and antiseptic boxlike structures that seem plunked down regardless of locale. Wright claimed that each of his designs could be built only on one particular spot, meaning that its setting was an integral part of the overall conception. He also relied on colors, wood grain, the outside coming in, and anything else he could muster up to fashion machine-made products into restful and intimate human forms (without sacrificing efficiency). The Internationalists, however, were proud of encasing their clients (and themselves) in fastidious, almost medicinal, surroundings.

Two of Wright's own houses—for Richard Lloyd Jones (1929) in Tulsa and the Mesa project (1931) in Denver—were closely related to Mies van der Rohe's scheme for a brick country home (1923), and served as transitions between the prairie and Usonian periods. In Mies's project, an open-plan building core on three distinct levels was carried out horizontally in vigorously stated brick, glass panels, and a contrasting vertically articulated fireplace stack. Wright's disastrously ugly Lloyd Jones House, with vertical rows of plain concrete blocks alternating with similar rows of windows of the same width and height, was also a three-level, horizontal structure with glass walls and modularly related rooms given separate expression on the exterior, as in the Mies van der Rohe project. The House on the Mesa was happier aesthetically and closer to the German's model. From a second-level living area above a billiard room, modular axes radiated out as a service wing with employees' L, a bedroom wing, and a covered swimming pool. With concrete block and glass panels stretched along a low-slung, multilevel plan, the House on the Mesa would have been an outstanding luxury home. Wright's two designs were the principal links between a one-floor building like the W. A. Glasner House (1905) in Glencoe, Illinois, and the Usonian home of the 1930s.

His few designs in the early 1930s revealed an interest in one- (or one- and two-) floor structures with expanses of glass and open plans, although the finished product evolved slowly. In the Walter Davidson Sheet Metal Farmhouses (1932), for example, he eliminated the dining room for the first time, replacing it with a table in the corner of a large kitchen. In the first scheme for Malcolm Willey the same year, the dining table became an extension of the living room L, and in the Minneapolis home finally built for him in 1934 the kitchen and living room spaces were essentially united, with only a dining table and an open wall of shelves between. The first Willey plan featured a horizontally lapped upper-level terrace, whereas the second was a single story of brick and wood, really a rectangle with embellishment.

Wright brought all the elements—the one-floor plan with raised sections, overpowering horizontality, sheets of plate glass, slab roof, and open plan—together successfully in 1936 in the projects for Robert Lusk in Huron, South Dakota, and for H. C. Hoult in Wichita, Kansas. Although the latter is frequently called the first Usonian house, the Lusk project is also L-shaped, with bedroom wing, floor-to-ceiling windows, roof and foundation slabs, and the other distinguishing features of the Herbert Jacobs House.

The social posture of the Usonian plan, embodying Wright's final thoughts on the family and its relation to the rest of society, struck a median between the prairie house and the textile-block designs of the 1920s. The former, which had usually faced the street with numerous windows, seemed to address the community, even with its sheltered doorway. The Usonian house did not shun social contact after the manner of the textile-block homes, but it, too, guarded its privacy. Turning away from passers-by to face the interior of the lot, with limited streetside window space and entry hidden under overhangs at the corner of the L or to the rear, it was an introspective building, protecting itself even in the country or on large lots, where it was relatively secluded. But with its rich materials, its reverence for the land, and its out-reaching overhangs, which at the entrance seemed inviting, the Usonian house did not attempt self-segregation. After two decades of unhappy relations with the outside world, Wright could not easily assume the optimistic detachment of the prairie house. But total withdrawal was even more undesirable, and so the Usonian residence drew on Wright's various domestic experiences to form a new synthesis.

In its own quiet way, however, it did not entirely abandon the notion of the family residence as a defense mechanism. Combined with plantings or topography, its L-shape (and later the Y-shape) was ideally suited for forming a kind of compound, open and spacious within, but closed to the neighbors. The concrete homes of the 1920s had been formidable and sometimes undomestic inside and out, but within its compound the Usonian house was precisely the opposite, making its statement of privacy and group protection only to nonresidents. On first encounter the visitor may have difficulty finding the entrance (trial and error is the only course), but once inside he is immediately drawn into the life of the household as he walks through a low reception area toward the glass walls of the living room. As he proceeds, the subtly changing vista is an exciting architectural experience, and by the time he arrives he is predisposed to like what he finds there. United by its open plan but sheltered and made secure from the outside world by real and symbolic devices, the residents of the Usonian house were, in Wright's words, "a little private club." The modern American family had no need to "box up or hole in for protection." Security in every sense is best found, he wrote, in "wide free spacing and integral construction. . . . Spaciousness is for safety as well as beauty." No longer fortifications, he stated in 1931, homes should be "shelter in the open."[4]

The Usonian house floor plan reflected changes in living habits since the 1900s. Born in the Progressive Era and come of age in the Roaring Twenties or the Great Depression, Wright's clients were impatient with many of the old formalities and social conventions, with wasted space and time, and they were also sexually more egalitarian. The changing role and status of women was undoubtedly an important factor in the internal arrangement of Wright's architecture in the 1930s. No longer the fragile, retiring, speak-only-when-spoken-to, headache-prone irrelevancy of William Dean Howells, the modern woman was the competitive, strong-willed, efficient careerist (in or out of the house) of John Dos Passos and Willa Cather. "The housewife herself became the central figure," Wright later explained; "she was now [a] hostess 'officio,' [instead of] . . . a kitchen-mechanic behind closed doors."[5] Since she wanted a compact, efficient home without servants, Wright moved the kitchen from the back of the house to the center, calling it the "work-space," from which she could run the entire operation.

The evolution of the dining room indicates changes in Wright's perception of family organization from the 1890s to the 1930s. Once the most stately and formal room in the house, it passed out of existence altogether, replaced by strategically located table and chairs en route from the living to the kitchen space. In many Usonian homes it was almost impossible to have an old-fashioned meal, for the table, permanently fixed in place and size, could accommodate only small gatherings. "Guests for any one dinner are limited to two or at most four," the former owner of a 1940 Wright house wrote, "because where can dishes for a proper dinner be put . . . ?" The new arrangement also reflected the increased informality of American home entertainment, wherein the cocktail party, the leisurely evening, and the buffet supper replaced the elaborate occasion. The best way to conserve space, Mrs. Marjorie Leighey continued, was to dispense with old formalities: salad could be served from a large bowl on the table instead of from the kitchen on individual plates.[6] The Usonian house was

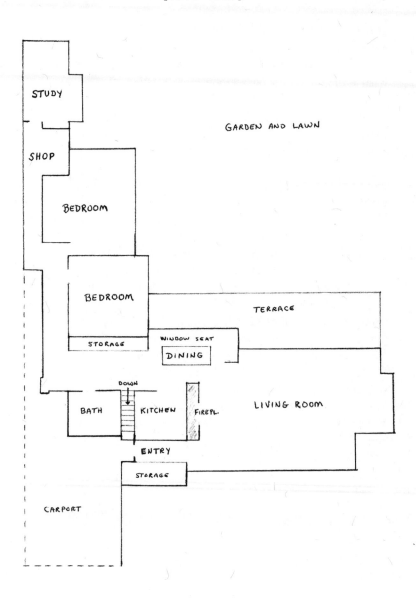

STUDY

GARDEN AND LAWN

SHOP

BEDROOM

BEDROOM

TERRACE

STORAGE

WINDOW SEAT

DINING

DOWN

BATH

KITCHEN

FIREPL.

LIVING ROOM

ENTRY

STORAGE

CARPORT

Floor plan of Herbert Jacobs House

also informed by a heightened concern for efficiency. Since the entire main area was now a single multipurpose space, the problem for the housewife was no longer where to do things, but when, in what order, and in what relation to each other; she became more of a manager than a servant, in other words. Without a dining room, her steps were reduced, and Wright usually designed things in such a way that from her "work-space" she could observe her children everywhere, except in the bedrooms.

The effect of all this was to increase family togetherness even more than in the prairie house. If that building had weakened the identification of particular rooms with prescribed purposes, the Usonian house did away with several rooms altogether, uniting more family activities in one place. The "living room" in a Wright house was apt to be a place for eating, relaxation, play, entertaining, and cultural enrichment, and with kitchen and patio appended, for virtually all other family functions. Of course, the Usonian and post-Usonian houses separated the bedroom wing from the living area, making adequate provision for personal privacy, according to Herbert Jacobs. Even in the busy family space there was often a quiet corner tucked away under a light-shelf, and the concrete floors reduced the children's noise considerably. Hence the Usonian house provided a margin for individuality sufficient to offset the stifling family mutuality Wright had rejected in 1909. Despite its protection of the independent interests of individual members, however, it affirmed that a family should be a tightly knit unit, separate from but not rejecting the community, in its compound close to nature.

The structure of the group might be egalitarian or authoritarian, depending on how vigorously the parents chose to exercise control. At once Victorian and modern, the Usonian house could accommodate either traditional or progressive living styles. "Either the children get left or must get spanked into place," Wright remarked in reference to his homes, "else they have the whole house and the grown-ups do what they can do to make themselves as comfortable as [possible]." The very choice, however, was a modern notion. At least one father saw no dilemma, believing the progressive concept of mutuality to have been beneficial: "The temptation is to be together more," Herbert Jacobs recalled in 1956. "I think it does something to you subconsciously. I think it did something to my children. . . . Living in that house was fantastically wonderful." But another Usonian father admitted that family togetherness could as easily enhance parental authority as increase the equality of members. Wright himself understood that with children constantly in the living room they were apt to turn the house upside down in the process of taking it over. But he was willing to take that chance:

Back in farm days [he wrote in 1954] there was one big living room, a stove in it, and Ma was there cooking—looking after the children and talking to Pa—dogs and cats and tobacco smoke too—all gemutlich if all was orderly, but it seldom was; and the children were playing around. It created a certain atmosphere of a domestic nature which had charm and which is not, I think, a good thing to lose altogether.

And so with the kitchen a part of the living area in the Usonian house, Wright sought to bring order to the old-fashioned family in a dignified modern setting.[7]

In his autobiography he asserted that he went on to design twenty-six more Usonian homes between the Jacobs House and 1943. Like so many other figures he cited, that too may have come out of his hat, but it is true that the house type rapidly proved its popularity. In the eight years from 1928 through 1935 Wright had executed only two buildings for paying clients, one of whom was a relative. But in the first eight years of the Usonian house, from 1936 through 1943, he executed thirty-six buildings, thirty-four of them by 1941, an average of six annually. Nineteen-forty was a banner year, with twelve completed commissions, his largest output since 1907, half of them Usonian houses.[8] Although parts of the structures—the walls especially—were designed to be prefabricated or shop assembled, in fact very few were, and after the Second World War, when Wright's practice grew to unprecedented dimensions, he built larger and more expensive buildings.* The bedroom wing and the open plan continued to characterize his work, but costs rose and clients grew more affluent, so that he never accomplished his objective of providing middle-income families with low-cost housing. Nevertheless, the Usonian house was the model for his later residences, and the catalyst for his professional recovery.

At the other end of the economic and architectural spectrum from the moderately priced house was "Fallingwater," the luxury weekend retreat Wright designed in 1936. Cantilevered over a waterfall at Bear Run, Pennsylvania, for Pittsburgh millionaire Edgar Kaufmann, the small vacation home has been photographed, analyzed, and described perhaps more than any other Wright building. Not only did it win him enormous acclaim at the time, but it has since come to be regarded as one of the finest structures ever built. One critic calls it "the most famous modern house in the world," while another says it is "one of the complete masterpieces of twentieth-century art."[9] Given an unlimited budget by an admiring client (one might say a patron, in fact, since the house has for some years been a public monument), Wright exploited his opportunity to the fullest, producing his most magnificent and creative residence since Taliesin in 1911.

The suggestion by one historian that the house in Bear Run is without precedent in Wright's work or in that of any other architect[10] is an exaggeration, since the building has elements—but only elements—of the International Style and of the prairie house. Its siting on the brink of a precipice and its organization of surface and mass recall Richard Neutra's Lovell House (1929–1930) in Los Angeles, except that Wright's far superior building is of canti-

---

* In *The Natural House* (p. 97), Wright claimed to have built over one hundred Usonian homes, a term he was then (1954) applying, however, to all his residences. I have chosen to use "Usonian" the way he originally intended: a moderately priced, partially prefabricated wood, glass, and brick slab-roof structure, and, unless one includes his completely prefabricated designs (see Chapter 10), he built no more after 1941.

lever construction while Neutra's has the steel frame his former mentor abhorred. Fallingwater's horizontal terraces suggest the raised second level of Le Corbusier's Savoie Villa (1930) at Poissy-sur-Seine, France, but while Wright's house planted its roots firmly into the rocky hillside, Le Corbusier's villa sits gingerly on its pole supports, seemingly afraid to tickle its bottom on the flat, grassy site. Some of Wright's own buildings also anticipated Fallingwater, for example the crossed cantilevered balconies of the Elizabeth Gale House (1909) in Oak Park, and the abstract modular composition and soaring roof lines of the Robie House. Fallingwater was not unprecedented, but it is virtually unmatched.

One of its most salient characteristics is an absolute refusal to be confined. The Robie House cantilevers had soared off in two directions, but Fallingwater seems to take flight every way at once, making it exceptionally difficult to reproduce in one's mind or to describe to someone who has not seen it. (Most photographs are also inadequate.) And that may have been one of Wright's purposes: to defy description, to destroy categories. "It has no limitations as to form," he once remarked.[11] So difficult visually to comprehend—so impossible to harness, as it were—Fallingwater destroys assumptions of what a house should be and do. Visitors are surprised, for example, by its comparatively few rooms. Most of its floor space—as well as materials and expense—is devoted to a massive living room, and to terraces, walls, and canopy-slabs that shoot out in four directions. The three bedrooms and the usual service functions take up a small proportion of the three levels. Fallingwater was not a family residence but a weekend entertainment retreat, and, like the Guggenheim Museum in New York, is a study in the interrelationship of sculptured forms. It is not subject to criticisms of "impracticality," for, as Henry-Russell Hitchcock has wisely stated, architecture lives not only "through the solution of generic problems but quite as much by the thrill and acclaim of unique masterpieces."[12]

Like few other buildings before or since, Fallingwater exploits site to advantage. Two unbelievably cantilevered balconies, shel-

"Fallingwater," the Edgar Kaufmann House, 1936, Bear Run, Pennsylvania

tered by a slab roof-canopy, cross axes very close to a waterfall, and seem to float in space without support. Horizontal sweeps of reinforced concrete, and the vertical thrust of the stone and glass fireplace core, tie the house securely to its rocky plateau, while mirroring the plunge of ledge and stream. Overhanging roofs, far-flung cantilevers, and out-reaching walls root the house to its site, but without appearing to restrict it. Without Fallingwater, Bear Run would have remained an attractive forest glen, like thousands of others, but, with it, the place became uniquely beautiful. Here was an unsurpassed example of art improving nature, of man making the world a better place. Fallingwater also proved Wright's contention that an organic building was appropriate only in its specific location, and nowhere else.

But Fallingwater achieves its greatness in the way it transcends site to speak to universal human concerns. In its unprecedented freedom from traditional architectural forms and composition, it reveals the aspiration of the human spirit, and in its successful partnership with environment it stands as a guidepost to man's sympathetic domination of nature and himself. Fallingwater is a matrix of opposites. At once incredibly stable and dangerously ephemeral, it is securely anchored to rock and plateau, but seems to leap into space. It embodies change and changelessness simultaneously, for its imperishable stone, steel, and concrete forms constitute an entirely different building from each new angle of vision. The solid rock and the rushing water reflect the permanence and the impermanence of man. Fallingwater sinks its roots deeply into the ground to grow out of its site more like a plant than most other buildings, yet it is a masterpiece of sophisticated technology. Composed of myriads of rectangles, it is never redundant, of innumerable individual pieces of varying size and material, it nevertheless achieves a unity few structures approach. Fallingwater is a study in the dichotomies—fluidity and inflexibility, motion and stability, permanence and change—that make the human condition a paradox of welcome adventure and anxious uncertainty. The house at Bear Run may have been a comment on the ambiguity of wealth and power in times of depression, but it was undoubtedly Wright's nature poem to modern man.

Along with the Usonian house and Fallingwater, Wright's third notable achievement during the depression was the Administration Building (1936) for the Johnson Wax Company in Racine, Wisconsin, a streamlined package with old-fashioned contents. If Wright viewed the contemporary household as a little private club, he conceived of the office force as an extended family. The Administration Building, in keeping with the Johnson Company's philosophy, offered a traditional interpretation of working relationships. Johnson Wax was family owned and managed, anti-union, paternalistic, and small town. The Johnson family was Racine itself, and as the largest local employer its relationship with workers and community was almost feudal. Unlike the impersonal giant corporations that were tightening control over American industry, the Johnsons considered their organization a large happy family. Taking pride in their civic improvements, and in their social and cultural contributions, they thought of Racine as protectively as a father does his children. Wright's design, therefore, was not only a place to work, but "to live in" as well; speaking solely to the situation at Johnson Wax, it was a totally inappropriate model for labor-management relations elsewhere.[13]

The Administration Building is a windowless brick rectangle, lit by skylights and two strips of translucent Pyrex tubing encircling it just below the roof line and a few feet above eye level. Like the 1904 Larkin Building in Buffalo, it sealed out the noise, odor, and ugliness of its shabby industrial location, and, like its parent structure, its main office space was a single large room (20 × 128 × 228 feet), ringed by a balcony. (Wright liked to say that the "masculine" Larkin Building "sired" the "more feminine" Johnson Building, where rounded corners and curved lines presumably carried sexual overtones.)[14] Indirect lighting, rich textures, integral furniture, and a scattering of structurally unnecessary but psychologically and aesthetically pleasing pillars combined to create unusual warmth and quiet for such a large and busy office.

Since the main entrance led to a covered parking area at the interior of the lot, the entire composition was completely self-enclosed. Secure within its beautiful surroundings, the Johnson family could ignore the gloomy social and economic conditions outside. Perhaps that explains Wright's attempt to make the building "as beautiful to live in and work in as any cathedral ever was to worship in," for during the depression a job, like religion, was an effective opiate. Both employer and employee, at any rate, applauded the success of Wright's efforts. The Johnson Company estimated their headquarters to be worth millions of dollars in advertising. Prospective employees were willing to wait a year for a position (even after the depression), and once hired their efficiency steadily increased. Many preferred to come early and linger after work rather than return to their less attractive homes. In keeping with the atmosphere of the place and with the philosophy of the owners, the office force began serving tea after it moved into the new quarters.[15]

Literally and symbolically, the organization of the Johnson Building reinforced time-honored labor-management relations. The president's suite was at the top center of the structure, at the juncture of the two oval penthouses that contained the other officers. Below them, on the mezzanine overlooking the large main room, were the junior executives and the department heads. At the bottom of the social and business hierarchy came the clerical staff,

Administration Building, Johnson Wax Company, 1936, Racine, Wisconsin

grouped together where their superiors could observe them. And, finally, all the services in the basement underneath the workers were directly accessible to them. Since families should play together when labor is done, the recreational aspects of this home away from home were also expressed architecturally, with terraces, squash courts, and a theater on the roof.

Office buildings of the period were tall, masonry-encased steel frames whose areas of glass increased as time passed. Apparently uninterested in stating the similarities between his clients and other businesses, Wright chose to stress their differences by making the Johnson Building low and windowless. This unique, marvelously successful, unusually beautiful edifice, therefore, had little architectural or sociological impact on American commercial civilization. Land in Racine was not as scarce as in the large metropolitan areas, so the Johnson Company could afford to expand out instead of up. Yet, ironically, when Wright designed a supplementary research laboratory in 1946, he created a fourteen-story tower, which not only reversed the usual order of things (an upright office slab with a low companion, like United Nations Plaza), but was altogether unnecessary. The only explanation is that Wright wished to state the local prominence of his clients, and in the complex as a whole to suggest that, unlike the giant corporations, they had not debased human relationships in a bureaucratic maze.

If the Johnson Building was not a precedent for subsequent corporate architecture, it did speak reassuringly to contemporary problems. Encouraging a spirit of togetherness in happy surroundings, it was a pleasure to be in, even during the depression. By recalling preindustrial working conditions, it defined everyone's place in an old-fashioned hierarchy, shunning the impersonal vagaries of the modern corporation. In an age of rapid and uncertain change it reduced anxiety by stating maxims from simpler days, when social and work relationships were easily understood. Conditioned by the shared perceptions of architect and client,[16] the Johnson Building was a product of hard times, and of the

Research Tower, Johnson Wax Company, 1946

ethics of paternal enterprise in a small midwestern city. For the future it was irrelevant, but it helped make work palatable in an organization somewhat outside the mainstream of modern capitalism.

If during his lifetime Wright had designed only the Johnson Building, Fallingwater, and the Jacobs House, his place in architectural history would have been secure. The three were largely responsible for increased critical attention after 1937, and probably determined Howard Myers, editor and publisher of *The Architectural Forum*, to devote his entire January 1938 issue to Wright, who planned or wrote most of it. *The Forum* was read by only a few, unlike *Life* magazine, which commissioned Wright to design a Usonian house for its September 26, 1938, issue, or *Business Week*, which reported the Johnson Building's formal opening the following May. Having recently been consigned to unwilling retirement, Wright was now acknowledged to be as vital as Le Corbusier or Mies van der Rohe. Publicity accompanied his every move, and he obliged by designing a number of remarkable new buildings. Not since the first decade of the century—thirty years before—had he been so prolific, or so creative.[17]

One of Wright's most important legacies is his architectural adaptation of elemental geometric shapes, and their manipulation into new arrangements challenging preconceptions about the most appropriate forms for certain kinds of structures. During this period of great productivity and accomplishment—from 1936 into the Second World War—he began to explore seriously the possibilities of the triangle, the hexagon, and the circle, all of which, combined with the Usonian open plan, made Wright's later homes more complex but less dependent on rectangular predictabilities. His first important departure from the ninety-degree angle was the hexagonal house (1936) in Palo Alto, California, for Professor Paul Hanna of Stanford University. Wrapped around the crown of a gently sloping hill, its V shape enclosed a pool and interior court, and the spaces inside seemed to flow into each other more naturally without right angles. The guest wing forming the third side of a hexagon emphasized the house's impulse toward self-enclosure, making the circle the next logical step in Wright's exploration. Only two years later, in fact, in 1938, all the rooms in the plywood Ralph Jester project in Palos Verdes, California, were circles, united by free-flowing space under a squarish roof that projected far over a large round swimming pool. And in 1942, when he designed a second home for Herbert Jacobs, in Middleton, Wisconsin, Wright dug a fieldstone semicircle with a two-story interior glass arc into a hill-sized berm at the back. During the remainder of his career he often relied on triangular and hexagonal modules, and, in the 1950s particularly, made increasingly greater use of circles.

From 1936 to 1940—which after the prairie period might be called Wright's second golden age—he designed so many outstanding structures that enumeration becomes an exercise in frustration. As the Usonian house evolved it grew longer and lower, like the Stanley Rosenbaum House (1939) in Florence, Alabama, with farther-reaching overhangs to resolve it more gently than the somewhat abrupt Jacobs residence. Nineteen thirty-seven saw the magnificent "Wingspread" in Racine, Wisconsin, for Herbert F. Johnson of the wax company, a luxurious living room in a central stack with four wings spinning off toward the compass points. The next year there followed Taliesin West, the Midway Farm Buildings at Taliesin East (perhaps the world's most avant-garde bovine domicile), the first of four versions of the abortive but brilliant Monona Terrace Civic Center for Madison, Wisconsin, and the sixteen-unit master plan for Florida Southern College at Lakeland, which over the years grew into the largest collection of Wright's architecture in any one location. He designed several more exciting commissions in 1939, including a magnificent guest-house addition to Fallingwater, the dramatically cantilevered George D. Sturges House in Brentwood Heights, California, and "Suntop Homes" in Ardmore, Pennsylvania, a compact but spacious arrangement of four three-level apartments, each in its own quadrant of the structure, separated by a cross-axial brick partition.

Gregor Affleck House, 1941, Bloomfield Hills, Michigan. A Usonian house closely integrated with its environment

In 1940 came the concrete- and steel-walled Community Church in Kansas City; the Lloyd Lewis House in Libertyville, Illinois, floating on its short stilts above the Des Plaines River; the John C. Pew residence, jutting out daringly from the wooded slope of Lake Mendota in Madison; the Rose C. Pauson House in Phoenix, a masonry, boulder, and wood oasis in the desert; the $15 million Crystal Heights apartment and commercial center project in Washington, D.C.; and several more outstanding Usonian homes. Many of these buildings were given individual attention in the professional journals and in local newspapers, so that Wright's stature and his achievements grew apace. In January 1938 *The Architectural Forum* and *Time* magazine, which had begun to give him extensive coverage, both dubbed him the nation's greatest architect in feature stories. And from 1937 through 1940, *The Saturday Review, Scientific American, The Christian Science Monitor Magazine, The Nation, Newsweek, The New Republic,* and *Science News Letter* were among the other nonprofessional journals favorably discussing him and his designs. So it was not entirely surprising when, in 1941, the author of Wright's first entry in *Current Biography,* commenting on his recent exhibition at New York's Museum of Modern Art, where many of the new structures had been displayed, should have quoted *Time* to the effect that his was "as exciting a body of architectural thinking as has come from the brain of anyone since Michelangelo."[18]

Official honors accompanied the praise. In 1937 he accepted an invitation to be the United States representative to the International Convention of Architects in Moscow, forcing him to postpone the reception of an honorary degree—his first—from Wesleyan University until the following year. In a brief exhibition at the Museum of Modern Art in January 1938, he displayed twenty drawings and photographs of Fallingwater, and toward the end of the year he launched a two-week speaking tour, including an address to the one thousand members of the Federal Architects Association in Washington. Supervision of the Johnson Wax Building put off his Sir George Watson Lectures of the Sulgrave Manor Board at the University of London until 1939, when his talks for a £500 stipend were immediately published as *An Organic Architecture.* During the extensive retrospective exhibition of his work since 1905 at the Museum of Modern Art from November 1940 to January 1941, he was awarded King George of England's Gold Medal and made an honorary member of the Royal Institute of British Architects. He was also inducted into the National Academy of Architects in Uruguay and Mexico in 1941 and 1942 respectively, prior to the generally friendly reception accorded the expanded edition of *An Autobiography* in 1943.[19]

Wright continued to crisscross the country—a self-appointed critic and debunker—saying what he pleased no matter whom he offended. The buildings in Los Angeles were "a dish of tripe," but no worse than the "fire traps" and "vermin-catchers" of New England. In Chicago he accused real estate brokers of ignoring health and beauty for profit when they selfishly chopped up land into tiny house lots. He ridiculed the restoration of colonial Williamsburg, argued that housing projects only institutionalized poverty, and blasted the District of Columbia's architecture as "symbols of authority out of a pontifical past."[20] A typical virtuoso performance, at the Woman's Club in Whitefish Bay, a fashionable suburb north of Milwaukee, began when Wright accused his hostesses of inviting him, not because he was a great architect with an important message, but because notoriety had made him picturesque. "You have to be a thriller or a shocker to be noticed" in America's pervasive mediocrity, he told his perturbed audience, as if to explain his own behavior. "If people thought your idea meant any actual change in their lives they'd put you in jail. The United States is the least liberal, least inclined for free speech in open forum, least inclined to give an honest man the benefit of the doubt of any nation in the world." Woman's organizations in particular paid little attention to speakers' remarks, he asserted, only to their clothes and personalities, present company included. He finished by telling the women they were all overdressed, and, when he asked them their purpose as a club, no one ventured a reply.[21] Wright may not have believed half the things he said, but he obviously enjoyed saying them, and intimidating his listeners. And they, no matter how outrageous his comments, invariably invited him back.

Speaking frequently on a great variety of subjects, it was inevitable that Wright would become embroiled in political controversy, and he did so often after 1937, when he became involved in the "mini" Red Scare. To accusations in 1936 that he showed too many Soviet films at the Taliesin Playhouse, he replied that Russian movies were no more propagandistic than American westerns, and that as citizens of the world the Fellowship had an obligation to explore other cultures. He did not agree with everything about the Soviet Union, to be sure, but he believed it to be a "sincere . . . experiment" producing worthwhile art. Being much intrigued by the country, he had been happy to accept the invitation in 1937 to the International Convention of Architects in Moscow. Arriving in June for a two-week visit as a guest of the Soviet government, he inspected architecture, talked with as many citizens as possible, and gave a few speeches. Except for one incident—he refused to permit border guards to inspect his luggage—Wright enjoyed the experience immensely.

If he was predisposed to admire the young nation before his excursion, he returned an enthusiastic apologist. Russia and the United States were the world's best hopes for democracy and happier living conditions, he said, and if she could learn industrial techniques from us, we could profit from her sense of dedication, her communal spirit, and her commitment to the goal of a better life for all. Pointing to the fate of conservatives in the American and French revolutions, Wright explained Stalinist repression as the natural and unavoidable result of any social upheaval. He admired the premier as a great leader, and prophesied that with economic success terror would subside. Except for the xenophobists, Wright charged, Russia's worst enemies were American Communists, self-seeking politicians who totally misunderstood the Revolution and whose objectionable behavior helped prevent an alliance between the two great nations. His several public statements concerning Russia prompted rejoinders from the political Right and Left. The faculty branch of the party at the University of Wisconsin acknowledged its admiration for Wright, but, compelled to criticize his attack on Communists, asked him to explain his characterization of them as "racketeers." He replied rather lamely that any group with "ist" or "ism" in its name was only a cult, languishing in formulae, unable to think for itself.[22]

Denunciation from the Right was less appropriate and more irrational. On the occasion of the unveiling of Abraham Lincoln's head at Mount Rushmore, South Dakota, on Constitution Day, 1937, Sen. Edward R. Burke (D.-Neb.), an opponent of President Franklin Roosevelt's court-packing plan, condemned the administration's "attack" on the Constitution. Apparently supporting the President's scheme, Wright criticized Burke at a press conference following the dedication, saying that the day should have been sculptor Gutzon Borglum's, not the senator's. Wright speculated that the four men on the mountain (Lincoln, Washington, Jefferson, and Theodore Roosevelt) would not have hesitated to tinker with the Constitution—a tentative, hastily thrown-together document—had they thought it necessary, and furthermore would have frowned upon propagandists invoking their names for partisan advantage. He could not remember, he claimed dramatically, ever being so outraged at a politician. Burke retorted that, until the sculptor expressed displeasure with the speech, Wright's views did not matter. It was really his condemnation of "dictators"—Roosevelt and Stalin—not a concern for Borglum that had prompted the architect's remarks, the senator maintained. And anyway, whatever Wright said could be dismissed, since his "strong advocacy of communism" was well known.[23]

As his comments at Mount Rushmore suggest, Wright was an early supporter of Franklin D. Roosevelt and the New Deal. Although the President's recovery measures fell short of Wright's solution for the depression—government-subsidized transportation to country homes, the cost of which he did not discuss—the architect was happy to admit that Roosevelt had tried to get some of the needed work done. "I was with him in the early days," he wrote to a Madison, Wisconsin, newspaper editor in June 1941. "I talked and wrote in his defense." He broke with Roosevelt, he averred, over foreign policy, when "with only hearsay information, he misjudged the world situation and did universal harm" by becoming entangled in the European conflagration.

As late as July 1939 Wright insisted there would be no war: wishing to preserve the accomplishments of which he was so proud, Adolph Hitler would never risk them in battle. After years of brutality and murder, the architect speculated, Hitler would want respectability and serenity, like Al Capone. In May 1941 Wright still believed that the United States could coexist with

Germany, that our example of democracy was the best weapon against her, that we had at least five years to arm if need be, and that Hitler could not last that long anyway. Wright's opposition to American entry in the Second World War was not based on sympathy for the German dictator, but on fear that the equalization of wealth at home, which he believed Roosevelt had begun, would be undermined by the huge profits from armaments manufacture, and that the United States would inevitably become imperialistic from its role as "world savior." In the end Wright sided with the America First Committee and publicly endorsed Charles A. Lindbergh's isolationist sentiments.[24]

His commitment to unfettered individualism, plus his opposition to American entrance in the first place, accounted for his strong endorsement of conscientious objection during World War II. The force of Wright's convictions undoubtedly influenced his apprentices, twenty of whom declared their opposition to compulsory military training in April 1941, claiming it would destroy the Fellowship, and that the "indigenous American culture" they were developing was actually a form of "interior defense." Their statement went unnoticed until September 1942, when one of their ranks, Marcus Weston, refused to report for induction. Federal Judge Patrick T. Stone quickly accused Wright of poisoning his students' minds, called for the FBI to investigate his possible obstruction of the war effort, and ordered Weston to "stay away from that man." Replying publicly that Stone was "another one of the things that is the matter with America," Wright suggested that for the safety of the nation "such men as yourself should be deprived of any . . . authority whatever. . . ." He had not counseled his apprentices politically, he claimed, and unlike the judge, respected a man's right to his own opinions. He would be pleased to turn Taliesin into a haven for war resisters, and insisted that if he were forty years younger he, too, "would be a c. o." In private Wright was even more irate. Stone and men like him, he wrote to a friend, were "yelping maddened animalistic 'patriots.' . . . When the pack runs with blood on its chaps and froth flecking

from its chest there is nothing but shame and futility. . . . Democracy's real enemy," he contended, "is not the Axis but Bureaucracy here at home in the War for Gold." Marcus Earl Weston
was convicted of draft evasion and sentenced to three years at the
Sandstone Penitentiary in Minnesota.[25]

Fearing by 1941 that federal authority, poisoned by militarism,
had lost all concern for the people, Wright suggested a complete
political restructuring of the nation. "The United States of North
America" would be divided into three sections along geographic,
economic, and cultural lines: New England—also including New
York, New Jersey, Pennsylvania, Delaware, and Maryland—the
industrial and financial center; Usonia South, the Old Confeder-
acy and staple-producing region; and the remainder, the *real*
America, with a new national capital on the Mississippi River, to
be called Usonia. Each section would have its own president, and
the three congresses would elect a federal congress, which in turn
would choose a federal president. This arrangement, Wright
thought, would enable each region to pursue its interests with a
minimum of foreign influence; New England, of course, would
probably remain an English satellite, but the rest of the nation
would develop its own culture. And with the federal capital—also
called Usonia—at the geographic and spiritual center of American
civilization, indigenous values and institutions could emerge un-
hampered by international pressures. Removing the selection of
important officials from the people, Wright believed, would improve the quality of government, since voters were easily stam-
peded into making the wrong choices. He insisted that his
reorganization was the only way in which the 1776 ideal of
national independence could be truly realized.[26]

In spite of his opposition to President Roosevelt's foreign policy
and his call for the dissolution of the presently constituted United
States, Wright was awarded a commission from the Federal
Works Administration in December 1941 to design one hundred
homes for defense workers in Pittsfield, Massachusetts. And in
spite of his militant stand against rearmament and government

centralization, he accepted it even at a fee considerably lower than his customary ten percent. He had almost completed his plan, an adaptation of the Ardmore, Pennsylvania, "quadruple house" by the New Year, but before he could submit it the government withdrew the commission, preferring to build temporary demountable shelters. Instead of hiring nationally known architects (Walter Gropius, Eliel Saarinen, and Richard Neutra were also chosen), FWA decided to rely on local practitioners, the better to conform to regional building codes and traditions, it said. The administration, however, was reported to be under pressure from several congressmen who wanted to keep the architectural fees within their constituencies. Wright urged federal officials at least to look at his plans before abandoning them, claiming they would be cheaper, easier to erect, and more beautiful than the proposed demountables, but his conviction about bureaucratic ineptness was reinforced when they refused.[27]

Another commission received during the war ultimately grew into one of his most controversial and spectacular buildings. Solomon R. Guggenheim's intent was to build a suitable home for his extensive collection of nonobjective art, and in 1943 Wright offered three proposals. The first, a variation of which was later executed, featured a continuous spiral ramp with each turn smaller than the one above, attached to an apartment for the museum director at the north end. The second scheme—recalling the Sugar Loaf Mountain Planetarium project of 1925—inverted the first, placing the widest turns at the bottom, while the third arrangement was composed of flat hexagonal floors connected by ramps. The first proposal was unveiled in New York in 1945 amidst much fanfare and the familiar inflated Wrightian rhetoric. At a Plaza Hotel luncheon given by Guggenheim, the architect declared that no decent museum had ever been built. His million-dollar structure, however, would remedy that situation, while offering unique extras—like the possibility of seeing the entire collection from a self-propelled wheelchair, or viewing movies projected on the ceiling from reclining chairs on the main floor several stories below. Construction was postponed until 1957, but from the very beginning Wright conceived of the Guggenheim as a piece of architectural sculpture, and in many ways it was the most imaginative structure he ever created.[28]

In 1942, 1943, and 1944 Wright executed no commissions, but after the war his practice reached unprecedented dimensions as he flooded the country with his buildings, the press with his comments, the journals with his articles, and the public consciousness with his flamboyant activity. He designed his most lucrative and spectacular projects in the 1950s, including a number of engineering marvels and futuristic fantasies, but by then the formative period of his philosophy was over. During the 1930s he had published a number of books that represented the culmination of his architectural and social thought, a philosophical swan song that carried him through the remainder of his career.

9. MAKING STRUCTURE
EXPRESS IDEAS

[1930–1959]

During the last three decades of his life, Frank Lloyd Wright's innumerable appearances in the mass media and professional publications gave considerable exposure to his ideas. But he undercut his credibility with outrageous remarks, obscure jargon, and abysmal prose. His doubt that he was making an impact occasionally left him frustrated. "Here I am at it again," he confessed to an audience in 1939, "trying, trying, trying, but what is the use?"[1] While his verbal excesses obscure the import of his message, his monumental achievements demand that his teachings be taken seriously, that an effort be made to sift the kernels of his ideas from the chaff of his rhetoric. With the exception of "The Art and Craft of the Machine" speech, his autobiography, and a few other works, his vast literary output has been neglected, even though much of it merits serious attention.

Especially in his last years Wright ventured opinions on almost every imaginable subject. His sweeping pronouncements were undoubtedly stimulated by a monumental ego, and by his belief that accomplishment and acclaim obliged him to dispense his wisdom. But the most urgent motivation was his messianic insistence on spreading the philosophy of organic architecture. If properly understood, this Hegelian-like overview bestowed universal insight, at least to Wright, who measured the value of everything by its degree of "organicness." Despite his wide-ranging sallies, however, he devoted most of his attention to one problem at a time: to the nature of materials during the 1920s, to Broadacre City in the early thirties, and to American culture in the 1940s and 1950s. He would focus tenaciously on a theme, then move to another, yet it was uncharacteristic of him to abandon an idea completely or let it slip from his intellectual storehouse.

From the 1930s to the end of his life, Wright devoted most of his literary effort to expounding his philosophy and to criticizing American life and culture, especially urbanism. Despite his rambling and disjointed presentations, however, his discussions of the organic lent a certain consistency and imposed a certain order on everything he said, no matter what the topic. "The creative facilities of the human race," he told a group of admiring students in 1954, are "intimately linked to the relationship of man to the cosmos." This Emersonian suggestion that the artist represented the divinity of man was the basis of Wright's contention that a kind of structure—a coherent pattern—characterized all human affairs: "Organic architecture feels at home with the ideal of unity," he once remarked.[2] In fact, one of the two key words in his philosophical vocabulary was "unity," a determining attribute of the second word, "nature." From these two concepts all others flowed. The link between natural variety and cosmic unity, Wright believed, was organic structure, the only proper model for man's social relationships.

"Nature" was so central to Frank Lloyd Wright's philosophy that in 1954 he entitled a book The Natural House. As he defined it, the concept had two meanings, the first and more common being the out-of-doors, "the visible world," or "external" nature. One of the most widely appreciated objectives of Wright's architecture—to integrate buildings with site and environment—was initially attempted during the prairie period, when he incorporated the Midwest's level terrain into the lines of his houses. An intimate relationship between inside and out was as symbolic as it was real during those early years, for although his homes nestled closer to the ground than their neighbors, and although their outreaching walls, casement fenestration, overhanging eaves, decorative urns, and far-flung terraces made overtures to the outdoors, the buildings themselves were planted on top of the prairie. The distinction between art and nature, between inside and out, remained quite apparent.

The few notable exceptions were not sited on flat plots. The unexecuted portions of the W. A. Glasner House (1905) and the Sherman Booth project (1911), both in Glencoe, Illinois, would have made excellent use of plummeting ravines. The Thomas Hardy residence (1905) in Racine, Wisconsin, perched over the edge of Lake Michigan's bluffs, and Wright's own Taliesin (1911–1914) near Spring Green, were both outcroppings, not mere acknowledgments, of the land itself. In the twenties his projects for Edward Doheny (1921) in California's Sierra Madre Mountains and for the San-Marcos-in-the-Desert resort (1927–1928) near Chandler, Arizona, both incorporated streams, hills, crevices, and woods into their very structures. The 1920s textile-block homes in California were interpretive expressions and literal extensions of their rugged hillside locales, while Fallingwater in 1936 was the culmination of all his efforts. It was difficult in these cases to determine, as Wright often said, "where the ground leaves off and the building begins. . . ."[3]

After World War II he utilized sloping, undulating, or otherwise irregular lots more often. Some of his designs faithfully reproduced nearby topographical features—the Wyoming Valley Grammar School (1957) near Taliesin, for example, and the Marin County Civic Center (1957–1959), north of San Francisco—while others were so well blended into their sites they could not possibly have been built elsewhere in the same form. Even in the flat regions of the Middle West Wright often found (or made) variegated terrain so that structures became almost one with their surroundings. After the 1930s he supplemented casement fenestration with floor-to-ceiling plate glass panels and, by utilizing cantilevers, introduced the corner window, further eliminating the post and beam construction that impeded view and acted as a barrier between inside and out. Steel and glass made wider spans possible, he wrote, "therefore more open spaces . . . and a closer relation to nature. . . ."[4] The prairie house had established the value of designing according to the features of terrain, but the "natural house" did not reach maturity until well into his Usonian phase.*

Wright's insistence on the importance of living close to nature is perhaps an area for psychological investigation. It may have sprung from his childhood summers on the farm or from his positive associations with rural Taliesin, his refuge after 1911. In any case he found the country desirable and, after the 1930s, decided the best thing he could do for his clients was to move them as far from the city as possible. In *The Natural House* (1954), for instance, he urged his readers to "go way out into the country, . . . and when others follow, . . . move on." (There is a certain irony in the fact that he built only one home for an actual farm client: Robert Muirhead in Plato Center, Illinois, 1952.) When television interviewer Mike Wallace asked him the rather conventional question: "When you're out in nature, don't you feel small and insignificant?" he replied, in true Whitmanesque fashion: "On the contrary. I feel larger, I feel enlarged and encouraged,

* The second house for Herbert Jacobs in Middleton, Wisconsin, illustrates the way Wright sometimes manufactured "natural" sites. To create the berm sheltering the rear from northerly winds, he dug a shallow circular depression in front that now serves as a slightly below-grade patio-lawn, giving the impression that the house projects out of a tiny hill. At the partially prefabricated Arnold Jackson House (1957–1958) a few miles away in Madison, Wright made two small hills with the soil from the excavation, and wedged the building lengthwise between, further enhancing a sloping plot already memorable for its distant view of Lake Mendota.

intensified, more powerful."⁵ Critics have claimed that his ode to nature was cynical posturing, since he spent a great deal of time in cities. But the fact remains that, after Thomas Jefferson, Wright was probably the best known American architect to make his home outside the metropolis.

Living in the great outdoors may have been a blessing, but it was also a source of architectural inspiration. So another way in which Wright utilized external nature was as a model for the content and the processes of his work. Trees, for example, suggested the "tap-root" foundation of the Johnson Wax Company research tower (1946) in Racine, Wisconsin, wherein the floors were cantilevered like branches from a hollow central core (of elevators, stairs, and utilities) sunk fifty-four feet below grade and stabilized underground by a sixty-foot-in-diameter annular slab, which transmitted to the subsoil most of the load of seventy thousand square feet and fourteen stories—the whole arrangement analogous to a trunk and root system.⁶ Snail shells, Wright liked to remark, inspired the form of the Guggenheim Museum (1943–1957) in New York City, and folded hands the triangular facade of the Unitarian Meeting House (1947) in Madison, Wisconsin. Wright's fieldstone homes closely resembled the rock strata surrounding his Spring Green estate, and the way some flowers opened informed the floor plans of certain prairie houses. There was a mine of information available to the architect, Wright insisted, if only he would observe nature carefully.

In addition to external nature, Wright ascribed a second and more fundamental meaning to the concept: "internal" nature. Every thing that existed, he had explained in *The Japanese Print* (1912), had its own unique nature, its inner harmony, determining character, or essential reality. In inanimate objects, nature in the "interior sense" was inherent structure, while in abstract or more complicated phenomena—ideas, for example, or people—it was "the working of principle." When Wright talked about nature study, therefore, he not only meant bird watching or a trip to the arboretum, but also a probe into the essence of something to determine exactly those characteristics making it itself. By penetrating beneath the surface, he explained, "the creative mind sees the basic patterns of construction in the form of whatever is," in other words the "principle, . . . the ever-moving, basic inner-rhythm of all being." Although internal nature was eternal in the Platonic sense of existing as idea or form before perception, it was constantly evolving ("ever-moving") and therefore its consequences were discoverable by patient observation. Man-made objects also had natures, and the shifting sands of human need and aspiration made change an inherent part of his creations. Change was indeed the measure of all things.[7]

Consequently, the nature of a tree was the same and yet different as time passed. It always had its "treeness," those attributes that made it what it was, yet its leaves, its bark, and its roots evolved continuously. "Life itself is a splendid unfolding," Wright wrote in 1949; "there can be no real *beginning* . . . on this earth. Nor . . . [any] end to be foreseen." The implication for architecture was that "no organic building may ever be 'finished.' The complete goal . . . is never reached. Nor need be. What worthwhile ideal is ever reached?" Refinements during planning and construction could always be made, of course, but Wright also meant that, even after the client took it over, an edifice continued to be the architect's responsibility. "We must and will see that every building becomes as we intended it to be . . . even if we have to help." Furthermore, organic designs were perpetually called upon to perform new functions and house new activities—in other words, to grow. Therefore, Wright tried to provide for change in his architecture, if he could anticipate its future. What a residence should be and·do when the whole family lived together was entirely different from when the children married and departed. So for Paul R. Hanna in Palo Alto, California, for example, Wright designed a large home in 1937 that was easily adapted to the needs of the middle-aged couple years later by making a few adjustments and shifting a few partitions. In *The Natural House* he suggested ways to accommodate family growth by preplanning for expansion and alteration without distorting the home's essential character.[8]

Not only should buildings "grow" from sites as natural consequences of topography, and in character and purpose as human situations changed, but also as ideas in the mind of the architect. Wright defined a building as enclosed space, revealing its reality or nature not on the facade but inside. The purpose of architecture, therefore, was to "unfold an inner content—express 'life' from the 'within,'" so that the room space might "come through" on the outside. A building could grow organically in the mind of the architect only if he conceived it "from inside out," that is, only if he began by grappling with the problem of enclosed space, moving later to the exterior expression. Wright's most illuminating description of this process is his autobiographical account of Unity Temple (1905–1906) in Oak Park, Illinois. The first step in his thinking, he remembered, was to determine the philosophy of the building and the purposes of the interior space. With these firmly in mind, he tried to visualize the appearance, proportions, materials, and construction methods suitable for their expression, and not until he had completed all this did he begin to sketch, struggling through dozens of studies until the design finally came true. The facade of the building, in other words, was the last step of the conceptual process, taking shape only as the consequence of an organic development, in which the building and the *idea* of the building grew as if in nature. What fundamentally separated him from the practitioners of the International Style, he insisted, was his belief that the interior accommodation of human needs should take precedence over the exterior purity of architectural form.[9]

Just as an organic building grew in the mind of the architect, so should it grow from the nature of its culture. As the historian Raymond Williams has insightfully demonstrated, "culture" developed new connotations in the late eighteenth and early nineteenth centuries throughout the English-speaking world. On the one hand, it referred to "the general body of the arts," Wright's meaning on occasion, and on the other hand to "a whole way of life, material, intellectual, and spiritual," his most frequent definition.[10] If the United States was really a democracy, Wright argued, it must produce democratic buildings, by which he did not mean a drab egalitarian style, like early Soviet design, or popularly chosen architects, although that would have characterized Broadacre City, but that the nation should develop architecture especially suited to its institutions, values, and goals that in principle exalted freedom and individualism. If democracy in fact meant maximum personal liberty and minimal government restraint, its residences would assert the supreme importance of privacy, human difference, self-esteem, and unpretentiousness, while its state edifices would substitute symbols of citizen participation for those of traditional authority. A democracy, Wright believed, could not in good conscience sanction princely styles or pompous forms.

Nature's principle of continuous change by no means implied disorder or disarray. Quite the contrary. The first principle of growth, Wright insisted, was "perfect correlation." Nothing that evolved naturally—trees, ideas, or buildings—could be a mere aggregation, for "integration was its first essential." "Perfect correlation" or integration, he argued, is life itself, meaning that "nothing is of any great value except as naturally related to the whole." Wherever the whole is to the part as the part is to the whole, the goal of harmony would be reached, and "the nature of the entire performance becomes clear as necessity." Each part, its relation to the others and to the whole, and the whole itself, were necessary and purposeful when harmoniously integrated. In organic architecture, therefore, as in nature itself, growth and change characterized the perfect correlation of parts and epitomized, furthermore, the unity of form and function.[11]

This unity was based on another of Wright's central concepts, the idea of plasticity or continuity. From Louis Sullivan's ornament and from his many discussions with the Master, Wright had learned to appreciate architectural "flow," the notion that a composition should be internally consistent, complete within itself, and should develop logically and steadily without interruption or irrelevancy, in other words, that it should begin, proceed, and end smoothly. Wright's second model of plasticity was exterior nature. Cactus, he noted, "employs cell to cell or continuous tubular or often plastic construction." Skin on human hands, sheathing functional attributes in free-flowing materials, was another example. Wright had reasoned that by eliminating post and beam construction he could make an entire building plastic, not just its ornament or its facade. "Instead of two things," he proposed "one thing. Let walls, ceilings, floors become part of each other, flowing into one another, . . . eliminating any constructed feature." Plasticity or continuity meant that "materials are seen 'flowing or growing' into form instead of . . . built . . . out of cut and joined pieces." Plastic forms, he emphasized, are not composed, but, "inasmuch as they are produced by a 'growing' process," they are *developed* and *created.* From the prairie house wherein he tentatively achieved this unity with monomaterials and carefully placed trim, he went on in the Usonian house to merge entire rooms and floors. Continuity in his architecture manifests itself in the gradual opening up of vista, in the consistent treatment of materials, in horizontal lines of expression, and in the organization and flow of space, especially from outside in.

Wright's teaching, that "form and function are one," was an extension of Sullivan's famous precept, "form follows function." For Sullivan, the key word had been "follows," implying that function *suggested* form, that any architectural problem might have several intelligent solutions. But Wright took the Master a step further, maintaining in good Platonic fashion that the correct form for an organic building existed, as it were, a priori, and therefore was the only possible solution. In nature, every part depended upon and was a consequence of the whole. Likewise, airplanes, ocean liners, locomotives, automobiles, and the best industrial designs that "are perfectly adapted to their function,"

Wright explained, "seem to have a superior beauty of their own. . . . All features in good building, too, should correspond to some necessity for being . . . found in their very purpose."[12] If a structure was organic, it looked the way it did in large measure because of the way it was used.

Although Wright stoutly insisted that all his designs revealed the unity of form and function, the Guggenheim Museum in New York may have come closest to achieving the ideal. His objective was to display a unified collection and at the same time show the development of a painter or a movement over time—in other words, to express continuity, change, and totality simultaneously. The traditional rectangular organization of fixed rooms and corridors was poorly adapted to logical sequence or artistic maturation. In the Guggenheim Wright twisted a three-quarter mile gallery into a spiral ramp of three percent grade, down which the viewer ambled after an elevator ride to the top. Thus it became possible to trace the unfolding of an artist's career during a pleasant downhill stroll, to gain perspective on the entire collection by turning to the center, or to leave at any point without retracing one's steps. An overhead skylight-dome (and window slits under the ramp that were not executed as Wright planned them) enhanced proper viewing with unusually abundant natural lighting. With complex engineering Wright offered a deceptively simple solution to problems that had plagued museums for years.

The facade of the Guggenheim was a direct expression of internal space, its spiral form being literally the outside of its inside functions. But Wright had arrived at his solution only after considerable experimenting. His hexagonal plan with ramps connecting flat floors was a weak version of what finally emerged, while placing the larger turns on the bottom made the building squat and dull. The cone shape that he ultimately settled on increased ground space and visibility, and actually was structurally sounder than if the largest ramp had been at ground level. (Poured concrete has a contraction coefficient equal to the expansion coefficient of the stressed steel cantilevers holding the ramps. Coiled spirally for unimpeded vista, they held the building in a kind of tension, its thrust inward through steel and concrete piers down to the ground. If the larger turns had been on the bottom, the thrust would have been outward, with a great amount of non-transferable dead weight weakening the dome supports, perhaps making cantilevering impossible, and thereby necessitating interior columns.) An edifice so shaped was appropriate only on a flat site that would not compete aesthetically. Although the Guggenheim might have been more visible across the street in Central Park, it nonetheless serves as a foil for the many high-rises surrounding it, making Fifth Avenue that much more interesting. Windows are unnecessary in a museum, of course, and poured concrete was the best material for a curved surface. Given the circumstances and Wright's objectives there were no other alternatives for the Guggenheim. If architecture was enclosed space, and if that space was to be expressed honestly on the exterior, the museum could only look the way it did.

The Guggenheim is more plastic than any other Wright structure. There are no posts and beams, no boxy rooms, no obstructing columns, and no obvious terminal points, only continuity and rhythm. As the sun moves slowly across its facade, it subtly changes tones and its hanging vines and landscaping make it anything but hard and menacing. Inside, change is its very definition. From every point the visitor is aware of the pervasive ebb and flow of activity, and as he follows the ramp his perspective constantly shifts. From the outside the museum is a tone poem of fluctuating color, while inside it becomes a preserve for human and architectural motion. Yet it is obviously an orderly, self-contained, solid, and enduring structure. Here in one statement, a culmination of many of his ideas, Wright combined the universal human respect for stability and strength with the equally insistent impulse toward change and variety. Every component in the Guggenheim has a

The Solomon R. Guggenheim Museum of Non-Objective Art, 1943–1957. New York City

Interior of Guggenheim Museum

compelling raison d'être, and its form and function are indeed one. Like Fallingwater, it successfully embodies many of the most important implications of organic architecture.*

Wright never offered a totally satisfactory definition of his famous term, "organic architecture," perhaps because he did not have the patience or see the necessity for it, or perhaps because in many ways it was too personal and vague a concept to be defined. Yet an attempt to put it succinctly seems appropriate. If a building is organic, it is harmonious in all its parts, a coherent expres-

---

* Comments on the Guggenheim Museum—many quite thoughtful, many not—have been legion. Its critics argue that rectangular paintings cannot be shown properly against walls that slope backward from the floor and down from left to right. They say that the ramp hurries patrons along faster than they want to go, that it tires the leg muscles, that the lighting is insufficient, that the building is too small, and that viewers cannot stand far enough away from larger works for necessary perspective. The guard rail at the center well, they allege, is too low, creating the psychological impression of danger, thereby forcing people even closer to the paintings. The notion also persists that the Guggenheim is actually Wright's mammoth practical joke on New York and modern art, both of which he despised.

Personally, I find most of these arguments rather specious. It is true that large works are handicapped, except on the top ramp (which has often been closed, however) and in the annex, which houses the permanent collection. Picasso's *Guernica* obviously could not be shown here, but the Guggenheim was not intended to replace the Museum of Modern Art, only to feature small unified exhibits. As for lighting, it is true that the museum directors supplemented the mirrored ribbon-windows under the ramps with artificial lights after Wright's death, but the fact remains that the natural light from above is quite generous, making the Guggenheim in fact brighter than its local rivals. Regarding perspective: as far as I know the ratio between size of painting and distance for proper viewing has never been determined, and seems to me a matter of taste; it may be that, in the Guggenheim, one can achieve a certain intimacy with the art, an intimacy enhanced—as a friend pointed out—by the dividers that periodically interrupt the downward slope.

The other criticisms appear to be reflections of personal whim or misinformation, and while I do not maintain that the Guggenheim is flawless, I find it after many visits a continually fresh and exciting experience. As architecture many museums can be taken for granted, indeed forgotten entirely, but in this building the art lover gets two shows for the price of one. For a totally different assessment see Peter Blake, *Frank Lloyd Wright: Architecture and Space* (Baltimore: Penguin Books, 1964), pp. 117–122.

sion and unification of its environment, its inhabitants, materials, construction methods, site, purpose, cultural setting, and of the ideas which called it into being, each being a consequence of the others. An organic structure defines and prophesies life, grows along with those who use it, assumes its own "essential reality" or "internal nature," and, by including everything necessary and nothing unnecessary for solving the immediate architectural problem, is as unified and as economical as nature itself. "*A building can only be functional,*" Wright stated emphatically, "*when integral with environment and so formed in the nature of materials according to purpose and method as to be a living entity. . . .*" Its tangible and intangible aspects, in other words, should strive toward unity and naturalness, all the while "making structure express ideas."[13]

Wright believed that the principles of organic architecture were applicable to personal and social life, both of which could benefit from the impulse toward unity that characterized his buildings. He tried to adapt his architectural philosophy to politics and social science, and, although he may have stretched his ideas so thin that they lack conviction and precision, the comprehensiveness of his world-view has seldom been matched. Sounding like an existentialist philosopher, he affirmed that life could be trusted, perhaps "life is all that can really be trusted." It was perfectly sensible, therefore, not to be overly concerned with the past or the future, and there was indeed a persistent strain of presentism in his thinking. He had once eulogized his mistress, Mamah Borthwick, because she had "seized the present" and lived according to the imperatives of the moment, disregarding possible consequences. "As far as we can see," he wrote, the future *is* the present, the "ever-moving" point in time when tomorrow becomes today, and so "it is for us to *act*, now. . . ." "Every day life is the important thing," he wrote to his daughter, Catherine Baxter, in 1921, "not tomorrow or yesterday, but *to-day*. You won't reach anything better than the 'right-now' if you take it as you ought."[14]

And the best thing about life, Wright maintained, was the

process of becoming. "Human affairs are of themselves plastic in spite of . . . man's ill advised endeavors to make them static. . . ." "Does not all live to change?"[15] If so, life was incompatible with architecture that assumed certain kinds of movement and habitual living styles. Boxlike rectangular structures with major and minor axes, he contended, virtually dictated predictable patterns, with traffic flow, furniture arrangement, room usage, and social behavior almost the same as in grandmother's day, the antithesis of the change and "becoming" that defined human existence. Consequently, organic architecture rejected "every building that would stand in military fashion, . . . something on the right hand and something on the left . . . ," favoring instead "the reflex, the natural easy attitude, the occult symmetry of grace and rhythm. . . ." Since social relationships ought to be "a profession of freedom," he told an interviewer in 1953, "there should be free expression in building. The box was merely an inhibition and a restraint," "never intended to serve life [and] mainly an imposition upon it." Architecture would not be free to evolve according to the organic growth of life until it abandoned exclusive dependence on the right angle. Then, he said, we will see "entirely new forms of living. . . ."[16]

Shortly before his death in 1959, Wright asserted that "there is no square in nature—nature knows only circular forms." While not suggesting that all buildings should be without corners, he nevertheless utilized every opportunity in his last years to dispense with them. During the prairie period he had moved beyond the architectural and psychological confines of the cruciform plan, and by the late 1930s was frequently experimenting with triangles, hexagons, and circles. In the 1950s his rectangles were often asymmetrically related, hardly ever crossed or balanced in the classical manner; he thought nothing of designing Y-shaped and round houses, spiral, hexagonal, and circular public buildings. As old age overtook him he may have subconsciously been attracted to forms symbolizing infinity or self-perpetuation. But his reliance on nonrectangular shapes was more than likely an attempt to escape the limitations that corners and straight lines imposed on living styles and on design possibilities, for he was continually in search of new means of artistic expression and of anything to eliminate the mundane aspects of living. When the box was abolished, Wright contended, we were "no longer tied to Greek space but were free to enter into the space of Einstein."[17]

Free expression in building meant the accommodation of human variety and unpredictability so inadequately contained in boxlike structures. Reflecting the nature of man's activities, free expression was "simply the human spirit given appropriate architectural form" in which, for example, defining walls and room arrangements were shaped by, but did not themselves shape, the human preferences that the architect had carefully ascertained. Every organic building, Wright constantly stressed, "is necessarily expression of the life it is built to serve directly," therefore "a humane and intensely human thing," potentially "the most human of all the expressions of human nature." In his 1901 Hull House lecture he had defined architecture—"the principal writing—the universal writing of humanity"—as the point of convergence for all the intellectual and artistic forces of a people. By 1930 he broadened his definition to include not only the buildings that had already been erected but also "life itself taking form."

Yet Wright went even further, ultimately maintaining that his structures *improved* life, that they were therapeutic and morally uplifting, the embodiment, in fact, of the "house beautiful" ideal to which he had committed himself in 1896. "About all my clients have testified to the joy and satisfaction they get from their own particular building," he claimed in his autobiography. They acquired "a certain dignity and pride in their environment; they see it has a meaning or purpose which they share as a family or feel as individuals." Not only did he insist that his designs "affect our conduct," but also that they had a "salutary effect morally." When a person knew he was becomingly housed, he found himself living "according to the higher demands of good society, and of [his] own conscience"; freed from embarrassment he grew rich in spirit.

"When you are conscious that the house is right and honestly becoming to you, and feel you are living in it beautifully, you need no longer be concerned about it," Wright assured potential clients. "It is no tax upon your conduct, not a nag upon your self-respect, because it is featuring you as you like to see yourself." He did not mean to be facetious when he added that if organic architecture spread over the land, the national divorce rate would drop.[18]

When that day came, everyone would be living organically in a Broadacre City situation, fulfilling their natures in a unified democratic society. It all seemed simple enough—if his teachings and his buildings were universally accepted, America would be better off—but Wright contradicted himself when he discussed how the new way of life would actually come into being. At times he insisted that organic architecture would be the agent of organic culture: "an architecture upon which true American society will eventually be based. . . . An architecture upon and within which the common man is given freedom to realize his potentialities as an individual. . . ." But at other times he argued exactly the opposite: "We cannot have organic architecture," he told a London audience in 1939, "unless we achieve an organic society!" "It is useless to free humanity by way of architecture . . . so long as humanity itself is inorganic." His confusion on this point— whether organic architecture would precede or follow organic culture—did not blunt his message that something was terribly wrong with the way Americans lived individually and in groups. At the very least, organic architecture was a relevant *ideal* for the nation since "a sense of valid structure in our culture is what we most lack," and Wright firmly believed that a whole society, like a building, should work toward the goal of unity.[19]

Wright liked to shock his audiences by saying that the United States was the only nation to pass "from barbarism to degeneracy never having known a civilization." Unguided by any national purpose, it had copied its culture from others already decaying, and was thus left with "no sense of the whole, nothing of real integrity of concept or structure [with which to] grow its own way of life, and by ways of its own establish a culture belonging to itself. . . ." America's ancient goals had been lost sight of, and somehow its promises had remained unfulfilled; it was "losing, completely losing, that dignity and quality of character which was common to our forefathers—the dignity of the individual." Since it had no "forms true to its own nature," which itself remained undiscovered, it searched for meaningful "inner experience," longing for a common life to provide a cultural base. Without sociocultural cohesion, America had nothing to offer its citizens or mankind. If archeologists were to excavate the continent a thousand years from now, Wright half seriously told a college audience in 1932, they would find nondegradable bathroom fixtures, but very little else, from which they would conclude that although Americans had been a sanitary lot, they probably led empty lives.[20]

Without cultural or social unity, America had developed certain widely applauded but harmful characteristics. The triumph of indiscriminate private wealth, for one thing, had turned the masses into "wage-slaves" and the nation itself into an economic despotism. Wright believed the United States to be the most materialistic society since Rome: the sturdy yeomen envisioned by the Founding Fathers had devolved into a "mobocracy" admiring quantity more than quality, brainwashed by bureaucracy and Big Business into thinking that the accumulation of goods was life's objective. The country had become a "cash-and-carry" nation, with a "Broadway-creed" of salesmanship and boosterism. Wright also castigated America's blind and unreasoning worship of science, the national substitute for art, religion, and philosophy. In an organic society the scientific method would be related to the creative spirit in the same way as a paint box to an artist, but, without a culture to adopt and adapt its discoveries, without a sense of the whole, science was socially destructive. The detonation of the first atomic bomb represented to Wright the fallacy of purposeless scientific inquiry. "A ghastly revelation of the failure of our educational, economic and political systems," he concluded in 1947, it had thrown us "completely off our base, undoubtedly making all that we call progress obsolete overnight. Prone to our own destruction, we may be crucified on our own cross! . . . This push-button civilization over which we gloated has suddenly become nameless terror."[21]

Improperly restrained science and materialism were also to blame for inorganic social organization, Wright insisted, specifically for American cities and governments, which invariably destroyed human life. Greed and technology (in the form of skyscrapers) exacerbated urban congestion while government, controlled by those responsible for the plight of the cities, stifled creativity and individualism. A knowledge of organic structure—which in architecture integrated individuality of parts with a harmonious whole—would be useful to statesmen and politicians whose objectives ought to be the simultaneous preservation and extension of social order and personal liberty. The nation's salvation, Wright claimed, would be the application of organic architecture to social organization along the lines of Broadacre City. Short of that event, he could only hope that decentralization would begin to mitigate urban problems.

Although Wright is frequently remembered for his bitter anti-urban diatribes, his relationship to the city was actually quite ambivalent, a kind of love-hate affair resembling the reverberation of a compass needle between two magnets. The city came to represent for him all that was unnatural and fraudulent in America, but he arrived at that view gradually, and even in his last years, at the height of his invective, he enjoyed occasional encounters with the urban fleshpots. He began his professional career in the 1880s an enthusiastic urbanite; fresh from the farm and a small town he entered a kind of premature second childhood, reveling in Chicago with his new friend Cecil Corwin. But when he opened his independent practice in 1893, four years after he had assumed the responsibilities of marriage and home ownership in suburban Oak Park, he declared that the architect should find an environment "that conspires to develop the best there is in him, . . . a place fitted and adapted to the work . . . outside the distractions of the busy city." In an 1899 letter he confessed that his spirit had become "somewhat hardened in the hustle of this great western city," revealing both his admiration and his distrust of metropolitan pleasures.[22]

But Chicago was a jealous mistress, and Wright eagerly continued his love affair with hustle and bustle. Throughout his Oak Park years he remained a patron of the arts, taking full advantage of the specialty shops, restaurants, galleries, and concert halls his urban colleagues, clients, and friends frequented. Only after he left the city hastily in 1909 did he begin to condemn it, covering his departure and perhaps his regrets with recrimination. In 1918, after seven years in rural Wisconsin, he stopped in Chicago during a respite from his labors on the Imperial Hotel to criticize its lack of culture, which he defined broadly as soul, life-spirit, and sense of destiny. Yet he did not indict *all* cities, nor was he particularly harsh even with Chicago, for he also praised its artistic, literary, and industrial achievements, and extolled the good life to be had there.[23] Not until after marital difficulties frightened away his (largely urban) clientele did Wright become single-minded about metropolitan evil. But even then his two Taliesins were located within easy commuting distance of Chicago and Phoenix, and in the 1950s he regularly visited New York, where he kept a permanent suite at the Plaza Hotel. Heaping abuse on almost every town he visited, he could not avoid languishing in their attractions.

Wright developed a similarly ambivalent attitude toward technology: eager to exploit its architectural possibilities, he feared its social impact. Making an appropriate intellectual leap, he began to describe the city as a machine, in terms recalling Frank Norris and others who feared technology's destructive impact on agrarian America. "This greatest of machines, a great city," Wright declared with mixed metaphors in "The Art and Craft of the Machine," his 1901 Hull House lecture, was a "monstrous leviathan" with "fetid breath" reddening the sky. With lights for eyes, streets for veins and arteries, and communications for nervous and sensory systems, the city was like a living organism. At its very heart, industry sent energy to every "tissue and cell" of its "flesh." This city—this "monstrous thing"—grew and functioned in "blind obedience to organic law," but whether it would work for humanity's good or ill was unclear to Wright at the opening of the new century. Thirty years later, however, when he described the city as "a mechanical conflict of machine resources," he was certain that evil had triumphed.[24]*

Wright offered his first extended analysis of the urban plight in the last of six Kahn Lectures at Princeton University in 1930, published the next year as *Modern Architecture,* followed by *The Disappearing City* (1932), *When Democracy Builds* (1945), and *The Living City* (1958). Beginning with prehistory, he divided mankind into two groups: "cave-dwelling agrarians and wandering tribes of hunter-warriors." The former, who later built towns and cities, were static and conservative, ultimately becoming the first establishmentarians. The wanderer, on the other hand, was an adventurer "following the laws of change." When enmity erupted between the two the cave dweller, seeking strength in numbers, developed a fortification mentality and in the course of time became a statist, while the wanderer, relying on ingenuity and mobility for defense, evolved into the prototypical democrat. In the end the cave dweller was victorious because, as civilization emerged, man placed a premium on centralization to solve the problems of defense, transportation, and communication and to facilitate commerce and technology. Having originally been established to accommodate man's actual needs, cities "grew naturally

---

* Wright's descriptive adjectives for the city-as-machine are strikingly similar to those Frank Norris used to characterize the railroad in his novel, *The Octopus,* also published in 1901, although the author was more pessimistic than the architect about the destructive impact of technology. Whereas Norris was convinced that the machine (his symbol was the railroad) had already crushed humanity, Wright embraced it as a liberator, being one of the first American social thinkers to do so. Thirty years later, however, he was less certain.

as the organism of our own body grows; the natural result of proper feeding." This was no less true of America, which had modeled itself after, and been an outgrowth of, late medieval Europe. Before the nineteenth century, Wright thought, cities rewarded and were "in scale true to human life"; in other words, they had developed organically.

Then, with the Industrial Revolution, disaster struck. When Wright reviewed urban problems he did not concentrate on air, water, and noise pollution, on crowding, crime, poverty, and corruption, on the hectic pace, or on the other obvious ills. Nor did he dwell on "the poles and wires, tracks and sheds, stumpage and erosion, barbed wire fences, sign boards and dumpage"—"the ugly scaffolding of a civilization," he called it—for the American junkyard was not a cause but an effect, a product of closed minds and base instincts. Cramped and confined by "the landlord's ruse"— buildings jammed together on small lots to extort exorbitant profits—and by his own lack of self-confidence, the average citizen was denied his birthright. "Instead of freely going in and out and comfortably round about among the beautiful things to which their lives are related in horizontal lines on top of this green earth," Wright commiserated, people were marched "six floors up, and up six floors again. And none may know just why they go, so narrowly up, up, to come narrowly down, down, down. . . ." Urban superconcentration, he thought, would eventually destroy its residents, for the "human motions of the city-inhabitant become daily more and more compact and violent" until the frenetic pace would finally culminate in a great internal collision, an implosion on a gigantic scale. By exploiting the individual's fear of being alone and his misguided belief in the safety of the group, the real estate agent, the landlord, and the politician greedily perpetuated an inhumane arrangement. The epitome of all that was wrong with the city, Wright maintained, was the skyscraper, an easily copied box, designed to "pig-pile" people on top of each other. Lined up in rows along narrow streets, it also created an architectural wasteland.

"The modern city," Wright once charged with typical exaggeration, "is a place for banking and prostitution and very little else." On another occasion he prophesied more seriously that it would soon be purely utilitarian, invaded three days a week at ten in the morning and abandoned at four in the afternoon by workers employed largely in financial houses, international trade, travel, and commerce. The metropolis might even become a museum of an older way of life, for some day no one would want to work or be able to live there. And this was entirely in keeping with the imperatives of human evolution, for Wright insisted that the very factors that once made the city necessary and desirable now made it obsolete. In an age of nuclear weapons and long-range delivery systems, for example, it was considerably less defensible than in medieval times; the only salvation from attack now lay in population dispersion. With advanced means of transportation and communication, furthermore, business and social life no longer depended on proximity. Indeed, a revolutionary change had occurred in which space had become more valuable than time. But with time conquered and space available elsewhere, urbanism was rendered meaningless.[25]

Wright therefore urged small towns to remain small, to shun the boosterism that signaled growth and congestion, for the wave of the future, he thought, was away from the city. He took heart when his reading of the 1930 census showed people already leaving, and predicted that by 1940 the trend would be obvious. Mass communications, superhighways, and the automobile were to his way of thinking the advance agents of decentralization, and he often cited the gas station as the embryonic regional distribution center. During World War II he argued rather cold-bloodedly that the bombing of London was not an unmixed evil, since it opened the possibility for planned decentralization, and later suggested that returning veterans be given transportation to free land to inaugurate the process. He also urged clients to build outside urban centers, "just ten times as far as you think you ought to go," he replied when asked. But "of all the underlying forces working toward emancipation of the city dweller," he wrote in 1958, "most important is the gradual reawakening of the primitive instincts of the agrarian." Like the ancient wanderer, the modern American would reject the urban cave for the freedom of the plains, once again making the natural life a real possibility.[26]

Wright was equally critical of American governments, claiming that they had evolved, like the city, into unnatural, tyrannical structures unresponsive to popular needs. His two major civic center designs—for Marin County, California (1957–1959), and especially for Madison, Wisconsin, which he revised several times (1938, 1941, 1953, 1956), and in which he invested an unusual amount of thought—reveal his grievances with the status quo and his suggestions for a more organic state. Wright objected vigorously to the symbols that traditionally appeared on government buildings, particularly to the Renaissance dome, which over time had come to represent unchallenged state power and the hegemony of outmoded institutions, not only in the capitals of Europe, but also in every state, county, and municipality in the United States, not to mention Washington, D.C. Like the Pope's miter, the ubiquitous dome symbolized the absence of citizen participation and popular control and was therefore totally undemocratic.[27] In his own public architecture Wright consistently avoided emblems of traditional authority, even in updated form, as well as materials like marble or granite not equally suitable for residences. Indeed, the most notable feature of his government buildings is how little they resemble centers of jurisdiction and how much they emphasize civic pleasure. They envision the state not as a locus of power but as the repository of human virtue and the coordinator of social harmony.

Even though Monona Terrace grew more elaborate with each revision, its informing idea remained the same. (This analysis is based on the 1956 final version.)[28] Approached along a two-block mall from the state capitol, the street level—the roof of the five-floor structure extending over Lake Monona—was a seven-and-one-half-acre semicircular park, with fountains, formal gardens, walkways, and benches. But, viewed from the lake below, the terrace was an expanse of glass above a municipal boat launch, and Wright emphasized its recreational facilities by including pleasure craft and excursioners in his numerous perspective drawings. The railroad station, a city auditorium, art galleries, a community center, and other services not requiring natural lighting or lake views were buried deep inside. Although many governmental agencies were given outside exposure, the courts, the jail, law enforcement offices, and other regulatory functions were not stated architecturally on the facade. Wright's many delineations clearly show that the community aspects of the project were uppermost in his thinking. An uninitiated visitor coming to Monona Terrace from the center of town might have thought he had discovered an attractive public gardens, so well camouflaged were the government facilities, while from the lake he would never have suspected that the airy glass and concrete semicircle also housed the punitive aspects of local authority. There was nothing about the place to suggest that the state coerced as well as served.

Like a doting father expressing his love, Wright drew and redrew Monona Terrace—one of his favorite creations—many more times and from many more angles of vision than really were necessary, one of which—an astrological "Plan of Roof Garden"[29] —is a particularly important clue to his thinking. At midpoint along the chord connecting the ends of the semicircle, that is, at the most conspicuous point of entrance from the street, Wright placed a fountain labeled "earth," which, lighted at night and soaring into space, referred to the four fundamentals of human life: air, fire, water, and land. Near the lake, around the circumference, were twelve smaller fountains, one for each sign of the zodiac, and halfway on the diameters between earth and the perimeter, at ten and two o'clock, were fountains for the moon and the sun. Unlike the fourteen stations of the cross, which in the Church denote the humanity of God, these symbols from a pagan age paid tribute to the divinity of man. In Wright's construct, furthermore, the sun, the moon, and the constellations orbited earth, emphasizing man's cosmic importance. Centuries before, the Copernican Revolution had dealt a crippling metaphysical blow to humanity's ultimate supremacy, weakened even more by industrialization and the rise of the bureaucratic corporate state. But at Monona Terrace Wright reaffirmed that man was indeed the measure of all things, that his earth gave meaning to the universe. And, if man was supreme, of course the state was not.

The Marin County Civic Center north of San Francisco advanced a similar philosophy. On several hundred hilly acres with trees and lakes Wright arranged an administration building, a hall of justice, a national guard armory, a post office, a fairgrounds, a highway and entrance drive intersection, a memorial auditorium, a helioport, and a yacht basin. The dominating structure at Marin County—actually two connected buildings identical in style—is the four-story Administration–Hall of Justice complex, linking hills at either end and joining at a third hill, from which the two branch out at an approximate 120-degree angle. Although the Administration Building is 560 feet long and the Hall of Justice 850, the fourth floor of the latter is level with the second floor of the former, the greater height suggesting that service takes priority over punishment in county government. The Administration Building spans one roadway and the Hall of Justice two, hence its double archway leading to the rear parking area: although it is larger it faces away from the principal approach, yielding supremacy to the Administration Building, which overlooks the entrance and defines the premises.

Like the Monona project, Marin County's symbols and relative importance of articulated parts give clues to its political philosophy. The focal point of the entire scheme both visually and intellectually is the juncture of the Hall of Justice and the Administration Building, where overhead soars a 172-foot transmitting tower, beneath which is a 140-foot-long triangular terrace for employees with pool, fountain, and shrubbery. Both the tower and the terrace actually extend out from the front of a slightly elevated circular library, the precise meeting place of the two main build-

Administration Building, Marin County Civic Center, 1957-1959, San Rafael, California

Marin County Civic Center. Roof of Administration Building looking toward library, transmitting tower, and San Francisco Bay

ings. It is not by accident that at the architectural center of the project (the first thing motorists see on arrival) Wright provided for disseminating knowledge, for transmitting information, and for employee relaxation. The power and authority of the state, in other words, find their raison d'être in the wisdom of the citizenry from which, architecturally at least, their expressions emanate.

The buildings pay obvious tribute to the Spanish heritage of the region and in shape almost literally reproduce nearby hills, "growing," as Wright would have put it, out of their cultural and environmental setting. Unlike most of his designs, which have definite terminal points, these flow into the land, seeming not to end at all; indeed, doorless top-level entrances open directly onto patios molded into the hillsides. Snuggling into their gentle valleys, the long, low, ground-hugging buildings obviously reject the pomposity of traditional government architecture. The courtrooms, the jail, the sheriff's office, and the other vehicles of coercion find no articulation, even on the facade of the Hall of Justice. The exteriors of the buildings are made rhythmic by archways shading balconies along their length, every office having direct access to, and an unimpeded view of, the outdoors, an additional boon for the workers. And inside Wright grouped the offices around central wells in the manner of the Larkin and Johnson administration buildings, except that he did not indicate hierarchy, for each was given identical treatment, especially appropriate in a democracy. Like its Madison counterpart, the Marin County Civic Center anticipated a more egalitarian state, provided stimulating and pleasing working conditions, and advocated citizen participation in government. By not giving architectural expression to power and authority, it prophesied their ultimate abolition.

This idealistic view of government bore little relation to political reality. The humanistic, noncoercive state presupposed a harmonious society internally at peace, a Broadacre City where government regulation would be unnecessary. Although Wright was certainly an elitist in his personal life, occasionally revealing his contempt for lesser men by referring to "them asses" instead of "the masses,"[30] he nevertheless insisted that the greatest threat to the American experiment in democratic individualism was the "mobocracy" created by centralization, for which he blamed political and economic oligarchy. The framers of the Constitution, he claimed, had meant to abolish economic feudalism by reserving to Congress the right to issue currency, but "ever since [Alexander] Hamilton's money-lending schemes, our democracy has been leading toward greater and greater debt, subsistence on 'foreign' money and war." The state had been captured by commercial and financial giants who built an economic pyramid inverted on its apex, the rich few supporting and exploiting the rest. Authentic capitalism would reverse the situation by basing the pyramid firmly on universal ownership of private property along the lines suggested by Broadacre City. Political and economic centralization, Wright believed, were incompatible with the American ideals of individualism, equality, and opportunity.

Democracy was the best possible kind of government, and the American variety potentially the best possible kind of democracy. If practiced correctly it was "the highest form of aristocracy that the world has ever seen—the aristocracy of the man, the individual . . . ," a better and purer form than one based on lineage or wealth since it allowed men to rise by personal achievement. "Free growth of humane individuality," moreover, was perfectly consistent with social harmony, because in developing self-respect men learned respect for others. The result of true individualism, Wright believed, was the Jeffersonian ideal of government being best when it governed least. In an organic society "all controls" would be corrective, not preventive; "government, therefore, may not institute or lead . . . only execute policy, correct or punish the individual," and only "those matters incapable of individuality—say police powers"—would be entrusted to it. By 1949 Wright was convinced that the American state was "becoming an enormity." Yielding benefits only to the rich and powerful, it was rapidly approaching the "gangsterism" that now characterized the

Soviet Union. Already it took "a good one-fifth of [American] society," he complained, "to keep the other four-fifths . . . in order."[31]

Like architecture, cities and governments should model themselves after nature—where everything was in place and nothing out of place, where structure was absolutely harmonious, and where each component asserted its own individuality. "Internal disorder is architectural disease, if not . . . death," Wright asserted, and so in the proper social state each citizen would enjoy "less government, yet more ordered freedom." An authentic democracy would be organic, wherein unity—the harmonious integration of truly independent members—could be achieved because of universal acceptance of common values and goals. The primary duty of statesmen and artists was to discover the character, or nature, of the people and then fashion a social state that would preserve the polar opposites of individualism and group harmony. This was obviously an idealistic, perhaps naïve, notion, and Wright, who always spoke abstractly on the subject of social organization, was concrete only in the assertion that his architecture would somehow lead the way. But he knew what he wanted: "the electric spark of popular curiosity and surprise to come to life again, along the highways and byways and over every acre of the land." Someday, "the salt and savor of individual wit, taste and character . . . will have come into its own and the countryside far and near will be a festival of life—great life." To that end, every one of his designs, he said, was "a missionary."[32]

10. A GIANT TREE
IN A WIDE LANDSCAPE

[1946-1959]

During his last years Frank Lloyd Wright was often in the lime-light. Like fireworks making their exit in a blaze of glory, his performance grew more dazzling as death approached. He de-signed more buildings than ever, some of which were so spectacu-lar and announced with such fanfare that his every move became an object of public curiosity. His ofttimes outrageous remarks and his irreverence for authority enhanced his reputation as an eccen-tric genius (or crackpot, as his detractors preferred to believe), and he seemed to relish controversy. His comments were often windy and uninformed, but his buildings continued to amaze his ad-mirers and confound the skeptics. By the end of his life he was a personage of monumental proportions, a national institution that few could ignore. His death in 1959 at ninety-one years was head-line news. So ubiquitous had his influence become that many people could not believe his life had finally run its course.

Frank Lloyd Wright's contribution to architectural theory actu-ally ended before World War II. Most of his writing after *An*

Organic Architecture in 1939 was anecdotal, redundant, and vague, and with the exception of The Living City in 1958, itself an elaboration of earlier work, was of little intrinsic value. Few of his buildings after the 1930s offered constructive new suggestions on how to organize individual and social life. But if his philosophical and sociological creativity had ebbed, his artistic daringness flowed as never before. Many of his buildings were indeed amazing to behold, each one seemingly more spectacular than its predecessor, as if Wright, knowing the end was imminent, seized every opportunity to memorialize himself in brick and mortar. Although a greater proportion of his designs were for public use—more than thirty percent from 1952 to 1959 compared with twenty percent overall—and although he built no single dwelling to match the Robie House, the Coonley Estate, or Fallingwater, Wright was still primarily a residential architect. From 1946 through 1959 he received 270 house commissions, 38 in 1950 alone.[1] None was more luxurious than the Harold C. Price House (1956) in Phoenix, which sold in 1964 for $500,000, and few surpassed the Charles F. Glore House (1955) in Lake Forest, Illinois, offered the same year for $125,000.[2] But most were larger and more luxurious than the Usonian homes, whose open plan and other architectural devices they elaborated. Wright had often said he would "rather solve the small house problem than build anything else I can think of,"[3] but in the 1940s and 1950s he found lucrative commissions more compelling than social service.

Yet, with a kind of compulsion, he periodically returned to the low-cost house, offering a variety of unusual but unsatisfactory ideas. In 1951 he announced he would soon make available an attractive and livable home for $5,000–$6,000, better than anything on the market for twice the price. Using nonunion labor, he would pour "a few teakettles of grout" over a stack of concrete blocks tied together by steel rods, and presto!—instant beauty. The first "Usonian Automatic"—in 1953 near Phoenix for Benjamin Adelman—used plain hollow blocks, which were far lighter and much cheaper than the solid, highly decorated textile blocks of the

1920s, and therefore suitable for the roof. Construction was simple and comparatively inexpensive but unless relieved by decoration the Automatic was stark, mechanical, and rather ugly. Wright was as unrealistic on the matter of cost as he was in thinking he could circumvent the unions, and his attempt to improve the Automatic with wood trim only raised the price higher than the $25,000 Adelman residence, clearly out of reach of the common man.[4]

Between 1956 and 1958 Wright designed four types of prefabricated homes, with synthetic-fiber wall panels and concrete blocks, which could be modified according to individual taste by rearranging their modular units. With three bedrooms, a sunken living room, a carport, open plan, and other Usonian characteristics—except that prefab number two, of decidedly Oriental flavor, split four levels on two stories—they were manufactured by the Marshall Erdman firm of Madison, Wisconsin. In 1958 Erdman claimed to have built nine homes in five states with ten more on order, and as many as two dozen may ultimately have been erected. Nevertheless, these designs were also unsuitable for the low-cost housing market. Model number two (1957) at $16,000, for example, required another $19,000 to $22,000 to ship and assemble, and the complete price of the others averaged between $30,000 and $50,000, considerably more than most standardized homes. Of course, they may have been more elegant than their competition, but Wright conceded that they were usually purchased by comfortable admirers who could not otherwise afford him. In 1958 he raised his estimate for a good inexpensive home—with three bedrooms and adequate lot—to $15,000, a figure he never reached.[5]

His final suggestion for cheap housing was certainly provocative, but it stood little chance of popular success. For the International Home Show in New York's Coliseum in 1957, Wright designed a portable, inflatable "Air House," made from vinyl-coated nylon by the United States Rubber Company. Its two units—one thirty-eight feet in diameter by nineteen feet high, the other twenty-four by twelve—contained a large living room, a bedroom, and a kitchen area, supported by a low-pressure heating and air-conditioning blower. Anchored to the ground by 1,750 pounds of sand in fifteen-inch tubes around the perimeter, the structure could withstand strong winds, a heavy snow load, and a man walking on the surface. US Rubber said that air-supported warehouses were already in use, and that Wright's display model was intended to demonstrate the technique, not to replace conventional dwellings. A company in Lexington, Kentucky, however, stood ready to take orders at $2,245, plus $75 for the blower and $100 for the front door. Weighing 200 pounds (without sand) and capable of storage in a three by three foot package, the Air House would have been perfect for living in the Arizona desert.[6]

Wright lent his name to other merchandising projects during the 1950s. After considerable persuasion, he reluctantly consented to design furniture for the Heritage Henredon Company in 1955. Although he freely admitted having been "black and blue in some spot . . . almost all my life from too intimate contact with my own early furniture,"[7] and although the idea violated his teachings on the unity of architecture and accessories, he undertook the project, perhaps rationalizing that by this means he could benefit more people. Some of the rectilinear pieces were quite pleasing, but the chests and tables were overly trimmed, and as usual the chairs were awkward and clumsy. In 1955 and 1956 Henredon manufactured $1 million worth of goods that sold quite well but, due to high development and promotion costs, were "barely profitable." To complement the furniture, Wright offered a "Taliesin line" of wall fabrics (from $3.40 to $13.50 a yard) and wallpaper (from $5.95 to $7.45 a roll) through the F. Schumacher Company, and a selection of carpets by the Karastan Rug Company—all attractive enough but sometimes rather overpowering. Wright's other business venture, a 1957 partnership with Michael Todd, Sylvester "Pat" Weaver, and Henry J. Kaiser to manufacture aluminum theater domes, apparently failed to materialize.[8]

Wallpaper and end tables were only sidelines, of course, for Wright's major business during the 1950s was spectacular build-

Furniture ensemble, 1955

ings, of which the most famous is undoubtedly the Guggenheim Museum in New York City. First conceived in 1943, its construction was postponed fourteen years, by World War II, the death of Solomon R. Guggenheim in 1949, the slow process of buying up real estate along Fifth Avenue between 88th and 89th streets, and by the long wait for leases to expire before demolition could begin. After the property had been purchased, the Guggenheim Foundation filed building plans in April 1952, beginning more than four years of bickering between Wright and the city. Officials contended that the spiral ramp, which was originally to extend six feet over the sidewalk, necessitated a variance they could not grant, and that the glass dome, the few exits, and the windowless facade were fire hazards. When they would not suspend their regulations and when, doubting the safety of the thing, they scratched heads over the whole conception, Wright publicly ridiculed them, so it is not altogether clear if their reservations represented actual code violations or pique at his arrogance. Wright, of course, had a point, that bureaucracy—in this case the Board of Standards and Appeals and the Department of Housing and Buildings—was unresponsive to innovation, but he damaged his own cause with his lack of tact.

He was equally unkind to the twenty-one artists, including Robert Motherwell and Willem de Kooning, who claimed that since paintings could not properly be displayed on sloping surfaces the Guggenheim would do them an injustice. Perhaps fearing that the spectacular surroundings would detract from or overpower their art, they condemned in architecture the very spirit of adventure they claimed for themselves. But Wright's reply was characteristically uncharitable: "I am sufficiently familiar with the incubus of habit that besets your minds to understand that you know all too little of the nature of the mother art—architecture." Artists would paint better pictures, he told an interviewer, under the influence of his museum. In the end Wright agreed to changes that satisfied city officials, and with everyone apparently reassured, with the last of the old buildings demolished, and with the removal of the "obscure reasons" the *Times* said had delayed the project, construction began in 1957. Wright kept close watch on proceedings, occasionally scrambling over the scaffoldings while leading tours of admirers, but he did not live to attend the dedication, in October 1959.[9]

The Guggenheim was only one of many unusual buildings Wright designed during the 1940s and 1950s. The range of his ideas and the daringness of his conceptions surpassed all his previous efforts, and perhaps because of their showiness, sometimes dwarfing their virtues, they received considerable attention in the mass media. His 1954 Beth Shalom Synagogue in Elkins Park near Philadelphia, for example, irritated those who felt it alien to Judaic traditions and those who thought the architecture too improbable. Construction was delayed until the congregation

Beth Shalom Synagogue, 1956–1959, Elkins Park, Pennsylvania

found a contractor, in Oklahoma, willing to attempt the avant-garde scheme: an inverted hexagonal fiber glass cone perched atop a triangular poured-concrete base, altogether forming an abstract Star of David.[10]

Other nonresidential commissions stirring comment were: the sealed Johnson Wax brick and pyrex tubing Research Tower (1946) in Racine, Wisconsin, with fourteen stories cantilevered from a central core of utilities; the triangular glass and fieldstone Unitarian Meeting House (1947) in Madison, Wisconsin—with crisscrossed light baffles above the rostrum—built by the parishioners themselves; the windowless brick gift shop (1948) with a sweeping spiral staircase for V. C. Morris in San Francisco; the octagonal tower (1953) for the H. C. Price Company in Bartlesville, Oklahoma, based on the Saint Mark's in the Bowery scheme (1929), but with one quadrant devoted to two-story apartments; the Annunciation Greek Orthodox Church (1956), a bowl-shaped auditorium supported by piers forming an abstract Hellenic cross, in Wauwatosa, Wisconsin; the monolithic hexagonal Kalita Humphreys Theater (1958–1959) with a revolving stage in Dallas; the massive multistructure Marin County Civic Center (1957–1959) north of San Francisco; and the several buildings at Florida Southern College (1940–1959), Lakeland. These and many others were reported by The New York Times, Time, Life, Look, or Newsweek, the architecture journals, and the various local papers, yielding Wright enormous publicity.

There were also dozens of fantastic projects that never saw the light of day: a saucer-shaped resort hotel suspended from a mountaintop, a floating garden, houses tacked to the sides of cliffs, a space-age church and a mushroom wedding chapel on stilts, a sports pavilion, a trailer court, a drive-in mortuary, government buildings, theaters, a radio station, an airplane hangar, department stores, bridges, a laundry—virtually every imaginable kind of structure in every imaginable form, some of which generated extensive discussion even though execution was never a possibility. The Masieri Memorial (1953) for the Grand Canal touched off a heated exchange between those who felt it captured the grandeur that was Venice and those who felt it too radical for its "sacred" (that is, traditional) setting. Commissioned by the parents of an architectural student, an admirer of Wright who had been killed in an auto accident, it was a vertical three-story project with concrete balconies cantilevered over the water. Ernest Hemingway, recuperating in the city from two airplane crashes during an African safari, suggested the disputants would be placated if "as soon as it is finished it is burned." The Municipal Building Commission decided the memorial would violate hygienic regulations (which could only have meant that it was too sanitary for the area), and that the neighbors must first agree to it before approval could be granted, but, when it was finally rejected by a second commission on the grounds of aesthetic incompatibility, Wright declared that tourism had won another victory.[11]

The Masieri Memorial was a believable building that provoked a lively controversy, but "Mile High Illinois" was an unbelievable building that produced more amusement than anger. He had never been more serious in his life, Wright said, when he announced in 1956 that he was preparing plans for a 528-story structure for the 100,000 employees of Chicago, Cook County, and the state of Illinois. For $300 million he would provide 24 million square feet of floor space (later reduced to 13 million at no specific cost), parking for 15,000 cars, a landing pad for 75 helicopters, and nine floors of television studios with a transmitting tower that he claimed would reach both coasts. Built on the principle of the Johnson Wax and Price Towers with a central core sunk 150 feet underground, it would be pressurized like an airplane, and have atomic-powered elevators attaining speeds of a mile a minute. Located in a park along Lake Michigan, with its employee hours staggered, the "Illinois" would not add to congestion even if it served for the next hundred years. Wright at first maintained and then denied he had financial backing, saying only that he had conceived the scheme after someone came to him with a proposal for a half-mile edifice, to which he had scornfully replied, "The hell with that!" No one took him very seriously—although buildings now in excess of a hundred stories make the notion less improbable—but many were no doubt impressed when he unveiled the drawing, itself twenty-two feet high.[12]

The federal government was even less taken with Wright than the state of Illinois. Violating his highly touted principle of non-collaboration with other architects, he joined with seven colleagues in July 1954 to form the Kitty Hawk Association, a cabal competing with eighty others to design the $125 million Air Force Academy at Colorado Springs, "the commission of my career!" he exclaimed in anticipation. A year later, after Kitty Hawk for no stated reason had withdrawn without making a bid, Wright told the House Appropriations Subcommittee that the winning Skidmore, Owings, and Merrill plan was a "shocking fiasco," a "half-baked" wayside market "utterly without a soul, utterly without a spirit," "a glassified box on stilts," and suggested that the teenagers of America could have made a better choice of architects. Political pundit Drew Pearson charged that brick and stone lobbyists successfully placed more of their materials into the project as a result of Wright's testimony. The architect denied the allegation and nothing further was heard on the matter. During the imbroglio, Wright submitted an unsolicited plan for a restaurant at Yosemite National Park. To Conrad Wirth, Director of the Park Service, who dismissed it as "a mushroom type of thing" that would block the view, the architect replied only, "It's politics."[13]

Wright's associations with foreign governments were equally unrewarding: none of the projects he designed for outside the United States after World War II were erected. Perhaps the best known and most elaborate was the $45 million Plan for Greater Baghdad, commissioned in 1957 by King Faisal as part of a nineteen-year, $9 billion public works development. Wright's contribution was to have been the cultural buildings—an opera house, a civic auditorium, public gardens, and a university—on Edena Island and the adjacent banks of the Tigris River. The plans he unveiled at the Iraqi Consulate in New York in May 1958, although decidedly Middle Eastern in flavor, were not unlike his other circular projects at the time, particularly the Grady Gammage Auditorium for Arizona State University completed in 1962 by William Wesley Peters, his son-in-law. A week before Peters was scheduled to leave for Baghdad to supervise the beginning of construction, the King was overthrown in a bloodless coup. At first the revolutionary government said it would honor the contract, but early in 1959 announced that Wright's plans were "rather grandiose." The people needed food, clothing, and shelter more than floating gardens, gold fountains, and a mammoth zoo, and although the new leaders wanted a university they decided to look elsewhere for an architect. In Eastern eyes, Wright represented Western imperialism, an irony, considering his reputation in American government circles.[14]

Wright's difficulties with his adopted state of Arizona culminated in yet another controversial project that was never built.

When, in 1951, the state constructed a power line near Taliesin West, interfering with his view of the Superstition Mountains, he demanded its removal lest he take his home and his practice elsewhere. Neither he nor the wires gave an inch, and the bitter memory undoubtedly lingered until 1956, when the Technical Board of Registration announced that Wright would have to obtain an Arizona architect's license or face prosecution for a misdemeanor. He had met all the requirements and would not have to prove his qualifications, the secretary of the board said, presumably with a straight face, but there could be no exceptions, and Wright had to abide by the regulations like everyone else. Obviously miffed, he refused to comply, and the issue was settled only when the Board granted licenses to him and a number of other architects and engineers because of their eminence.

Wright was probably carrying a grudge a few months later when Arizona announced its plans for a new state capitol. "Not anything I've ever seen betokens incompetence as much as this proposed building," he charged with his usual understatement, and, in an attempt to embarrass the authorities, offered his own design directly to the people. Endorsed by Henry and Clare Boothe Luce, and by former Connecticut Senator and Mrs. William Benton—all winter residents there—"The Oasis" was a hexagonal, crenolated skeleton-canopy of concrete, glass, and blue copper, pierced by jet fountains and elaborately decorated transmitting towers. Rejecting the pompous symbols of authority, the design was nevertheless overpowering, and probably too fussy and ornate for popular taste. Wright's suggestion that the public circumvent the "pole-and-wire" politicians (he had not forgotten the power lines near Taliesin West) by selecting their capitol from three offerings—including his, of course—at a referendum, met with an equally unenthusiastic response. Many people think of him as "an egomaniac, [an] egocentric, [and] a crackpot," one observer noted, expressing the general sentiment somewhat accurately. But a man "has to be a little of all those things," he admitted, "to be creative. . . ."[15]

Wright's skirmishes with Arizona paled in comparison to those with his native state of Wisconsin, which were responsible for much of his final reputation as an irascible ne'er-do-well. The first occurred in 1947, when, with the solid support of Spring Green, he asked the State Highway Commission to replace a steel-truss bridge scheduled for demolition with one of his concrete butterfly designs (a single row of piers fanning out to form the underside of the roadway), and to consider his highway rerouting and landscaping scheme, which would have beautified the area, removed busy thoroughfares from the village limits, and facilitated transportation for nearby farmers. In his first public address to his neighbors—some six hundred, the largest crowd in Spring Green's history—he said he could design three bridges at 120 percent the cost of one old-style, and that his would be safer, larger, and easier to construct. He also advocated periodic town meetings where citizens could discuss mutual problems and circumvent bureaucratic mismanagement. Despite considerable support—four hundred signatures on a petition and newspaper endorsement—Wright's effort was tardy. The contract was let for a steel-truss bridge on a roadway cutting through a corner of town, and Highway Commissioner James R. Law, a Madison architect who disliked Wright intensely, stated gratuitously that his proposals had not been taken seriously anyway. Whereupon Wright fired off "Bureaucracy Jumps the Gun," an indignant editorial accusing the state of neglecting the people while knuckling under to the "interests," but failed to secure an injunction to halt construction.

Four years later, in 1951, Wright renewed his offer to build a butterfly bridge, this time free of charge at the state's most famous tourist spot, the Wisconsin Dells. Modestly assuring everyone that his work would attract international attention, thereby increasing local business, he failed to mention the primary motive for his magnanimity: having unsuccessfully sought the commission for the Bay Bridge connecting San Francisco with Oakland, he was willing to take a financial loss to demonstrate the efficacy of one of his favorite conceptions. Governor Walter J. Kohler and the Sauk

County Board of Supervisors endorsed the plan, but they met stiff opposition from Highway Commissioner Raymond Jensen—"We are not looking for beauty"—and influential business interests. Demanding full control over construction, Wright wanted to locate the span at scenic Echo Point, but pressure from area merchants forced the commission to insist it feed the town of Wisconsin Dells, half a mile away. Furthermore, Jensen's colleague, James R. Law, again declared that, if Wright designed it, there would be no bridge. After further consideration, he withdrew his offer and Wisconsin lost a second opportunity to become the first state to commission him.[16]

His third encounter with Wisconsin had been festering ever since he opened the Taliesin Fellowship in 1932. Contending that part of his estate—the Hillside School, eighty acres, and later the Midway Farm buildings—was used for educational purposes and should therefore be tax exempt, he had twice, in 1937 and 1939, protested his local real estate levies, which he always left in arrears anyway. In 1939 Iowa County officials voted to take possession of Taliesin if he did not pay up. Apparently he did, for nothing further was done about the issue until the Frank Lloyd Wright Foundation (incorporated in 1940) renewed the claim to exemption in 1950, and the next year filed in circuit court asking that $3,642 accrued since 1942 be dismissed. In response, Iowa County and the town of Wyoming claimed that Wright owed $13,477.67 in unpaid taxes, penalties, and interest covering the last ten years.

Circuit Judge Arthur Kopp handed down a decision in 1953 denying the Foundation's request. After studying Taliesin's financial records, which revealed that Wright's fees were $80,000 to $100,000 a year, that apprentice tuition brought in $18,000 to $36,000, and farm income $4,000 to $12,000 more, leaving an annual average profit of $20,000 to $30,000, Kopp decided that the Foundation was actually a business venture. Wright might have accepted the verdict and paid his taxes had not the governor's Educational Advisory Committee less than a month later approved Taliesin as an architectural training school for veterans.

Claiming that this supported his original contention, Wright petitioned for a new trial, which Judge Kopp denied on the grounds that the advisory committee decision was not retroactive. Now owing the county and the town well over $14,000, Wright decided to appeal to the state supreme court.[17]

When the case came up in September 1954, Wyoming Township argued that, since Wright used his apprentices to reduce his expenses, he was primarily engaged in business, while he on the other hand claimed that architecture was not a business at all and that he spent much of his time teaching. Speaking for a court unanimously agreeing with Wyoming, Chief Justice Edward Fairchild decided in November that the Foundation "is completely dominated in every detail of its life by Frank Lloyd Wright, the individual," and that apprentice training was only incidental to "the main purpose of continuing [his] architectural business." Wright was ordered immediately to pay $886 in back personal property taxes to the town for 1944 to 1948, leaving the remainder for further determination. Even though he seems to have been treated quite reasonably, Wright announced to the Madison *Capital Times* that, since Wisconsin obviously did not appreciate him, he would henceforth conduct his practice from New York and Arizona. The next day he told *The New York Times* that he planned to move into the Plaza Hotel; that all his income—sometimes as much as $200,000 annually—went into the Foundation, a nonprofit organization that would presumably foot the bill for his expensive New York lodgings; that he could not even write a ten-dollar check without borrowing money to cover it; and that he did not have full control over Taliesin's expenditures. Then, in a dramatic gesture, he threatened to burn Taliesin to the ground, move to another state, and leave the ashes as a memorial to Wisconsin's stupidity.[18]

We can "take no pride in directing tourists to ruins," the editor of Spring Green's *Weekly Home News* wrote. "The home-town folks don't want him to leave. . . . We hope we'll always have a Taliesin." His neighbors need not have worried, for a few days later Wright confided to his friend William T. Evjue, editor and publisher of The Capital Times in Madison, that he would not follow through on his theatrics. He did not have as much money as people thought, he said, and if the town decided to collect back taxes it might very well have to confiscate his property. The reason he objected to the supreme court's decision was that he feared the payment of local taxes might be used as a precedent for rescinding his federal and state exemptions. He said he wanted nothing more than the same financial relief as others in his position. Evjue's talk with Wright convinced him that the architect would neither leave the state nor destroy Taliesin. The editor failed to speculate in his column, however, whether Wright had retained the spending habits from his Oak Park days, when, as he put it in An Autobiography, "I hardly knew which were necessities and which luxuries." Close scrutiny may well have determined that Wright's liquid resources were not overwhelming.[19]

Without questioning his intentions or his financial situation, a group of Wright's admirers organized a testimonial dinner at the University of Wisconsin's Memorial Union in February 1955. Three hundred seventy well-wishers from around the nation, including Evjue, Governor Kohler, Herbert Jacobs, and New York architect Ralph Walker, presented Wright with a $10,000 check to pay his debts and to express their appreciation. "After the demonstration of feeling and affection last night," he commented the next morning, "I don't think it would be possible for me to leave my native state." The guests and the many others unable to attend may not have known that ten days before the banquet Wright had paid $5,000 in real estate taxes to Iowa County to forestall a foreclosure sale on his cattle and to remove attachment orders on some of his personal property, having already paid more than $4,000 to Wyoming in January. But they probably would not have cared, for they were as eager to honor Wright as he was to receive adulation. What he wanted more than money, and what he got, was an expression of concern, a public recognition that he was indeed Wisconsin's leading citizen. In almost half a century of residence, the state had never commissioned a building, given him an honorary degree, consulted him professionally, or acknowledged his presence except by spurning his design offers and battling him over taxes, morals, and politics. And, as if to corroborate the point, neither the state nor the university sent an official representative to the testimonial. The situation was somewhat remedied, however, when State Senator Gaylord Nelson cosponsored a bill to grant local tax exemption to the Wright Foundation. At a Taxation Committee hearing in May, Wright confided that he had everything out of life he wanted "except the respect of my neighbors," but then confessed he had never gone out of his way to get it.[20]

This was not altogether true. A footnote to this extended imbroglio was that in 1956 Wright designed a grammar school free of charge for Wyoming Township, supervised its construction on land he himself had purchased and donated, and contributed some $7,000 to the building fund. His only rural schoolhouse consisted of two classrooms separated from a gymnasium-cafeteria-assembly hall combination by a skylit central corridor under a forest of crossed beams. Its roof line almost exactly reproduced the contours of the hill behind it, and in its bucolic setting it was a quaint and simple expression of organic architecture. Most of the twelve hundred people who came to the open house in January 1958 agreed that it might be nice to attend school again in such a fine building. The favorable reaction was not unlike that prompted by the equally unorthodox Hillside Home School more than half a century before, underscoring the point that Wright's work was not unappealing to the unsophisticated in rural America. Although the two buildings were only a few minutes apart down a quiet country road, they were separated by half a lifetime of tumult. In the end, however, he became his people's architect.[21]

Wright's arduous relations with Wisconsin and his outspoken political ideas adversely influenced the fate of one of his finest designs—the Monona Terrace Civic Center in Madison—itself the basis of another dispute. Originally conceived in 1938, Wright modified it at least three times (1941, 1953, 1956) before another

Wyoming Valley Grammar School, 1957, Wyoming Valley, Wisconsin

revision by William Wesley Peters after his death. When a citizens group revived his fifteen-year-old proposals during the early stages of discussing new city-county facilities in 1953, the architect offered $20,000 to prove his scheme could be built for less than $20 million. Publication of the plans in four daily installments of *The Capital Times* inaugurated a year or more of public debate, settled by referenda in November 1954, when Madison voters agreed overwhelmingly (22,500 to 6,300) to float a $4 million bond to finance a civic center, decided convincingly (16,800 to 11,700) to erect it at the Monona Terrace site, and consented reluctantly (15,100 to 13,800) to hire Wright as the architect. Some nineteen months later, after numerous unexplained delays, he signed a disadvantageous contract principally because the terrace was a favorite design he wanted to build.

Stipulating a low fee, severe budgetary limitations, and inadequate planning time in a maze of legal technicalities, the contract also included a provision that came back to haunt him: he would not be paid for preliminary work if the project were prohibited by law. Revised plans unveiled in August 1956 transformed an issue into a controversy. Endless budget cutting efforts, political haggling, nitpicking over architectural details, and lawsuits to prevent construction—stalling tactics by the "Wrightophobes," according to editor Evjue—all combined to stymie progress. A leader of the opposition, local Assemblyman Carroll Metzner, finally thwarted the project completely in 1957 by securing passage of a law prohibiting construction of anything on the terrace site over twenty feet tall, thereby activating the seemingly innocuous clause in Wright's contract. The Metzner Law remained in force until March 1959, a month before the architect's death, and as a result Madison was denied the civic center it voted for. Of course, Wright did little to bring the opposing factions together. By reiterating how much his project would rehabilitate a lakeshore the "foolish" city had allowed to deteriorate, he antagonized many potential supporters, not so much by his candor as by his patronizing tone. If Madison preferred to remain "commonplace" by rejecting the terrace, it would be the "stupidest" place in America. Wright advised it how to vote in the referenda, campaigned against an anti-terrace mayor, and then said he was "ashamed" of the town of his boyhood. Few other architects would so closely identify themselves with civic virtue in order to build one of their own structures.[22]

Another factor contributing to the polarization over Monona Terrace, as well as to Wright's controversial stature in Wisconsin, was his attitude toward the Red Scare of the 1950s. He spoke out loudly and frequently against hysterical anti-Communism, which he recognized as a political stratagem, as a threat to personal liberty, and as an incorrect analysis of Soviet intentions. He had been a target of right-wing vitriol ever since the 1930s, when he publicly endorsed the "great Russian experiment." But the attacks increased after 1951, when he replied to a House Committee on Un-American Activities accusation that he had once been a member of an unspecified subversive organization by branding the committee itself un-American and the charge part of a broad political ploy to reelect its members. He argued that the underlying basis for anti-Communism was America's lack of national self-confidence, which caused her to assume a belligerent (and preposterous) attitude toward the rest of the world. The most convenient vehicle for achieving collective ego-reinforcement during the 1950s, Wright believed, was red-baiting, and, as far as he was concerned, the chief baiter was the former country judge from Appleton, that "political pervert," Wisconsin's own junior senator, Joseph R. McCarthy.[23]

"Not so long ago," the architect remembered in 1952 of the two Robert M. La Follettes, the father and son who had dominated local, and influenced national, politics for over half a century, "Wisconsin had the reputation of a great and noble state." Today, it "is a stench in the nostrils of decency everywhere . . . stand-[ing] more for damage to America . . . [than] any other State in the world." Wright's ultimate solution to the McCarthy problem was a typical blend of sarcasm and fantasy: "As an architect," he wrote in Madison's *Capital Times,*

I submit a simple design for a suitable and perhaps salutary memorial to the chief demagogue. . . .

Here it is: At all principal cross-roads of the State set up, on a solid concrete base, a large cast iron pot of simple but chaste design, say 6 feet in diameter. Pour into it a powerful charge of $H2S$ or carbon dioxide. On the birthday of the chief demagogue . . . light a blaze under every pot and raise such a prodigious stink that the true character of such a "patriot" will be brought to the noses of the voters. . . . This realistic celebration to last for 24 hours. . . .[24]

In more serious moments Wright proposed reconciliation with the Soviet Union, disarmament, a one-term limitation on the Presidency, and the revitalization of local government as ways to restore power to the people and sanity to the state.

These and similar remarks on Communism stimulated much of the opposition to Wright in Wisconsin and to the Monona Terrace in Madison. Carroll Metzner, the legislator responsible for the law prohibiting its construction, was also conspicuous in right-wing Republican circles. Carrying his single-mindedness to considerable lengths, he turned up unexpectedly in 1957 at a public hearing in San Raphael, California, during a "vacation," to lobby against the choice of Wright as architect for the Marin County Civic Center. Metzner claimed to have proof of his "incapacities" for the job, but his specific charges were not revealed. Coincidently, one of the five county supervisors released a document prepared by former HUAC Staff Director J. B. Matthews, purporting to show that Wright had given "active and extensive support to Communist enterprises." The architect's pithy reply—"Oh rats!"—apparently mirrored the general consensus, for the Board of Supervisors voted 4 to 1 to hire him, and he went on to design his only executed government structure.[25]

Although he never won a comparable statewide victory in Wisconsin, he was able during his last years to build friendly relations with his Spring Green neighbors and, despite his unorthodox life-style and opinions, to win from them a certain respect. Their strong support for his 1947 "General Plan of Highway and Bridge Relocation" and their appreciation of his Wyoming Grammar School indicate a communality of interest which found public expression on several other occasions. In 1949, for example, at the request of the local Businessmen's Association, Wright designed a fourteen- by twenty-eight-foot stone and wood sign for a triangular plot at the intersection of two highways feeding Spring Green. With white lettering on a green background, a gold directional arrow, and red spaces for civic claims, its design and construction would have been his gift to the community. Although the project never materialized, it was revived in spectacular fashion in 1957, when a new proposal for the same intersection called for a ninety-foot lighted shaft rising from a landscaped base, with three fountains flowing into pools representing a spring. Someone suggested adding "teaser" markers all the way to Madison (forty miles) and an equal distance to the west. Wright's death ended the scheme, which was nothing more than high-class boosterism, much too grandiose for so small a town. The shaft was primarily intended to aid local commerce, but its unique design, word of mouth, and the American Automobile Association's guidebook would inevitably have made it an advertisement for Taliesin as well, linking the destinies of home and community in a way Wright would have approved.

His several projected buildings for Spring Green—a state bank (1914), a Methodist Church (1940), an artist's studio (1941), a restaurant and service station (1943), a bridge (1947), a post office (1957), a commercial building (1957), and an auditorium (1958)—were all deemed too expensive for the available resources and never constructed, even though the village wanted a Wright design very much, according to its president in 1957. Good relations were cemented in other ways, however. When the fire department extinguished a small blaze at the Fellowship's buildings in 1952, the architect thanked it with a hundred-dollar check, suggesting the men blow it on a good time. (They refurbished their equipment instead.) Spring Green reciprocated his many gestures in 1957 by giving him a number of saplings, which he promptly planted along a state highway near the business district, and then in turn offered twenty twelve-foot elms for the main street. Although Wright was a strange and difficult man in many ways, most residents of Spring Green understood that his name lent prestige and commercial value to their community, and they were reasonably happy with his presence there.

The high point of good relations came between 1957, the year of Spring Green's centennial, and 1959. Eager to honor their most prominent citizen, and noting the long hours donated by the Fellowship to the planning, the town fathers decided to hold a Frank Lloyd Wright Day during the celebration, and to put his picture on the cover of the commemorative booklet. Between June 28 and 30, the apprentices gave a free concert, presided over open house at Taliesin and an architectural exhibit at the high school, while on his day, the twenty-ninth, Wright was feted at a luncheon, a banquet, and a parade. Things went so well that it was decided to make the festival an annual event, and there was talk of Wright designing a civic center or a summer theater. Two senior Taliesin Fellows, Eugene Masselink and Wright's son-in-law William Wesley Peters, were included on the four-man planning committee for 1958 (Peters was chairman), symbolizing the kind of working relationship with his neighbors the architect had long envisioned. His announcement that he was "eager to put every effort into building Spring Green's future" prompted the newspaper editor to note that Wright had always hoped the town and the Fellowship might collaborate, a hope, he added, now being realized. "It's no longer a friendship between Taliesin and Spring Green," an enthusiastic apprentice observed after the successful 1958 festival. "It's a love affair."[26]

Wright died before there could be a third celebration, and slowly the bonds between Spring Green and Taliesin withered away. His continuous effort to design something for it—free of charge, if necessary—indicates a strong interest in its future, a desire to make it "an ideal community," as he once said. But, unfortunately, Spring Green was not unlike the fictional Gopher Prairie of Sinclair Lewis's *Main Street*. Just down the road and across the river from America's most famous architect with his international group of apprentices, it was actually in quite another world. Wright never found a way to reconcile the cosmopolite and the provincial, to make Art meaningful to the Common Man. Today Spring Green itself has but three small, second-rate structures to memorialize his name—a clinic, a cocktail lounge, and a remodeled theater—designed after his death by William Wesley Peters. Of course, there are the usual drugstore postcards and the souvenirs in the restaurant gift shop. Everyone knows the way to Taliesin and can repeat apocryphal stories about the Master.

Spring Green tends the Wright legend and trades on his name, but it never reaped the most lasting benefits of all.*

Nevertheless, more than any other Wisconsin community it recognized Wright's greatness, especially during the 1950s when, despite his outspokenness, his iconoclastic stance, and his politics, many organizations and institutions outside the state praised him lavishly. In his last years few who could have honored him failed to. The American Institute of Architects, the "establishment" of the profession he had attacked on so many occasions, finally awarded him its gold medal in 1949, long after several others with comparatively limited abilities had received it. Between 1947 and 1953 he accepted citations from the National Institute of Arts and Letters, the Cooper Union, the American Academy of Arts and Letters, the National Academy of Design, the American Institute of Arts and Letters, the Franklin Institute, the National Academy of Finland, and the Royal Academy of Fine Arts in Stockholm. He received Italy's Star of Solidarity in 1951, and honorary doctorates from Princeton University (1947), Florida Southern (1950), Yale (1954), the University of Wisconsin, and the Technical Institutes of Darmstadt, Germany, and Zurich, Switzerland (all in 1955), and from Sarah Lawrence (1958). A photographic exhibition of his houses by Ezra Stoller at the Museum of Modern Art in New York in 1947 was far surpassed in scale and splendor by "Sixty Years of Living Architecture," which opened in Philadelphia in 1951 and for the next three years toured Europe and the United States. Chicago held a Frank Lloyd Wright Day in October 1956, and labeled the Robie House an official landmark, shortly after *The Architectural Record* had selected it as "one of the seven most notable residences ever built in America."

---

* There was another monument to Wright in Spring Green, surely an un-appreciated one. At the intersection of Highways 14 and 23, at the outskirts of town on the triangular plot he planned to use for his markers, there stood upright for many years a huge fieldstone slab, once intended to point the way to Taliesin. It was unmarked and its purpose virtually forgotten, an appropriate symbol of Wright's ultimate impact on Spring Green. It is now (1972) gone altogether.

Basking in his glory, when he might have been more generous, Wright remained adamant on the subject of other architects. Occasionally he had a kind word—Edward Durrell Stone was "honest" and the Mormon Tabernacle in Salt Lake City was "a remarkable structure with an original and harmonious expression"—but generally he was uncivil. "He is a highbrow," he said of Philip Johnson. "A highbrow is a man educated beyond his capacity." Mies van der Rohe was "very nice," but was a reactionary, wasting his time trying to make the nineteenth century box frame beautiful. The giant firm of Skidmore, Owings, and Merrill he ridiculed as "Skiddings, Own-More, and Sterile," and for the leading Swiss architect he had nothing but contempt: "I think Corbusier should have been a painter," he told an interviewer. "He was a bad one but he should have kept on. No painter can understand architecture." Most contemporary designs, he insisted modestly, were "betrayals" of his own ideas:

Like those awful UN buildings. Or that Corbusier thing in Marseilles. Massacre on the waterfront, I call that. Or any of those skinny glass boxes. Why, I wouldn't walk on the same side of the street with them. Fool things might explode. There! That's from a fellow who knew what architecture was when these glass-box boys were just so many diapers hanging on the line.[27]

Having dispensed with all the others, he alone remained a great creative force. "I defy anyone to name a single aspect of the best contemporary architecture," he asserted hotly and sincerely in 1953, "that wasn't first done by me." One commentator on an NBC radio program remarked, "I don't think you could find a building constructed anywhere in the United States today, even a lunch stand, that doesn't show in some degree the influence of his architectural ideas," and Wright, who was also on the broadcast, smiled approvingly. "Once, after her husband had agreed on the witness stand that he was the world's greatest living architect," Look magazine reported, "Mrs. Wright protested, 'Frank, you should be more modest.' 'You forget, Olgivanna,' he replied

Frank Lloyd Wright, September 14, 1955, at the Merchandise Mart, Chicago, Illinois

quickly, 'I was under oath.'" His son John, also an architect, was a bit more objective: "My father, whose colossal ego is matched only by his towering ability, would be the first to agree that anyone who would choose the son when he could have the master ought to have his head examined. In fact, I once heard him say to one of

277

MY clients, 'Why fool around with the coupon when you can have the genuine bond?' " And Wright was the genuine article— "an American original," a friend called him. He lived life to the fullest, "at its central current," never wasting a moment, his sister Maginel commented. "If I felt any better," the architect declared in 1956, a month before his 89th birthday, "I couldn't stand it."[28]

By this time Wright was an established national celebrity. Appearing frequently on radio and television, giving scores of interviews, lecturing and publishing constantly, he was often in the news, a reliable source of material for *Life, Time, Look,* and *Newsweek.* "A great showman and cut-up," his friend Bruce Barton wrote, Wright "loves to say things that make headlines." He was an eternal fount of quotable quotes, but no matter how often he followed his bombshells with sensible analysis, the press focused on the outrageous, and few rose to take issue. Some he simply overpowered by the force of his personality. He would transform interviews into platforms for his current concerns, insult his audiences beyond the bounds of good taste, and intimidate almost everyone by the breadth of his views. So effectively had he cowed the public that he could, for example, barge unchallenged into board meetings or other private gatherings at New York's Plaza Hotel—where he kept a permanent suite of his own design—and with his malacca cane point out flaws in the decor. Or he would stride down Fifth Avenue from the Guggenheim construction site, entourage hurrying to keep pace, acerbicly analyzing the buildings en route, and scathingly commenting on diverse subjects. The Plaza itself, of course, was spared his wrath; although much of it had been ruined by "inferior desecrators," it still retained much of its "human sense." But the rest of the city upset him: after each visit, he said, he was "turned inside out, shaken, and returned—empty." He could get around faster by walking over the tops of the taxicabs than by riding in them, he sneered. Yet he loved it, especially his Plaza suite, which, he told his visitors, had once belonged to Diamond Jim Brady. "It's the best part of New York," he remarked proudly.[29]

In many ways the comparison was a good one, for there were obvious similarities between the gambler and the architect. Both lived high, wide, and handsome, unrestrained by the fetters that bound the common man. There was a drama and a flair to Wright's life: contact with the world's leading citizens, praise and adulation, headlines and travel, the finest automobiles, and mammoth birthday parties at Taliesin—a "small" affair might exceed a hundred guests—with replicas of Egyptian barques floating on the lake, candlelit Japanese lanterns bobbing in the breeze, and personages like Alexander Woollcott, Carl Sandburg, or Adlai Stevenson strolling about. His life was a whirlwind of activity. If he was not off on a crusade or blasting one or another national foible, he was turning out buildings at a furious pace, and if anything was even more prolific as he entered his tenth decade. In 1957, as he passed his ninetieth birthday, he received a career high of forty commissions, from 1946 through 1958 having averaged almost twenty-six a year, more than ever before. Even though apprentices did most of the busy work, Wright conceived the buildings and supervised the finished drawings, and that, with his five books and fifty or more lesser publications during the 1950s was a prodigious achievement, even for a much younger man. "How do you do it? How do you think of it all?" his sister asked him toward the end. "I can't get it out fast enough," he said.[30]

Underneath this supercharged exterior, however, was a quieter man, hardly the Diamond Jim known to the public. There was about him "none of the efficiency, the snap, the sense of speed and high-pressure salesmanship of the era he has endeavored to express in steel and stone," one interviewer noted. He was something of an anachronism, another reported, with his alpaca suit, white collar, and black string tie, "that turn-of-the-century ensemble of the romantic and aesthetic rebel." And in the privacy of Taliesin Wright was even less flamboyant. On a typical day he arose at seven-thirty, took breakfast in his quarters with Olgivanna, then read and sketched until ten, when he strolled the three-quarters of a mile to visit the apprentices in the drafting room at the Hillside

School. After lunch he napped until three o'clock tea, then held a staff meeting followed by an Old Bushmill with a water chaser to whet his appetite for dinner. In the evening he usually read, watched television, and talked with his wife before bed at ten, though on weekends he might indulge himself with an Irish whisky nightcap.

The schedule varied a little on Saturdays and Sundays. Every Sabbath morning at the tiny Unity Chapel he had helped his family build seventy years before, he preached a "sermon," a two-hour talk to the Fellowship on whatever issue concerned him. Sometimes guest speakers or apprentices substituted, but the service was always homey and simple. After evening dinner with the Fellowship on Saturday there would be a film, and on Sunday a musicale, both followed by refreshments and discussion. Taliesin was "a special kind of oasis," one observer recalled, "in which the raw and hostile forces of surrounding life had somehow been reorganized into a landscape of blessed peace and plenty."[31]

At the age of ninety-one Wright seemed to be a permanent part of the American scene. He was seldom sick, always active, alert, and very much evident. As March turned into April in 1959 he accepted a new commission, gave another interview, continued work on the Marin County Civic Center, and fired off an indignant letter denouncing his Monona Terrace opponents: everything business as usual. At Taliesin West, he and his wife celebrated Easter with the Fellowship. "Arm and arm we walked back to our rooms to talk," Olgivanna remembered, "to be in each other's presence."

It was their last Easter together. On April 4 Wright complained of abdominal pains and was rushed from Taliesin West to Saint Joseph's Hospital in Phoenix, where he underwent surgery for an intestinal block and accompanying hemorrhage. For the next three days he progressed nicely, apparently on the way to full recovery. Doctors marveled at his strength and resiliency. Then on April 9, fifteen minutes after a final check by his bedside nurse, "he just sighed and died."[32]

The body was flown to Spring Green, where, on April 12, scores of mourners gathered to hear the funeral oration delivered by Reverend Max Gaebler of the Unitarian Meeting House Wright had designed in Madison. Later, some forty relatives and friends walked behind the horse-drawn, flower-draped coffin to the tiny family burial ground next to Unity Chapel, where Wright's body was lowered into an unmarked grave near a fieldstone slab bearing the simple inscription, "Mamah Cheney."[33]

Well-spoken, well-placed individuals from around the world offered their eloquent regrets, too many for one architecture journal to include in a single issue. Mies van der Rohe's may have been the most appropriate: "In his undiminished power he resembles a giant tree in a wide landscape which year after year attains a more noble crown." But the most poignant tributes came from Spring Green, almost overlooked in the eulogizing. "We are much diminished in his passing," the newspaper editor wrote; we have "suffered a great loss." It won't be the same with Mr. Wright gone, a bank cashier remarked. "We always got a thrill when he came in here. . . ." The lady who owned the drugstore, however, said it most simply: "I just can't believe it. He was the kind of man you thought would live forever."[34]

11. HOW DO YOU SPEAK
TO A DIVINITY?

[AFTER 1959]

Even before his death in 1959 several of Frank Lloyd Wright's buildings were destroyed. After more than a decade of abuse, the Midway Gardens (1914) in Chicago was demolished in 1929. The Larkin Administration Building (1904) in Buffalo, one of Wright's most significant works, perished in 1949, followed the next year by the original Hillside Home School (1887) near Spring Green, Wisconsin. Others were lost or thoughtlessly altered after his death. The important early residence for Allison Harlan (1892) in Chicago burned in 1963, just before its scheduled restoration. The main house on the Coonley Estate (1907–1912) was divided into duplex apartments, and the stables, playhouse, and gardener's cottage remodeled as individual dwellings. Leaded windows and furniture from several prairie houses were sold by galleries and auctioneers, sometimes for hundreds of dollars apiece. The most publicized demolition was the Imperial Hotel (1913–1922) in Tokyo: after riding out the 1923 earthquake that killed over 90,000 persons and left another 42,000 homeless; after withstanding four hundred incendiaries, which gutted an entire wing during Allied bombing in 1945; and after surviving a number of attempts to procure its choice downtown location, the hotel finally succumbed to "progress" in 1967, and in 1969 was replaced by a seventeen-floor, $60 million "New Imperial."[1] At the time of Wright's death over three hundred of his structures remained, several dozen less than were built.

During the 1960s many more Americans than ever before awakened to their architectural heritage, organizing to fight developers impervious to cultural landmarks. Wright's legacy has benefited from this as well as from individual citizen efforts. His own Oak Park home (1889), for example, was purchased by an admiring middle-aged couple, who renovated the entire structure from the proceeds of conducted tours. The Elizabeth Gale House (1909) down the street was purchased in 1963 by an architect willing to undertake the "massive repairs" necessary for its refurbishing, and the Darwin C. Martin House (1904) in Buffalo was restored as a presidential residence by the local branch of the State University of New York, too late, however, to save its one hundred-foot pergola or any of its furnishings. Periodic public outcries saved the Robie House (1907) from destruction at the hands of the University of Chicago and its previous owners; in 1964 it became a registered historical landmark, and in 1966 was rehabilitated as headquarters for the Adlai E. Stevenson Institute of International Affairs. Public pressure forced Interior Secretary Stuart Udall to intervene in 1964 to save the relatively inconsequential Loren Pope House (1940) in Falls Church, Virginia, from highway bulldozers. By 1970 threatened Wright buildings were able to generate citizens lobbies, and an increasing number of his houses were being purchased by those interested in preserving or restoring their original characteristics.[2]

In addition to becoming causes célèbres, Wright's architecture has entered into the cultural mainstream in literal and symbolic ways. Many of his buildings have been opened to regularly scheduled tours: among others his Oak Park home, nearby Unity Temple, the Johnson Wax Building and Herbert F. Johnson's

"Wingspread" in Racine, Wisconsin, the Marin County Civic Center north of San Francisco, the Hillside Home School at Spring Green, Taliesin West in Arizona, the Beth Shalom Synagogue near Philadelphia, and the Greek Orthodox Church in Wauwatosa, Wisconsin. In 1963 Edgar Kaufmann, Jr. donated his late father's Fallingwater at Bear Run to the Western Pennsylvania Conservancy—with a $500,000 endowment fund and five hundred acres of land—and in the next four years over 185,000 people came to see it.[3] By the mid-1960s Wright's once controversial and unorthodox designs were so much a part of the American heritage that they were featured and used as backdrops for advertising in local newspapers and national magazines.[4] When his 1953 design for the Riverview Terrace Restaurant near Spring Green was finally executed in 1967, the President's wife, Mrs. Lyndon Baines Johnson, officiated at the dedication. Chicago and Oak Park collaborated in 1969 for a five-week festival to commemorate the architect's supposed centennial, exhibitions of his furniture and stained-glass windows have been held periodically, and collectors scramble for artifacts from his early buildings.[5]

In part, the structures that were lost have been offset by others erected after his death, some of which he left under construction: the Beth Shalom Synagogue, the Guggenheim Museum in New York, the Kalita Humphreys Theatre in Dallas, and about fifteen private residences. Several more important projects for which ground had not been broken were finished even later, including segments of the Marin County Civic Center begun in 1960, the Greek Orthodox Church dedicated in 1961, the Grady Gammage Auditorium at Arizona State University in Tempe and the Corbin Education Center at the University of Wichita, both opened in 1964. The forty to fifty buildings—mostly houses—he left in various stages of planning and construction were supervised after his death by his widow Olgivanna, and by his son-in-law, William Wesley Peters, president and vice-president respectively of the Frank Lloyd Wright Foundation. Established in 1940, this parent organization created two subdivisions in 1959: Taliesin Associated

Architects (TAA), a firm composed of Wright's assistants and former apprentices, and the Frank Lloyd Wright School of Architecture, staffed by TAA. The Taliesin Fellowship passed out of existence, but the name continued to be applied informally to the corps of student draftsmen.[6]

It was inevitable, of course, that without Wright significant changes would occur at Taliesin. Despite his insistence that organic designs could only come from the independent architect working alone, TAA followed the general trend and became a collaborative, even though some of the renderings bore only Peters's name. A second change was away from Wright's notion that architecture should be taught by the apprenticeship system and on-the-job training. TAA introduced a formal curriculum at the School of Architecture, including, predictably, a course in "The Art and Philosophy of Frank Lloyd Wright." The adoption of modern pedagogy may have been a tacit admission that Wright's methods had been deficient or that none of his disciples was an adequate replacement, but clearly the abandonment of the apprentice system as the sole means of instruction was a significant departure from the Master's practices. Thirdly, the Fellowship curtailed its attempts at "organic" living, preferring to purchase rather than grow its own food, and to contract rather than perform maintenance and repairs. And, finally, the Fellowship began to summer in Switzerland, and to spend most of its time at Taliesin West, where the climate was less rigorous, allowing Taliesin East to become quite dilapidated.[7] Only after plans for a TAA-designed resort complex for the Spring Green area were announced in 1967 did it return to Wisconsin for the summers and make token improvements on its property.*

---

* A day spent wandering over the entire Spring Green estate in April 1968 revealed to me its appalling condition. The Midway Farm complex—including a round tractor shed, a remodeled non-Wright cottage, the main building with its wing, and a few minor structures—was literally crumbling, as were the Romeo and Juliet Windmill and "Tanyderi," the Andrew T. Porter House. The Porter garage was almost beyond repair. Two small apprentice cabins near the Hillside Home School were open to the weather. The school itself, the

Even before TAA had executed Wright's unfinished designs it began to solicit new clients. Perhaps the continuing demand for "Wright" buildings was sufficient to justify this action, or perhaps the architects were shrewd enough to trade on his name rather than rely on their own. By 1963 they had accepted more than fifty new commissions, less than half as many as Wright had secured from 1955 to 1959, but obviously enough to stay in business. Most of TAA's early work was little more than mechanical reproduction of Wright techniques. The Lescohier House in Madison, Wisconsin, for instance, horizontally oriented but propped up away from its sloping site with the Corbusier-type poles Wright abhorred, culminated in triangular corner windows under cathedral roofs like the Unitarian Meeting House (1947) a few miles away, and was a disjointed, synthetic-looking, unresolved collection of elements from several of his other designs.

When it could not borrow directly from the Master, TAA relied on the device of dressing up uninteresting structures with excessively elaborate trim, substituting showy technique for creative content. The Lincoln Income Life Insurance Company, opened in 1966 in Louisville, Kentucky, for example, utilized a spectacular engineering concept conceived by Wright—its sixteen or seventeen floors hang from a deeply sunk utility spine without touching the ground—but it is so completely covered with intricate lacework trim that the windows cannot be seen, an entirely inappropriate treatment for a monolith, and an embarrassing architectural blunder. From the very beginning TAA lapsed into a

---

only building seen by the general public, was in fairly good condition. Silsbee's Unity Chapel across the highway was bare and filthy, but has since then been repaired. Most of the farm at Taliesin had gone to seed, the lake and the landscaping were unattended, and the dam was breaking up. And it was clear that at Taliesin itself, maintenance crews could not keep up with the deterioration. Hillsides under some of the most dramatic cantilevering were eroding, leaving glaring, unsightly gashes. The peripheral service quarters were faring quite badly, much of the wood was rotting, and the place generally showed signs of better days. The resident in charge specifically requests visitors not to photograph boarded-up windows, or other "winter precautions."

Lincoln Income Life Insurance Company by Taliesin Associated Architects

style, which Wright may not have condemned since it was more or less *his* style, but by emphasizing appearances his followers opened themselves—perhaps with more justification—to the very criticisms Wright had leveled against the Prairie School and the Internationalists years before. Although it moved somewhat away from him in the late 1960s, projects like the Monona Basin (1967–1968) for Madison, Wisconsin, indicate that most of its work is still eclectic, derivative, and not particularly distinguished, sacrificing originality for loyalty. (Seeing a TAA design for the first time can create an eerie sensation of *déjà vu*.) Despite the abandonment of the more rigorous aspects of life under Wright, his presence seems to linger everywhere at Taliesin, especially in the drafting room.[8]

One of TAA's largest projects illustrates the detrimental results of its inability to establish independence. In 1967 it announced plans to construct a resort community in the Spring Green area based, it said, on Wright's own ideas. Leaning on the Broadacre City model, William Wesley Peters and his associates laid out a four thousand-acre project along a four-mile stretch of the Wisconsin River for William Keland, head of the Wisconsin River Development Corporation, a former executive of the Johnson Wax Company and once a Wright client. With a golf course by Robert Trent Jones, the scheme also included a clubhouse, a three hundred-room hotel with convention facilities, ski runs and a lodge, a marina, a fishing village, shopping and crafts areas, and summer and permanent homes. TAA would have ultimate control over every detail, and a newspaper report gave the impression that the project had evolved from a Wright design especially for the region.[9]

The roots of the development can indeed be found in Wright's ideas but not one of such monumental proportions. In 1953 he had drawn plans for the Riverview Terrace Restaurant, cantilevered from a hillside overlooking the site of one of his proposed butterfly bridges of 1947. He promised it as "a gift to the people," and the Fellowship began construction in 1957, continued through the summer of 1958, but failed to resume after Wright's death. Eight years later, when TAA modified the original design, it changed the name to "The Spring Green" and opened it not as a gift, but as a commercial venture, the first stage in Keland's Wisconsin River Development. The restaurant is another measure of TAA's progress since 1959. Its variously shaped units are clumsily forced together, its cantilevered entry canopy and octagonal tea house are much too ostentatious for what should be a simple expression of an exciting site, and some of its most eye-catching components are purposefully nonfunctional, purely for show. Not only is The Spring Green an unresolved assortment of Wrightian forms, but all the major buildings in the proposed development are based directly on forty-year-old plans. The golf

"The Spring Green" restaurant, completed in 1967 by Taliesin Associated Architects from Wright's 1957 plans for Riverview Terrace restaurant

clubhouse turned out to be a resurrection of the Nakoma County Club project (1923) in Madison, other designs revive the tepee experiments of the 1920s, and the restaurant tower, duplicating another just out of sight at Taliesin's Midway Farm Buildings (1938), can also be traced to the Nakoma scheme. Even the name of the ski lodge—"The Winter Green"—is derivative.

According to Wesley Peters, the Wisconsin River Development "represents the realization of a dream Frank Lloyd Wright envisioned—the creation of an organic community with all facilities for recreation and resort living in the Wisconsin he loved so well." Not only does this contain an obvious contradiction as well as an important misunderstanding of Broadacre City, to which Peters alluded—that an "organic community" can be based on vacation facilities—but it also assumes that Wright would have accepted a colony of transients uprooting and commercializing an indigenous population and a relatively unspoiled countryside. Far from improving the lives of the people in any significant way, it will simply be an unusual resort, ministering to the whims of pleasure-seekers for a season, largely unavailable to the host community except for employment, and even then potentially destructive. Close architectural supervision will not insure the kind of social integration Wright knew could only evolve slowly. Although there will be permanent homes in the development, it is unlikely that the new settlers will be absorbed into Spring Green. They are more apt to have a disruptive impact similar to that of escaping New Yorkers on the once stable villages of southwestern Connecticut.

The appropriate conclusion about this project and TAA in general is that either it has not assimilated Wright's teachings or it lacks the capacity to carry them out. More than a decade after the Master's death, its designs are still derivative and distinctly second-rate, depending on unorthodox or elaborate surfaces for interest. It is very possible, of course, that Wright's concepts were so personal, so much the product of a supremely creative mind, that they cannot be taught, either by or to his followers, and it is also understandable if those close to him are unable to emerge from his overpowering influence. In any case it behooves TAA to acknowledge these facts, to admit that its only raison d'être is profit making, or to disband. It has not and cannot carry on Wright's work. No one can. Instead, it has confused architectural appearance with philosophical substance, institutional continuity with creative generation. Sculptor James Seawright once remarked that "the best ideas grow out of an understanding of the processes being used, rather than out of a preconceived notion of the effects to be achieved,"[10] a lesson TAA would do well to learn.

The Fellowship has also failed to fulfill two specific obligations it undertook at Wright's death. It has not built "Unity Temple," a memorial he had designed as a final resting place for himself and his family, a thirty-foot-square glass and fieldstone chamber of meditation for a spot next to J. L. Silsbee's Unity Chapel across the highway from Taliesin. Nor has it erected the air-conditioned, fireproof vault and museum to house his papers and his eight thousand drawings.[11] Perhaps these failures are blessings in disguise, for where the Fellowship has altered the Taliesins the results have been unsatisfactory. At Spring Green it placed a rather flashy swimming pool—with round doors cut through a highly decorated wall whose Sullivanesque motifs have no counterpart elsewhere on the estate—in such a way that the sunshield throws up a glare ruining the southern broadside view of the buildings. And in order to air-condition Taliesin West, TAA replaced the canvas roof and the magnificent redwood trusses in the drafting room with translucent plastic sheets and red steel beams, thereby destroying the ambience of one of Wright's finest conceptions. But if his disciples have failed him architecturally, they have more than fulfilled his expectations in public relations.

Under the aegis of Olgivanna Wright, the Taliesin Fellowship has performed one task with utmost fidelity. Perpetuating the myths and legends the architect originated about himself, and the flattering self-evaluations he broadcast, Mrs. Wright and her minions have stoked the furnaces of mystique to full capacity. Since his death she has published four books about her husband: *Our House* (1959), selections from her column by the same name that ran for several years in Madison's *Capital Times; The Shining Brow: Frank Lloyd Wright* (1960), biography, anecdotes, and recollections; *The Roots of Life* (1963), his addresses (some to the Fellowship) and "thoughts"; and *Frank Lloyd Wright: His Life, His Work, His Word* (1967), a "biography" based largely on *An Autobiography* and other familiar sources. In addition, she assisted in the posthumous preparation of *Architecture: Man in Possession of His Earth* (1962) featuring a biography by Wright's daughter, Iovanna.[12]

These twelve hundred pages do little more than reproduce writings and photographs that were reproduced before, and, although they add to the fund of Wright stories and apocryphal statements, they belabor the redundant. Except for what can be recognized from previous publications, the material in these anthologies is largely unidentified; the numerous talks to the Fellowship, for example, and the long private conversations supposedly reconstructed verbatim—complete with quotation marks—are generally undated, thereby diminishing their utility, and throwing their authenticity into question. By refusing to locate her husband's comments in time and place, Mrs. Wright shrouds him in eternal verities as if reluctant to concede his death. Unfortunately, her repetition, her vagueness, and her childlike adulation for his most banal observations and his most inconsequential remarks are ludicrous and embarrassing. She embalms his conscious levity in a reverential formaldehyde, draining off his life juices and reducing him to High Camp. She never questions his absurdities or corrects his inaccuracies but enshrines his every word as if it were Absolute Truth, thereby destroying the credibility of his serious and profound ideas.

Nevertheless, Mrs. Wright's prodigiousness has the singular merit of preserving and fleshing out the "official" interpretation of the architect's life. From her writings (and from his) it becomes apparent that two crucial factors were thought to have shaped his career: continuous confrontation with obstacles, and the certainty of predestined greatness. Anna Wright determined his destiny, so the story goes, when she willed her unborn son to be a famous architect, unburdening him of any responsibility in the matter. But the assurance of ultimate success did little to ease his way, for, when his father's desertion left the family impoverished social outcasts, young Wright found himself a modern-day Ulysses, a secular Pilgrim condemned to struggle for his own birthright. As he matured, his obvious talents added subtle dimensions to the paradox of inescapable hardship and inevitable triumph: he could follow the broad road to money and prestige, a chimeric victory at best, or he could labor along the narrow path of integrity, truth, and beauty to unassailable greatness in the long run. Choosing the difficult course determined his major life-decisions thereafter: leaving the university without a degree, refusing to design in the prevalent styles, leaving his wife and family when they limited his creativity, and fighting through years of yellow journalism, social ostracism, professional hostility, and government harassment—all in the name of principle. His work was maligned, ridiculed, misinterpreted, and purposefully ignored. The cause for which he fought was as unpopular as the cavalry at Little Bighorn, and Wright certainly believed himself a target for the slings and arrows of outrageous fortune.

When the material and the intangible benefits of his designs were finally recognized, the legend continues, inferior architects claimed his ideas as their own; first the Prairie School and then the Internationalists parlayed his innovations into fame and wealth while he suffered from neglect, taking consolation from the fact that he alone (sometimes he included Louis Sullivan) had created modern architecture. "When Sullivan and I came to architecture," he told an interviewer in 1953, "it had been slumbering for five hundred years. We woke it up. We gave it a fresh start." In order to save it from the death throes begun in the Renaissance, he had had to fight the profession every step of the way. "I was entirely contrary to everything they believed in," he said, "and if I were right, they were wrong. . . . It was a question at one time, I suppose, of their survival or mine."[13] But when the archenemy, the American Institute of Architects, awarded him its gold medal in 1949, Wright was forced to admit he had won the final victory. Despite William C. Wright's legacy—a lifetime of struggle against unimaginable odds—Anna Wright's prenatal decision had reaped its dividends, for the predestined greatness had been recognized by all. In the architect's own eyes and in his wife's he had become a kind of superman whose fantastic accomplishments defied belief.

If Wright had somehow conquered human limitations, if he really was another Jesus Christ, as Olgivanna has intimated, then she was entirely correct to label the Guggenheim Museum "The Miracle on Fifth Avenue." Not to be outdone, the pastor of the Greek Orthodox Church near Milwaukee once remarked, with questionable theology: "How do you speak to a divinity? I mean, I do that when I pray, but what about on earth? That's the way I felt about him." And Wright's son John, with a certain immodesty of his own, referred to "my father who is on earth."[14] This flighty rhetoric is all very flattering, but it dangerously obscures the man. Wright can hardly be congratulated for his accomplishments if he was predestined to greatness, if he possessed superhuman abilities. Awarding him honors would be akin to giving God a medal for designing the Grand Canyon. It is much more satisfying to presume that Wright was human—and there is evidence to suggest that indeed he was—for then his achievements stand as monuments to man's greatness. The more Wright is demythologized, the more believable he becomes.

How then is this man, this Frank Lloyd Wright, to be evaluated? Was he a conservative or a radical, a genius or a crackpot, a romantic or a functionalist? Was he immoral, as many believe, or did he have unusual, almost compulsive, integrity? Why did such a noted artist need to construct legends applauding himself? Why did he need to trumpet his own achievements when he accomplished far more than most men could ever dream?

The most important early documents in the development of

Wright's embattled and superhuman persona are the 1914 article, "In the Cause of Architecture, II" and *An Autobiography*, published in 1932 and expanded in 1943. Significantly, both were written during very trying times for Wright: when he was the object of public anger while living with his mistress in 1914, a difficult period for him in many ways, and then in the late 1920s, during years of financial hardship and his cacophonous battles with Miriam Noel. Adverse circumstances undoubtedly influenced his self-interpretation. Clearly Wright felt personally threatened and socially intimidated, and both these works utilize a spirited offense as the best defense. They blame others for all his difficulties and claim purity of motive for his every action. They enabled him to construct a more pleasant world, one in which he controlled his own destiny. When people were reluctant to purchase his services, these writings exaggerated his greatness; when the future seemed bleak, they reminded him of monumental obstacles he had already surmounted. By 1932 Wright was sixty-five, too old to change his analysis of events, his fixed convictions, or his self-image. He had been playing the role of harassed genius since 1914 or before, and it became increasingly difficult to separate role from reality. What began as a defense mechanism slowly and imperceptibly evolved into a pleasureful performance and then a way of life.

It has generally been forgotten, moreover, that his major obstacles were largely self-created. His popularity waned only when he followed architectural detours or traversed social conventions, most notably from the abandonment of his family and practice in 1909 until the resolution of his marital problems and the revival of popular interest in his work in the 1930s. The principal hurdles facing Wright during the prairie period were not lack of clients, critical hostility, or colleague rejection but were, on the contrary, his lengthy process of architectural maturation, the high standards he set for himself, and his insistence on reaching those standards. In 1909 he walked away from a profitable practice based on a popular art form, and in 1923 he failed to take advantage of international acclaim when the Imperial Hotel rode out the Tokyo earthquake. During the 1920s his buildings were as antisocial as his life-style, and it is little wonder that the public was uninterested. By choosing professional and personal unorthodoxy he denied himself the continued success that certainly awaited him. But the choice was his own. His insistence on reading public disapproval of his personal affairs as a rejection of his architecture violates the facts, but he used the contention to absolve himself of responsibility for the consequences of his actions.

Wright's interpretation of his life as a victory over insurmountable odds indicates that his ego must have been as fragile as it was monumental. To protect himself from criticism he transformed trivial skirmishes into cosmic encounters and mild critics into determined combatants. To assure himself that "they" and not he was at fault when he violated convention, he depicted himself as a besieged genius—ridiculed, exploited, and unrecognized—who ultimately prevailed over rivals, thieves, governments, skeptics, the ignorant, and the envious. The irony, of course, is that his life had more triumphs than tragedies, beginning with his successful apprenticeship under J. L. Silsbee. Fame and fortune more than compensated for a periodically hostile public or an aloof architectural establishment, both of which Wright offended and then used for his own purposes anyway. Toward the end of his life he surrounded himself with impressionable young admirers (including a wife thirty years his junior) willing to believe the myths, to offer the necessary ego-gratification, and to perpetuate the legend after his death. Olgivanna Wright and the Taliesin Fellowship have more than kept the faith, but their superfluous attempts to insure his immortality have only detracted from his name and tarnished his legacy.

Despite his own hyperbole and his followers' efforts to canonize him in a religion of their own making, the fact remains that in building matters Wright was an eminently practical man. To the extent that he was an experimenter, that he invented or was the first to use many new architectural devices, he was also a radical, willing to rethink his medium "from the roots," to introduce thoroughgoing change when necessary. He is generally acknowledged to be responsible for corner windows, built-in home and metal office furniture, early developments in air-conditioning and fireproofing, several aspects of prefabrication, dry wall construction, radiant heating in moderately priced homes, the elimination of cellars and attics, continuous fenestration, innovations in the use of concrete and, of course, the open floor plan. He was also among the first to popularize, though not to invent, casement windows, cantilevering, glass plating, textured concrete and horizontally oriented facades, overhanging eaves, minimal decoration, concrete block–tie rod construction, slab roofs, and carports. These are only partial lists, of course, but they indicate that in matters of implementation and technique he was an uncompromisingly progressive force.

He was also in the vanguard in more fundamental ways, challenging conventional wisdom on the aesthetics, shape, organization, and content of structure. Provision for merged interior space, for increased contact between indoors and out, and for the integration of architecture and topography required significant changes in form and appearance. Consequently, the prairie house simply did not look like its neighbors, and was a radical new departure, especially for the early 1900s. The fantastic cantilevering of the Robie House (1907), made possible by 100-foot-long welded steel channel beams, recently developed by Chicago shipbuilders, exemplified Wright's up-to-date technical knowledge and his aesthetic daringness.[15] He believed in change, in newness, in experimentation, and was never satisfied with the status quo. He tore down and rebuilt portions of his own Taliesin, for example, more times than can be recorded, all in an effort to make it even better, and one of his very last designs was for yet another alteration. The way he conceived his buildings, his manner of execution, and the appearance of the finished product challenged prevailing assumptions and required open-minded clients.

Despite their radical aspects, his residences were purchased by solid citizens of conservative stripe—architecture, after all, is the province of the upper classes—who found them congenial to their own life-styles. His houses militated against certain twentieth-century trends by resisting the destructive results of urbanization and industrialization. By bringing the family together more often in happy surroundings, Wright hoped to counteract urban entice-ments, the absence of the father from home, public education, peer group associations, civic commitments, and other aspects of modern life that weakened kinship ties. The "natural," close-knit, mutually dependent, "old-fashioned" family of warm stove and glowing hearth that he tried to recreate may never have existed—despite the Lloyd Joneses—but it is significant that he invariably put fireplaces at the "heart" of his houses and, after the 1930s, located kitchens ("work-spaces") so that their influence perme-ated the whole. Referring to a simpler and more virtuous rural America, a collective remembrance his clients also cherished, especially during periods of rapid social change and national depression, Wright's residences used advanced technology and avant-garde aesthetics in what Norris Kelly Smith and the archi-tect himself affirmed as "a cause conservative."[16]

If Wright's views on man, government, and the state are taken into consideration, however, he appears to be more a romantic and a philosophical anarchist than a conservative. After the late New Deal, he became a staunch opponent of activist government, believing that centralization of power had undermined individual freedoms. But he opposed state authority in ways conservatives dared not; in matters of national defense, internal security, states' rights, and public education, he was unwilling to grant responsibil-ity to the levels of government they considered proper. His view of human nature was more optimistic than theirs, for he truly believed man capable of caring for himself if freed from the debilitating burdens of oligopolistic capitalism, and state and corporate bureaucracy. The conservatives who feared federal and foreign governments and the liberals who feared big business both believed in human depravity, differing only as to which groups were most depraved.

Wright understood that government could not be banished altogether, at least not immediately, for without a beneficial environment man would require considerable policing. Until Broadacre City arrived, when man would discover his true individuality and his innately harmonious social sense, Wright's public buildings could serve as examples of the therapeutic environmentalism he anticipated. Indeed, he regarded his Larkin and Johnson administrative offices not only as assets to managers and workers but also as models for future social organization. Built around the concept of the work force as an extended family, these structures reinforced group solidarity and traditional authority patterns. They combated business impersonality, bureaucratic compartmentalization, sterile working conditions, and man's alienation from his labor by encouraging a sense of participation and mutual endeavor, not simply to increase productivity, but because Wright believed that purposeful work was good, that positive environment mattered, that capitalism could be made humane, and that the old-fashioned family was the basis of community, on the job as well as at home. His office buildings were not copied by other corporations partly because they symbolized preindustrial America.

A third office structure—the H. C. Price Tower in Bartlesville, Oklahoma, designed in 1953 from thoroughly revised Saint Mark's in the Bowery plans (1929)—illustrates Wright's deeply ingrained romanticism, his faith in the union of family and business, his insistence that architecture must proclaim man's individuality, that it must express his aspirations, his feelings, and his spirit, as well as his intellect. The Price Tower is a twenty-story polygon divided into four quadrants, three for offices and one for eight two-level apartments. The several facades alternate between vertical and horizontal articulation, and no two are quite alike. Indeed, with continuous green copper mullions, concrete band-spandrels, decorative panels, and projecting window awnings variously arranged on the several sides, the building looks entirely different from every angle. The Price Tower illustrates Wright's romanticism in at least three ways. First, by completely rejecting box-frame construction, it is unlike most modern skyscrapers. With its soaring roof fins and its multidirectional facades, it is a free-form essay in human aspiration, refusing to contain or be contained in traditional ways. Its visual complexity would be too stimulating for an urban setting where it could not fully be appreciated and where it would deleteriously affect its neighbors. A street lined with Price Towers would be disastrous, and that is really the point, for the building is too unique to be copied, and was not meant to be. Proclaiming itself a bulwark of variety and human aspiration, obviously a singular approach to a specific situation, the Price Tower was not a generalized remedy for urban ills, or an artistic cliché for mass consumption, but a tour de force of individuality.

Its second romantic characteristic is its autonomy. As the only skyscraper in Bartlesville (population 27,000 in 1960), it could be seen from miles away in any direction, fulfilling Wright's contention that as works of art tall buildings (like all others) should be as accessible to viewing as paintings in a museum. To be fully appreciated and to enable inhabitants to see something other than their counterparts in neighboring structures, skyscrapers should have space enough to cast their shadows on the ground, in a park, for example, or in small towns, but certainly not in rows on city streets. From a commercial standpoint, of course, this was totally impractical, but to an artist anxious about his work it made good sense. Thirdly, by including residences in Price Tower—certainly a boon for company officials wishing to cut commuting time, but hardly necessary in Bartlesville—Wright probably meant to suggest that man need not be alienated from his work, that office staffs were really extended families, and that life functions should not be mutually estranged. Other office skyscrapers contain rental apartments but rarely so closely integrated with the business facilities, and even so the arrangement is used infrequently.

H. C. Price Tower, 1952, Bartlesville, Oklahoma

The Price Tower rejected technological and bureaucratic "fascism," as Wright often put it, that plugged men into identical compartments in homogenized monoliths. Mies van der Rohe's skyscrapers have been characterized as expressions of pure rationalism, so carefully were their proportions determined. Although Wright admired Mies's perfectionism, he believed "*heart-felt* simplicity instead of *head-made* simplicity" to be his own principal objective, in other words, that the architect and his buildings should take into account certain truths about life that could only be described as instinctual. "Without this essential *heart* beating in it," Wright insisted, architecture "would degenerate to a box merely to *contain* . . . objects it should itself create and *maintain*." "True romanticism in art is . . . the result of an inner experience," he explained, "and is the essential poetry of the creative artist that his exploring brother, tabulating the sciences, seems never quite able to understand nor wholly respect." He who condemns romance, Wright affirmed, "is only a foolish reactionary."[17] The symbols and the composition of Price Tower warned that architectural mechanism foreshadowed spiritual death.

As this language attests, Wright was in many ways a nineteenth-century man who used twentieth-century methods for his own peculiar purposes. Ever since his "Art and Craft of the Machine" speech in 1901, he had accepted technology as man's great liberator; indeed, he was one of the first artists and social theorists to recognize its human potential. Later, he often claimed that machinery had enslaved man, but his own career belied the assertion, "I believe that romance—the quality of the *heart*, the essential joy we have in living . . . can be brought to life again in modern industry," he declared in 1930.[18] Wright proposed to use technology to increase man's contact with the outdoors, thereby strengthening his "true nature." After all, organic architecture meant that buildings should bear similarities to, and embody the unity of, natural organisms. But as Fallingwater demonstrated, Wright also believed that art improved nature, that the relationship between the two was reciprocal. His description of the Price

Tower as "the tree that escaped the crowded forest" indicates that nature's random activity occasionally required intelligent pruning. Although his emphasis on the benevolence of nature was peculiarly American, during the first third of the twentieth century Wright was more highly regarded in Europe than its own architects, and his year there—from September 1909 to October 1910—was crucial for its artistic development. Even before he visited Berlin in 1910 to supervise publication of his two extensive retrospectives—*Ausgeführte Bauten und Entwürfe von Frank Lloyd Wright* (1910) and *Frank Lloyd Wright Ausgeführte Bauten* (1911)—the city's leading architect, Peter Behrens, had paid him tribute by quoting the 1904 Larkin Building in his local turbine factory (1908–1909). Of Behrens's three most promising employees in 1910—Le Corbusier, van der Rohe, and Walter Gropius—the latter was most directly influenced by Wright, whose City National Bank (1909) in Mason City, Iowa, clearly presaged the model factory (1914) for the Werkbund Exhibition. There is no evidence that Wright met the trio or their employer—his first introduction to Gropius was in 1937—but they probably pored over his German publications, which by all accounts had a profoundly liberating effect on the younger Europeans. The Dutch *de Stijl* movement, cubism in painting, constructivism in sculpture, and the International Style were all influenced by Wright, and by 1930 most critics agreed that his Continental impact had been enormous.[19]

Despite his warm European reception, and the simultaneous social hostility toward him at home, he never seriously contemplated expatriation, because above all else he was unabashedly American, glorying in its virtues, anxious about its faults. His heroes were Jefferson, Thoreau, Whitman, and Emerson, whose 1858 essay on "Farming" he partially reproduced as the appendix to his last book, *The Living City*, exactly one hundred years later, and whose views on democracy and individualism he read and reread. Throughout his life Wright continually proclaimed America the greatest nation in man's history. He insulted it, criticized it, and condemned it, but always out of love, hoping to stem its regression toward conformity and materialism. In his expansiveness, his faith in technology to solve man's problems, his optimism about human nature, his strange blend of practicality and idealism, his individualism, his ingenuity, his distrust of government, his restlessness, and his disrespect for authority, in all these things and more he was typically American. But he was *not* a modern man. Wright was as unlike Saul Bellow's Moses Herzog or John Updike's Rabbit Angstrom as Theodore Roosevelt, whose "strenuous life" he exemplified. He was not introspective or self-analytical, leaving it for others to explore his motivations and his assumptions. Most of all he believed in himself. He was an "innerdirected," uncommon man, an uncompromising individualist in a mass society, an authentic human being in a plastic landscape.

By preference he was also a midwesterner, a fact that shaped certain of his prejudices, themselves a part of the national character. "If English travelers want to see America as it really is," he told a London audience in 1939, they must ignore the East. "America begins *west* of Buffalo. The greatest and most nearly beautiful city of our young nation," he continued, "is probably Chicago. Eventually I think that Chicago will be the most beautiful great city left in the modern world." Why? someone asked, probably not alone in his skepticism. Because it has the greatest park system on earth, a properly developed waterfront, "a life of its own," and because it "takes pride in building things in a big substantial broad way."[20] His regional loyalties seem to have influenced the location of his architecture. Only 15 of his 135 executed structures from 1894 to 1914 and 29 of his 230 projects were outside the Middle West, and even when he was nationally known the pattern remained unchanged. One hundred sixty-eight of the 300 or more buildings still standing at his death were located in three states—37 in Michigan, 43 in Wisconsin, and 88 in Illinois—and with 11 in Ohio, 10 in Minnesota, 9 in Iowa, and 11 scattered elsewhere, the Midwest could claim 209 or roughly two-thirds of his entire output. With an additional 25 structures in

California, 9 in Arizona, and 12 in other states, fully 255 or approximately eighty percent of his executed commissions were in the West. (He built only 5 houses in New England, all after 1940.)[21] But like William Faulkner, another famous regionalist, Wright invariably spoke to universal human concerns.

Like Faulkner's Yoknapatawpha County, Wright's Broadacre City was a world of his own making; its geography was as fixed in the architect's mind as the author's was in his. In 1958 Wright completed a final series of Broadacre studies, which in effect catalogued his life's work. Scattered around his fictional countryside in one perspective drawing were a segment of the Doheny Ranch (1921), the Ennis House (1924), the Gordon Strong Planetarium and automobile objective (1925), a Saint Mark's tower (1929), the Rogers Lacy Hotel (1946), the Pittsburgh Community Center, the Huntington Hartford Hotel, a self-service garage, and a butterfly bridge (all 1947), the Beth Shalom Synagogue (1954), and a portion of the Marin County Civic Center (1957–1959), altogether a surreal futuristic montage. The drawings represent Wright's last attempt at synthesis, his ultimate depiction of America as he would have planned it. One critic was entirely correct in concluding that · Wright "could well have furnished the countryside with some of the most dazzling buildings ever seen."[22]

But this final drawing also reveals that Wright's personality was simply too forceful for the architectural integration he envisioned. If he had actually assembled his buildings in one place, if he had lined New York's Park Avenue with Price Towers or designed Spring Green in toto, the effect would have been overpowering, a mind-blowing collage too stimulating for his own purposes. Unlike his houses, which individually achieved the sought-for repose, many of his larger projects were defiantly vigorous and assertive, reflecting his own "absolute inability to endure confinement of any sort," as one observer put it.[23] Many were tours de force, visual and emotional challenges to the public, uncompromising expressions of his own romantic individualism. So it is perhaps a blessing that Usonia never evolved from a house into a new America, for life there might have been too lively, too electric, too exhausting. The ultimate irony is that by extolling human variety so energetically, he might have created a surfeit of sensory experience, a different kind of dehumanization. Indeed, the suspicion lingers that only Frank Lloyd Wright himself could have lived comfortably in a landscape of his own design.

SOURCE NOTES

CHAPTER ONE: NEARLY EVERYTHING TO LEARN [1867–1893]

1. Biographical data on William C. Wright are in Abbie Whitaker comp., "A Copy of a Small Part of the Genealogy of the Wright Family," the Jane Lloyd Jones Collection, Manuscripts Division, State Historical Society of Wisconsin (SHSW), Madison; *The First Half Century of Madison University, 1819–1869* (New York: Sheldon & Co., 1872), p. 295; Elmer William Smith, ed., *Colgate University: General Catalogue Number 1* (1937): 94. The latter two sources were made available to me by Howard D. Williams, university archivist at Colgate.
2. *Richland County Observer* (Richland Center, Wis.), June 11, November 19, 1861; ibid., June 20, 1862; ibid., August 27, September 10, 24, October 1, November 19, 1863; *The Richland Zouave* (Richland Center, Wis.), October 19, 1861. Unless otherwise noted, all local newspapers used in this study are on deposit at SHSW. Also see James H. Miner, ed., *History of Richland County, Wisconsin* (Madison: Western Historical Assoc., 1906), p. 169.
3. Information on Anna Lloyd Jones is extremely sparse and rather unreliable. See Frank Lloyd Wright, *An Autobiography* (1932; new ed., New York: Duell, Sloan and Pearce, 1943), bk. 1; Maginel Wright Barney, *The Valley of the God-Almighty Joneses* (New York: Appleton-Century, 1965), chap. 7; and *The Weekly Home News* (Spring Green, Wisconsin), December 10, 17, 1885. On the Lloyd Jones family the files of the *Home News* are invaluable. See also *History of Iowa County, Wisconsin . . .* (Chicago: Western Historical Society, 1881), p. 939; and George

and Robert M. Crawford, eds., *Memoirs of Iowa County Wisconsin*, vol. 1 (n.p.: Northwestern Historical Assoc., 1913), pp. 261–262.

4. *Richland County Observer*, April 7, 28, May 19, 1864; ibid., March 2, May 11, 1865. On William C. Wright's marriage and Frank Lloyd Wright's birth date see Thomas S. Hines, Jr., "Frank Lloyd Wright–The Madison Years: Record versus Recollection," *The Wisconsin Magazine of History* 50 (Winter 1967): 109–119. I am indebted to Mr. Hines–who collaborated with me on the McGregor, Iowa, research–and his article for other information on Wright before 1887. The 1867 birth date is further substantiated by a copy from a page of Catherine Lloyd Wright's family record, Frank Lloyd Wright Collection (FLW Coll.), Avery Library, Columbia University, New York.

5. "Architecture and Music," *The Saturday Review* 40 (September 28, 1957): 72–73; *An Autobiography*, bk. 1.

6. *Richland County Observer*, April 20, 27, 1865; ibid., October 1, 1866; *The Live Republican* (Richland Center), May 16, July 4, 11, 18, 1867. For other aspects of Wright's Richland Center career see the *Richland County Observer*, August 27, 1861; ibid., June 30, 1864; February 9, 16, November 23, 1865; *The Live Republican*, February 7, 14, 1867; *The Richland Center Republican*, November 28, 1867; ibid., March 19, May 7, 1868; *Richland County Republican*, May 21, 1868; ibid., January 14, 28, April 15, 1869.

7. Wright's McGregor career can be traced in *The Times* of that community (on deposit in the newspaper office), March 3, April 21, May 28, July 21, September 1, November 10, 17, 24, 1869; ibid., June 22, August 10, 1870; ibid., March 29, May 24, 1871. The two long quotations are from the May 17 and July 5, 1871, issues.

8. *An Autobiography*, p. 51.

9. Robert Grieve, *History of Pawtucket* . . . (Pawtucket: The Gazette and Chronicle Co., 1897), pp. 226–227; *Pawtucket Gazette and Chronicle*, November 24, 1871; ibid., October 4, 1872; ibid., January 23, 1874, on deposit at the American Antiquarian Society, Worcester, Massachusetts.

10. Ibid., April 6, November 22, December 6, 1872; ibid., April 4, 18,

25, September 12, 19, October 24, 31, December 12, 25, 1873; ibid., January 23, 1874. For further information on Wright's Pawtucket career see ibid., January 5, March 22, October 4, 11, 18, 25, November 22, 1872; ibid., May 23, August 29, September 5, November 14, 1873; ibid., January 16, 1874. See also the Annual Letter of the High Street Baptist Church to the Providence Association of the Rhode Island Baptist Convention for 1872 and 1874, both quoted in Howard E. Whitney, President, Blackstone Valley Historical Society, Pawtucket, to author, December 9, 1967.

11. The Weymouth years can be reconstructed from the *Weymouth Weekly Gazette*, September 4, October 30, December 4, 1874; ibid., June 11, September 24, October 8, 1875; ibid., October 12, 26, 1877; ibid., March 1, 15, 22, 29, 1878, on file at Tufts Library, Weymouth. See also Gilbert Nash, comp., *Historical Sketch of the Town of Weymouth* (Weymouth: Weymouth Historical Society, 1885), p. 122; Howard H. Joy, ed., *History of Weymouth Massachusetts*, 4 vols. (Weymouth: Weymouth Historical Society, 1923), vol. 1, pp. 279–80; vol. 2, pp. 864–65; *100th Anniversary—First Baptist Church of Weymouth* (1954), pp. 10–11; Records of the First Baptist Church, Weymouth, ledger pages 85–86. Unusual help and courtesy in gathering information on Wright's Weymouth years was extended to me by Mrs. Joan S. Green, Tufts Library, Weymouth.

12. *The Inter-County Times* (Spring Green and Lone Rock, Wis.), April 30, July 9, 1878; *The Times* (Spring Green), October 28, 1881; *The Dollar Times* (Spring Green), August 12, 1879; *Spring Green News*, November 4, 11, 1881; ibid., January 13, 27, February 10, 24, April 21, July 14, 21, 1882; *The Weekly Home News*, August 28, October 9, 1884. Wright was first listed in the *Madison City Directory* in 1880.

On Wright's association with the Wisconsin Unitarians see *Unity*, the organ of the Western Unitarian Conference (Chicago), edited by Jenkin Lloyd Jones, 3 (June 1, 1879): 194–196; 4 (December 1, 1879): 299; 4 (December 16, 1879): 314–15; 5 (June 16, 1880): 128; 7 (March 1, 1881): 11; 7 (May 16, 1881): 106; 8 (September 16, 1881): 271; 9 (August 1, 1881): 234; 14 (September 1, 1884): 274; 15 (May 23, 1885): 140; 15 (July 11, 1885): 241.

13. Wright's story of his Madison childhood is in *An Autobiography*, bk. 1; see also Hines, "Frank Lloyd Wright . . . ," pp. 114–115. On Conover see *Madison, Past and Present, 1852–1902* (Madison: Wisconsin State Journal, 1902), p. 139.

14. Wright's court statement of claims is in Hines, "Frank Lloyd Wright . . .", p. 112, fn. 10. After leaving Madison, the peripatetic William C. Wright renewed his law practice in Wahoo, Nebraska, then lived in Omaha from 1890 to 1892, directed the Central Conservatory of Music in Stromsburg, Nebraska, until 1895, and before his death in Pittsburgh on June 16, 1904, lived in Saint Joseph, Missouri, Des Moines and Perry, Iowa, and York, Nebraska. See Smith, *Colgate University: General Catalogue Number 1* (1937): 94.

15. Anna's version of the divorce is in Wright, *An Autobiography*, pp. 50–51. Wright's marital problems from 1909 to 1928 will be discussed in chapters 4 and 6.

16. Grant Manson, "Wright in the Nursery: The Influence of Froebel Education on the Work of Frank Lloyd Wright," *The Architectural Review* 113 (June 1953); *An Autobiography*, pp. 12–14.

17. Barney, *The Valley of the God-Almighty Joneses*, p. 12. The extent to which Anna's influence has been inflated is revealed in a review of Wright's autobiography: "In 1869 [sic] a young Wisconsin school teacher looked about her. She did not believe that one sensible building was to be found within a radius of 300 miles, but she did believe that the boy she carried in her womb would be an architect—a real one. She was of the sisterhood of great men's mothers." John Wheelwright, "Truth Against the World," *The New Republic* 71 (June 29, 1932): 186.

18. Hines, "Frank Lloyd Wright . . . ," pp. 115–118; Wright, *An Autobiography*, pp. 57–60.

19. Most of the information on Unity Chapel and Wright's role in its construction is in William C. Gannett, "Christening a Country Church," *Unity*, 17 (August 28, 1886): 356–357.

20. Wright's story of his arrival and career at Silsbee's is in *An Autobiography*, pp. 65–74; note also *The Weekly Home News*, November 10, 1887.

21. The most accurate listing of Wright's designs (to 1941) is Henry-

Russell Hitchcock, *In the Nature of Materials: The Buildings of Frank Lloyd Wright, 1887–1941* (New York: Duell, Sloan and Pearce, 1942), pp. 107–130. Another list extends through 1959, and, although inaccurate and highly doctored, is helpful in making statistical computations: Olgivanna Lloyd Wright, *Frank Lloyd Wright: His Life, His Work, His Word* (New York: Horizon Press, 1967), pp. 206–222. At appropriate places in the text, footnotes, and bibliography I have noted additions and corrections.

22. Wright's comments on Corwin are in *An Autobiography*, pp. 67–69, 75; the quotation is on p. 70. On Catherine and other women see ibid., pp. 48, 77–78, 85–89. Their marriage date is confirmed by a Xerox copy of a page from Catherine's diary, on deposit in FLW Coll., Avery Library, Columbia University, New York.

23. *The Weekly Home News*, April 12, 1888.

CHAPTER TWO: THE ART AND CRAFT OF SUCCESS [1893–1901]

1. Wright's comment on Oak Park is in *Two Lectures on Architecture* (Chicago: The Art Institute, 1931), reprinted in *The Future of Architecture* (New York: Horizon Press, 1953), p. 188. For Barton's comment see *Oak Leaves* (Oak Park, Ill.), June 30, 1906. All Oak Park newspapers cited in this study are on file in that city's public library.

2. Wright's neighborhood was evaluated in *The Reporter* (Oak Park, Ill.), April 14, 1893; also see *The Vindicator* (Oak Park, Ill.), September 3, 1897.

A geographically arranged list of Wright's buildings extant in 1960 in Edgar Kaufmann and Ben Raeburn, eds., *Frank Lloyd Wright: Buildings and Writings* (Cleveland: World Pub. Co., 1960), pp. 329–346, may be supplemented by Olgivanna Lloyd Wright, *Frank Lloyd Wright: His Life, His Work, His Word* (New York: Horizon Press, 1967), pp. 206–222, and Henry-Russell Hitchcock, *In the Nature of Materials: The Buildings of Frank Lloyd Wright, 1887–1941* (New York: Duell, Sloan and Pearce, 1942), pp. 107–130, which include demolished structures and unbuilt projects.

3. The Oak Park years are described in Frank Lloyd Wright, *An Autobiography* (1932; new ed., New York: Duell, Sloan and Pearce, 1943), pp. 109–120; John Lloyd Wright, *My Father Who Is on Earth* (New York: G. P. Putnam's Sons, 1946), *passim*; and Maginel Wright Barney, *The Valley of the God-Almighty Joneses* (New York: Appleton-Century, 1965), pp. 133–134. The passports for the 1905 trip are in the Frank Lloyd Wright Collection (FLW Coll.), Avery Library, Columbia University. Also see *The Caxton Club, 1908–1909* (Chicago: The Fine Arts Building, 1908–1909); *The Reporter*, March 30, 1899; and Frank Lloyd Wright, *Genius and the Mobocracy* (New York: Duell, Sloan and Pearce, 1949), p. 72.

4. On Catherine Wright see *An Autobiography, My Father . . . ,* and *The Valley . . . ,* cited above, as well as *The Weekly Home News* (Spring Green, Wis.), June 15, 1893; ibid., September 30, November 11, 1897; ibid., February 14, 1901; *The Reporter*, July 14, 1893; ibid., January 11, June 28, 1900. For her activities in later years see *Oak Leaves*, April 29, 1906; ibid., September 21, November 2, 1907; ibid., September 26, 1908; April 10, 1909; ibid., November 12, December 10, 1910; ibid., February 11, December 16, 1911; *The Chicago Tribune*, November 8, 1909; *Chicago Blue Book, 1912*, p. 450.

5. John Wright's remark is in *My Father . . . ,* p. 43. See also Barney, *The Valley . . . ,* p. 133; *The Reporter*, January 11, 1900; and *Oak Leaves*, May 24, 1906. The assessment by his neighbors is in *The Reporter*, July 18, 1901. See also ibid., August 23, 1900.

6. *The Architectural Review* 7 (June 1900): 75. (This is not the article by Robert C. Spencer, Jr., cited below.)

7. O. L. Wright, *Frank Lloyd Wright . . . ,* pp. 206–222.

8. "Architecture and the Machine" was delivered to the University Guild of Evanston, Illinois, in 1894, and "Architecture, Architect, and Client" to the same group in 1896. See ibid., pp. 206–207, and Frederick Gutheim, ed., *Frank Lloyd Wright on Architecture: Selected Writings, 1894–1940* (New York: Duell, Sloan and Pearce, 1941), pp. 3–6. The full texts of these speeches are not available.

9. *The Brickbuilder* 3 (September 1894): 181–182; *The Inland Architect* 24 (September 1894): 17; ibid. (December 1894): 48.

10. Grant C. Manson, *Frank Lloyd Wright to 1910: The First Golden Age* (New York: Reinhold Pub. Corp., 1958), pp. 215–216. The *Inland Architect* commented quite favorably on Wright's 1900 contribution (35 [April 1900]: 18–19).

11. On the Milwaukee competition see *The Milwaukee Journal*, November 23, 1893, and on the Madison boathouses, *The Wisconsin State Journal*, May 12, 13, 25, June 15, 16, August 9, 1893.

    Wright's Luxfer design was published in *The Inland Architect* 30 (January 1898): 63–64; Robert C. Spencer, Jr., a close friend, won the award: ibid. 32 (September 1898): 15–16. For a list of Wright's contributions to this journal see the bibliography.

12. *The Brickbuilder* 7 (May 1898): 107. If plans for the Trans-Mississippi house were completed, they have not been included in any compilation of Wright's work.

13. His collaboration with Perkins is noted in *The Brickbuilder* 7 (November 1898): 240; ibid. 8 (January 1899): 17–18. Wright's office sharing is discussed by Manson, *The First Golden Age*, pp. 46; he disagrees with Hitchcock, *In the Nature of Materials*, pp. 111–112, that Tomlinson actually collaborated on buildings in 1901 and 1902, suggesting that he was nothing more than Wright's office manager and publicity agent (p. 137). In this connection see *The Brickbuilder* 10 (January 1901): 20; *The Inland Architect* 37 (March 1901): 16; and *The Reporter*, January 24, 1901.

    There is also an extant letter on stationery bearing the names of Tomlinson and Wright that refers to "us" and "we" as well as "I" in connection with a proposed commission. The sketch and floor plan for a $1,000 studio-home are in the letter, in Wright's hand; apparently the project did not go beyond this stage of discussion, for the drawing has not been listed in compilations of Wright's work. See F.L.W. to M. H. Lowell, Matteawan, New York, January 30, 1901, FLW Coll., Avery Library.

    The original home for the River Forest Tennis Club opened July 4, 1905, and burned to the ground July 23, 1906. Vernon S. Watson, Charles E. White, Jr., and Wright immediately prepared plans for a new clubhouse, which opened September 23, 1906. See *Oak Leaves*, April 27, 1907.

14. George R. Dean, " 'Progress Before Precedent,' " *The Brickbuilder* 9 (May 1900): 96–97; "The Architect," ibid. 9 (June 1900): 124–128; Robert C. Spencer, Jr., "The Work of Frank Lloyd Wright," *The Architectural Review* 7 (June 1900): 61–72 (plus foldouts), quotes from pp. 61 and 72.

15. Gutheim, ed., *Selected Writings*, p. 25.

16. O. L. Wright, *Frank Lloyd Wright* . . . , pp. 206–222; FLW to Willard Jones, April 2, 1959, FLW Coll., Northwestern University Library, Evanston, Illinois.

17. These comments on Wright's family history are distillations of impressions based on his autobiographical writings, particularly *An Autobiography*, bk. 1, "Family," and other sources mentioned in chapters 1 and 2.

18. Norris Kelly Smith, *Frank Lloyd Wright: A Study in Architectural Content* (Englewood Cliffs, N.J.: Prentice-Hall, 1966), pp. 70–71. Here and elsewhere I am indebted to Professor Smith both for specific interpretations and for modes of analysis.

19. FLW to William C. Gannett, December 27, 1898, Gannett Collection, Rush Rhees Library, University of Rochester, Rochester, New York. Also see FLW to Gannett, January 30, 1899.

20. *The House Beautiful* is reprinted in John Lloyd Wright, *My Father Who Is on Earth*; the quotations are from pp. 157, 166–169.

21. "The Architect," *The Brickbuilder* 9 (June 1900): 124–128; the long quotation appears on page 126. O. L. Wright (*Frank Lloyd Wright* . . . , p. 207) says that her husband read three papers in 1900: "The Architect," "The Philosophy of Fine Art," and "What is Architecture?" Frederick Gutheim (*Selected Writings*, p. 6) says that "The Philosophy of Fine Art" was read to the Architectural League of America in Chicago in 1900, and reproduces it almost entirely (pp. 6–21). "The Architect," as published in *The Brickbuilder* (June 1900), coincides almost exactly with what Gutheim calls "The Philosophy of Fine Art." I have assumed therefore that the two are different versions of the same speech, or actually the same speech revised for publication. There is no other record of "What is Architecture?"

22. The most accurate version of the original speech is in Kaufmann and Raeburn, eds., *Buildings and Writings*, pp. 55–73.
23. *The Ladies' Home Journal* 18 (February 1901): 17; ibid. (July 1901): 15.
24. "New Idea for Suburbs," *The Reporter*, July 18, 1901.

CHAPTER THREE: A RADICALLY DIFFERENT CONCEPTION
[1901–1908]

1. Vincent Scully, *American Architecture and Urbanism* (New York: Frederick A. Praeger, 1969), p. 126.
2. "In the Cause of Architecture," *The Architectural Record* 23 (March 1908), reprinted in Frederick Gutheim, ed., *Frank Lloyd Wright on Architecture: Selected Writings, 1894–1940* (New York: Duell, Sloan and Pearce, 1941), p. 38.
3. *The House of Mirth* (1905; new ed., New York: Charles Scribner's Sons, 1961), pp. 159–160.
4. Wayne Andrews, *Architecture, Ambition, and Americans: A Social History of American Architecture* (Glencoe, Ill.: The Free Press, 1964), pp. 182–185.
5. John Burchard and Albert Bush-Brown, *The Architecture of America: A Social and Cultural History*, abr. ed. (Boston: Little, Brown, 1966), p. 110, photo following p. 178.
6. Norris Kelly Smith, *Frank Lloyd Wright: A Study in Architectural Content* (Englewood Cliffs, N.J.: Prentice-Hall, 1966), p. 14.
7. "In the Cause of Architecture," in Gutheim, ed., *Selected Writings*, p. 35; Frank Lloyd Wright, *An Autobiography* (1932; new ed., New York: Duell, Sloan and Pearce, 1943), p. 139.
8. Ole E. Rölvaag, *Giants in the Earth* (1927; new ed., New York: Harper & Row, 1965), p. 345; Willa Cather, *A Lost Lady* (New York: Alfred A. Knopf, 1923), pp. 10–11; Sinclair Lewis, *Main Street* (New York: Harcourt, Brace, 1920), p. 140.
9. Grant C. Manson, *Frank Lloyd Wright to 1910: The First Golden Age* (New York: Reinhold Pub. Corp., 1958), p. 60.
10. Wright described the prairie house in *An Autobiography*, pp. 141–145.
11. Leonard K. Eaton, *Two Chicago Architects and Their Clients:*

Frank Lloyd Wright and Howard Van Doren Shaw (Cambridge, Mass.: MIT Press, 1969), pp. 96–98.

12. Fred C. Robie, Jr., "Mr. Robie Knew What He Wanted," *The Architectural Forum* 109 (October 1958): 126–27, 206, 210. This article, which contains the quotation by the elder Robie, indicates that the house was designed in 1906–1907, rather than 1908, the date usually given.

13. Scully, *American Architecture and Urbanism*, pp. 60, 72.

14. "In the Cause of Architecture" and the Introduction to the 1910 Wasmuth edition in Gutheim, ed., *Selected Writings*, pp. 31, 74.

15. Wright, *An Autobiography*, p. 142.

16. Manson, *The First Golden Age*, 178.

17. Smith, *Frank Lloyd Wright* . . . , pp. 72–76, quotes Wright's autobiography (p. 145).

18. Leonard K. Eaton, *Two Chicago Architects and Their Clients* . . . , pp. 67–133, 252–254.

19. *The Weekly Home News* (Spring Green, Wis.), November 6, 1902.

20. Russell Sturgis, "The Larkin Building in Buffalo," *The Architectural Record* 23 (April, 1908): 311–321; "Current Periodicals," *The Architectural Review* 14 (July 1907): 184. The best contemporary descriptions are Charles E. Illsley, "The Larkin Administration, Buffalo," *The Inland Architect* 50 (July 1907): 4, and Wright's own article, "The New Larkin Administration Building," *The Larkin Idea* (November 1906), reprinted in *The Prairie School Review* 7 (1st quarter, 1970): 15–19. The building was demolished in 1950.

21. After touring Unity Temple the public may purchase reprints of a pamphlet containing descriptive material, sketches, and floor plans (Dr. Rodney F. Johonnot, *The New Edifice of Unity Church* [Oak Park: The New Unity Church Club, 1906]). Old Unity was burned June 4, 1905. Wright received the commission for its replacement in September and completed his designs by February 1906. Ground was broken in May and Unity House, the smaller cube, opened in September 1907. Construction halted for lack of funds from December to April 1908. The church proper held its first services October 25, 1908. See *Oak Leaves* (Oak Park,

Ill.), September 16, December 9, 1905; ibid., February 24, 1906; ibid., October 24, November 21, 1908; ibid., November 12, 1910; *The Oak Park Argus*, September 16, 1905.

22. *The Inland Architect* buildings are listed in the bibliography. His work was appraised in Robert C. Spencer, Jr., "Brick Architecture in and Around Chicago," *The Brickbuilder* 12 (September 1903); The editors, "Work of Frank Lloyd Wright—Its Influence," *The Architectural Record* 18 (July 1905): 61–65; Thomas E. Tallmadge, "The 'Chicago School,'" *The Architectural Review* 15 (April 1908): 69–74.

23. "Current Periodicals," p. 78.

24. F. W. Fitzpatrick, "Chicago," *The Inland Architect* 45 (June 1905): 47; Sturgis, "The Larkin Building in Buffalo," p. 312; Monroe, in *The Chicago Examiner*, April 13, 1907.

25. "Current Periodicals," p. 184; *Lake Geneva News* (Lake Geneva, Wis.), August 1, 1912.

26. Computations are based on the list of designs in Olgivanna Lloyd Wright, *Frank Lloyd Wright: His Life, His Work, His Word* (New York: Horizon Press, 1967), pp. 206–222.

27. On this particular intellectual mode of analysis see Richard Hofstadter, "Beard and the Constitution: The History of an Idea," *American Quarterly* 2 (Fall 1950), esp. p. 208.

CHAPTER FOUR: AFFINITY TANGLE [1907–1912]

1. Mark L. Peisch, *The Chicago School of Architecture: Early Followers of Sullivan and Wright* (New York: Random House, 1964), p. 34.

2. Olgivanna Lloyd Wright, *Frank Lloyd Wright: His Life, His Work, His Word* (New York: Horizon Press, 1967), pp. 208–209.

3. "A visit was paid to Oak Park to see the concrete church designed by Mr. Frank Lloyd Wright" (*The Inland Architect* 51 [May 1908]: 46).

4. Wright's participation in this show has not previously been noted (*The Western Architect* 12 [May 1909]: 54).

5. November 7, 1909.

6. *The Chicago Tribune*, December 31, 1911.

7. Lloyd Wright to Linn Cowles, February 3, 1966, Frank Lloyd Wright Collection (FLW Coll.), Avery Library, Columbia University, New York.

8. For relations between the Wrights and the Cheneys, and the events from September 1909 through December 1911, see *Oak Leaves* (Oak Park, Ill.), September 21, November 2, 1907; ibid., September 25, 1910; ibid., October 31, 1911; *The Chicago Tribune*, November 7–9, 1909; ibid., August 3–4, September 24, October 9–10, 1910; ibid., August 6, December 24–31, 1911; *The Chicago Record-Herald*, December 24, 28, 1911.

9. *The Chicago Tribune*, December 26, 1911. Wright's recollection of the personal problems are here and in ibid., December 31; *The Capital Times* (Madison, Wis.), November 1, 1926; *An Autobiography* (1932; new ed., New York: Duell, Sloan and Pearce, 1943), pp. 163, 167; and is emphasized by Peter Blake, *Frank Lloyd Wright: Architecture and Space* (1960; new ed., Baltimore: Penguin Books, 1964), pp. 60–61.

10. Wright's first statement of the martyr myth is in "In the Cause of Architecture, II," *The Architectural Record* 25 (May 1914): 505–413. It is concisely stated here—but not accepted—by Norris Kelly Smith, *Frank Lloyd Wright: A Study in Architectural Content* (Englewood Cliffs, N.J.: Prentice-Hall, 1966), p. 83. Neither Henry-Russell Hitchcock, *In the Nature of Materials: The Buildings of Frank Lloyd Wright, 1887–1941* (New York: Duell, Sloan and Pearce, 1942), pp. 59–60, nor Grant C. Manson, *Frank Lloyd Wright to 1910: The First Golden Age* (New York: Reinhold Pub. Corp., 1958), pp. 211–213, can decide whether personal or professional considerations were of greater importance in Wright's departure, although Manson (pp. 202, 211) weighs the "McCormick fiasco" heavily.

11. The review appeared April 13, and Wright's letter followed ca. April 18. Both are in the Harriet Monroe Poetry Collection, University of Chicago Library.

12. See, for example, *The Brickbuilder* 12 (September 1903): 187; *The Architectural Review* 10 (May 1903): 152; ibid. 15 (April 1908): 69–74; *The Inland Architect* 45 (June 1905): 46–47; *The Western Architect* 14 (October 1909): 32.

13. The same articles that discussed the prairie "school" usually cited Sullivan's leadership. See also "A Departure from Classic Tradition: Two Unusual Houses by Louis Sullivan and Frank Lloyd Wright, Architects," *The Architectural Record* 30 (October 1911): 327–338; and "Comparison of Master and Pupil Seen in Two Houses," *The Western Architect* 17 (November 1911): 95.

14. *An Autobiography*, p. 162.

15. "Work of Frank Lloyd Wright—Its Influence," *The Architectural Record* 18 (July 1905): 61.

16. On life in Oak Park and Wright's personal habits see Wright, *An Autobiography*, pp. 109–120; John Lloyd Wright, *My Father Who Is on Earth* (New York: G. P. Putnam's Sons, 1946), pp. 15–17; Maginel Wright Barney, *The Valley of the God-Almighty Joneses* (New York: Appleton-Century, 1965), pp. 133–134; *The Chicago Tribune*, November 8, 1909; ibid., September 24, October 10, 1910; *Baraboo Weekly News* (Baraboo, Wis.), January 18, 1912.

17. *The Chicago Tribune*, November 8, 1909; Otto McFeeley to Bruce Barton, February 6, 1956, Barton Collection, State Historical Society of Wisconsin, Madison.

18. On Catherine Wright see *The Chicago Tribune*, November 7, 8, 1909; *Oak Leaves*, March 24, April 29, 1906 and April 10, 1909; J. L. Wright, *My Father* . . . , pp. 15–57. In his autobiography (pp. 109–111), Wright claimed that he and Catherine led totally separate lives, which was an exaggeration.

19. On Mamah Cheney see *The Chicago Tribune*, November 7–9, 1909; ibid., August 16, 1914; *The Chicago Record-Herald*, December, 28, 1911.

20. Brochure announcing his practice in 1893, reproduced in J. L. Wright, *My Father* . . . , p. 22.

21. Ibid., pp. 27, 53, 54; *An Autobiography*, p. 111.

22. *An Autobiography*, pp. 113, 163; J. L. Wright, *My Father* . . . , p. 55.

23. J. L. Wright, *My Father*. . . , p. 27.

24. Wright, *An Autobiography*, pp. 168–169.

25. *The Chicago Tribune*, December 26, 1911.

26. Ibid., December 27–31, 1911; ibid., January 1, 1912.

27. W. R. Purdy, "A Prophet is not without Honor Save in His Own Country," *The Weekly Home News*, December 28, 1911; ibid.,

Letter to the Editor, January 4, 1912. For the family's quite negative reaction see *The Chicago Record-Herald*, December 28, 1911,
and Jenkin Lloyd Jones to Jane Lloyd Jones, December 28, 1911,
and January 4, 1912, Jane Lloyd Jones Collection, State Historical
Society of Wisconsin, Madison. Wright's presence apparently
jeopardized the financial integrity of the Hillside Home School,
forcing him to issue a notarized statement on February 3, 1912,
dissociating himself from his aunts' affairs. That document is also
located in ibid.

28. *The Weekly Home News*, June 10, 1926.
29. Although he kept his Chicago address, he seldom used it after
1913, and closed it when he went to Tokyo in 1916.

CHAPTER FIVE: SPIRITUAL HEGIRA, PROFESSIONAL HIATUS
[1910–1914]

1. Computations are based on Olgivanna Lloyd Wright, *Frank Lloyd
Wright: His Life, His Work, His Word* (New York: Horizon
Press, 1967), pp. 206–222. Wright's phrase, "spiritual hegira,"
was quickly appropriated by *The Chicago Tribune*, November 8,
1909, and December 25, 1911.
2. This essay is reproduced in Frederick Gutheim, ed., *Frank Lloyd
Wright on Architecture: Selected Writings, 1894–1940* (New
York: Duell, Sloan and Pearce, 1941), pp. 59–76.
3. Chicago: The Ralph Fletcher Seymour Co., 1912.
4. Gutheim, ed., *Selected Writings*, p. 21; Clay Lancaster, *The
Japanese Influence in America* (New York: Walton H. Rawls,
1963), pp. 85–89, 220.
5. Gutheim, ed., *Selected Writings*, p. 76; Frank Lloyd Wright,
*Hiroshige: An Exhibition of Colour Prints from the Collection of
Frank Lloyd Wright* (Chicago: The Art Institute, March 26,
1906).
6. Wright said he received the Imperial commission after rebuilding
Taliesin, or sometime in 1915 (*An Autobiography* [1932; new ed.,
New York: Duell, Sloan and Pearce, 1943], p. 193). On the 1913
trip see *The Sauk Country Democrat* (Baraboo, Wis.), January
16; *The Weekly Home News* (Spring Green, Wis.), May 8; and

the *Baraboo Weekly News* (Baraboo, Wis.), June 19. Harriet Monroe thought he had already finished the Hotel by April 1914 ("The Orient an Influence on the Architecture of Wright," *The Chicago Sunday Tribune*, sec. 8, April 12, 1914). The Imperial will be discussed in chapter 6.

7. On Midway see Wright, *An Autobiography*, pp. 175–184; Alan M. Fern, "The Midway Gardens," with contributions by Alfonso Iannelli, the collaborating sculptor, and John Lloyd Wright, who assisted his father, in the Lexington Hall Gallery Exhibition brochure (Chicago, 1961), on Wright and Iannelli; also *The Chicago Tribune*, October 4, 1914. Midway's neighborhood was beginning to attract a large black population (Allan H. Spear, *Black Chicago: The Making of a Negro Ghetto* [Chicago: University of Chicago Press, 1967], maps 1–4).

8. "The Art and Craft of the Machine," 1901.

9. Wright, *An Autobiography*, p. 180; Henry-Russell Hitchcock, *In the Nature of Materials: The Buildings of Frank Lloyd Wright, 1887–1941* (New York: Duell, Sloan and Pearce, 1942), p. 63.

10. Karleton Hackett in the *Chicago Evening Post*, quoted in *The Weekly Home News*, July 9, 1914.

11. Hitchcock, *In the Nature of Materials*, pp. 66–67.

12. Reproduced in Gutheim, ed., *Selected Writings*, pp. 46–58. "Persecuted genius" is this author's term.

13. Mark L. Peisch, *The Chicago School of Architecture: Early Followers of Sullivan and Wright* (New York: Random House, 1964), pp. 96–99.

14. Ibid., pp. 57–59, 96; Hitchcock, *In the Nature of Materials*, pp. 118–119.

15. Peisch, *The Chicago School . . .* , pp. 65, 154 f., 25; White, "Insurgent Architecture in the Middle West," *Country Life in America* 22 (September 15, 1912): 16–17.

16. *The Western Architect* 19 (February 1913): 12, 15, quoting *Construction News*.

17. Wright's two letters to Harriet Monroe, April 13 and 20, 1914, are in the Harriet Monroe Poetry Collection, University of Chicago Library.

18. "Art Gallery Designed by Frank Lloyd Wright, Architect," *The*

International Studio 39 (December 1909): xcv–xcvi; "City National Bank of Mason City, Iowa," *The Western Architect* 17 (December 1911): 105; "Current Periodicals," *The Architectural Review* 18 (January 1912): 11.

19. "The Studio Home of Frank Lloyd Wright," *The Architectural Record* 33 (January 1913); and "Taliesin, The Home of Frank Lloyd Wright and a Study of the Owner," *The Western Architect* 19 (February 1913). Even Taliesin was later cited as an example of "what might be called the Sullivan school of design" (Peter B. Wright, "Country House Architecture in the Middle West," *The Architectural Record* 38 [October 1915]: 385–421).

20. Schuyler, "An Architectural Pioneer: Review of the Portfolios [sic] containing the works of Frank Lloyd Wright," *The Architectural Record* 31 (April 1912): 427–436; Monroe, "The Orient an Influence on the Architecture of Wright"; "Architectural Philosophy of Frank Lloyd Wright," *The Western Architect* 20 (June 1914): 58.

21. *Baraboo Weekly News*, January 18, 1912; ibid., October 5, 1916; *Chicago Record-Herald*, February 21, 1912; *The Sauk Country Democrat*, January 16, 1913.

22. *The Weekly Home News*, June 19, 1913; ibid., August 14, 27, September 10, 1914.

23. See Wright, *An Autobiography*, pp. 184–190; *The Republican Observer* (Richland Center, Wis.), *Baraboo Weekly News*, *The Iowa County Democrat* (Mineral Point, Wis.), and *The Weekly Home News*, all August 20, 1914; *The Chicago Tribune* and *The New York Times*, August 16, 1914. See also John Lloyd Wright, *My Father Who Is on Earth* (New York: G. P. Putnam's Sons, 1946), pp. 79–85.

24. "To My Neighbors," *The Weekly Home News*, August 20, 1914.

CHAPTER SIX: A REGULAR LIFE IS CUNNINGLY AMBUSHED
[1914–1932]

1. John Lloyd Wright, *My Father Who Is on Earth* (New York: G. P. Putnam's Sons, 1946), p. 86.

2. Henry-Russell Hitchcock, *In the Nature of Materials: The Build-*

ings of Frank Lloyd Wright, 1887–1941 (New York: Duell, Sloan and Pearce, 1942), pp. 67, 121–122.

3. *Baraboo Weekly News* (Baraboo, Wis.), March 30, December 28, 1916; *The Weekly Home News* (Spring Green, Wis.), December 21, 1916; *The Western Architect* 25 (January 1917): 4.

4. John Lloyd Wright, *My Father* . . ., p. 86.

5. On Miriam Noel see ibid., pp. 110–111; Frank Lloyd Wright, *An Autobiography* (1932; new ed., New York: Duell, Sloan and Pearce, 1943), pp. 201–202, 204, 259; *The Chicago Tribune*, November 8, 1915; *The Capital Times* (Madison, Wis.), September 1, 1926; ibid., March 11, 1933; *Baraboo Weekly News*, December 3, 1925.

6. *The Chicago Tribune*, November 7, 1915; ibid., November 8 and 14.

7. Letter to Wright, n.d., published in ibid., November 7, 1915.

8. For the "Miriam Letters," Wright's statements, and the events surrounding the entire episode, see ibid., November 7, 8, 14, 1915; *Chicago Herald*, November 11, 1915; *Baraboo Weekly News*, November 11, 1915; *The Sauk County Democrat* (Baraboo, Wis.), November 17, 1915.

9. It is impossible to untangle the chronology of Wright's trips to Japan, or to discover the duration of his stays there, but on the Imperial Hotel and associated matters see Wright's, *An Autobiography*, pp. 193–201, 203–224; Hitchcock, *In the Nature of Materials* . . ., pp. 68–70, 122–123, plates 219–232; *The Weekly Home News*, December 21, 1916; ibid., October 2, 1919; ibid., February 19, 1920; *Baraboo Weekly News*, March 30, 1916; ibid., May 17, 1917; ibid., October 9, 1919; ibid., April 15, July 15, 1920; *The Capital Times*, September 5, 1923; "The Effect of the Earthquake in Japan upon Construction," *The Western Architect* 32 (October 1923): 117–118. Apparently Wright received $380,000 in fees, most of which he left in Japan in payment for prints (George Nelson, "Wright's Houses," *Fortune* 34 [August 1946]: 116).

10. *The Weekly Home News*, October 2, 1919; Wright to his daughter, Catherine Baxter, February 7, 1921, Frank Lloyd Wright Collection (FLW Coll.), Avery Library, Columbia University, New York.

11. *The Capital Times,* November 14, 1922; ibid., September 1, 1926; *The Weekly Home News,* February 19, 1920; ibid., February 15, 22, 1923; complaint filed by James J. Hill, attorney for Wright, July 10, 1925, Sauk County Circuit Court, Baraboo, Wisconsin.

12. One of the best descriptions of their relationship from Miriam's point of view, a document quite revealing of her mental and emotional composition, is an interview published in the *Baraboo Weekly News,* December 3, 1925.

13. John Lloyd Wright, *My Father* . . . , p. 111. An affidavit signed by Carl Sandburg, Robert Morse Lovett, and others states that Miriam left after five months of marriage, that is, in April 1924 (*The New York Times,* October 29, 1926; *The Capital Times,* November 1, 1926). Miriam said she left about May 10 (*The Capital Times,* November 28, 1925).

14. *The Chicago Tribune,* November 27, 1924; *Baraboo Weekly News,* December 4, 1924.

15. *The Capital Times,* April 21, 1925; *The New York Times,* April 22, 1925; *The Weekly Home News,* April 23, 1925; *Baraboo Weekly News,* April 23, July 23, 1925.

16. See the Wright divorce file, Baraboo Court House; *The Capital Times,* November 27, 28, 30, December 3, 1925; *The Milwaukee Journal,* November 29, 1925; *The Weekly Home News,* December 3, 10, 1925; *The New York Times,* November 27, 28, 1925.

17. Wright recalled meeting Olgivanna at a Sunday afternoon matinee of a Russian ballet; the Petrograd company performed in Chicago on November 30 (*The Chicago Tribune,* November 23, 1924). For information on Olgivanna see: Wright, *An Autobiography,* pp. 510–514; *The Capital Times,* November 28, 1925; ibid., September 2, 4, October 22, 1926; and Wright's article, November 1, 1926, wherein he candidly admitted Iovanna's birth out of wedlock, a fact known before that. See also *Who's Who of American Women, 1970–1971* (Chicago: A. N. Marquis Co., 1969), 1365.

18. *Baraboo Weekly News,* May 27, June 10, 1926; also ibid., March 4, 11, 25, 1926; *The New York Times,* January 17, June 4–6, 1926; FLW divorce files, Sauk County Court House, March 1, 5, 1926.

19. *Baraboo Weekly News,* September 2, 1926; *The New York Times,*

September 4, 1926; *The Capital Times*, August 30–September 4, 1926.

20. *The Capital Times*, September 4, 7, 8, 10, 28, 1926; *Baraboo Weekly News*, September 9, 30, October 7, 1926; *The New York Times*, September 6, 8, 1926.

21. *The New York Times*, October 10, 22, 31, November 2, 1926; *Baraboo Weekly News*, October 28, 1926; *The Capital Times*, September 10, 23, October 1, 8, 21, 22, November 18, 1926.

22. *The Capital Times*, October 9, 13, 20, 28, 29, 1926; *The New York Times*, October 23, 29, 1926.

23. Olgivanna was interviewed in *The Capital Times*, October 22, 1926; see also "Frank Lloyd Wright Tells Story of Life; Years of Work, Love, and Despair," ibid., November 1, 1926. The other quotations are from ibid., October 1, 25, 1926.

24. Ibid., February 1, 18, 23, March 1, 4, May 9, 1927; *The New York Times*, January 2, 7, February 8, 18, 20, March 5, 1927; *Baraboo Weekly News*, February 3, 24, April 18, 1927; *The Weekly Home News*, February 24, 1927.

25. *The Weekly Home News*, May 12, 1927; *Baraboo Weekly News*, June 23, 1927; *The New York Times*, July 3, August 27, 1927; *The Capital Times*, May 6, 10, 16, 19, 20, 25, 28, June 20, 21, 23, 27, 28, July 2, 20, August 26, 27, 29, 31, 1927.

26. *The Capital Times*, September 21, October 5–8, 10, 14, 19, 1927; ibid., July 14, 15, 17, 1928; *The New York Times*, July 15, 18, 20, 1928; *Baraboo Weekly News*, October 13, December 15, 1927; January 19, 1928. There was one additional contact between them. In November 1929 Miriam won a $7,000 judgment against Wright for dipping into the $30,000 trust fund. After her death in January 1930 attorneys of the estate secured Wright's arrest for having failed to keep the fund at maximum level, although the case was ultimately dismissed. See ibid., November 14, 1929; December 11, 25, 1930; ibid., February 18, 1932; *The Capital Times*, December 6, 19, 1930; March 11, 1933.

27. *The Capital Times*, July 30, August 27, October 8, 14, 1928; *The New York Times*, July 31, August 27, 1928; *Baraboo Weekly News*, May 31, October 11, 1928; *The Weekly Home News*, May 24, October 11, 1928.

28. Olgivanna Lloyd Wright, *Frank Lloyd Wright: His Life, His Work, His Word* (New York: Horizon Press, 1967), pp. 206–222; *An Autobiography*, p. 303.
29. Hitchcock, *In the Nature of Materials*, pp. 75–79.
30. See the bibliography for a list of these articles. The fee is discussed in "Frank Lloyd Wright, 1869–1959," *The Architectural Record* 125 (May 1959): 9.
31. *The New York Times*, September 17, 18, 1931.
32. *The New York Times*, September 30, 1931; ibid., February 2, 1932; *Baraboo Weekly News*, April 23, 1931; *The Capital Times*, May 17, 1927.
33. *The New York Times*, May 29, 1930; *The Western Architect* 29 (September 1930): 152. Wright's response to the Museum of Modern Art's exhibition was "Of Thee I Sing," *Shelter* 2 (April 1932). For another view see Catherine K. Bauer, "Exhibition of Modern Architecture: Museum of Modern Art," *Creative Art* 10 (April 1932). Johnson and Hitchcock discussed Wright in their book—an outgrowth of the exhibition—*The International Style: Architecture Since 1922* (New York: W. W. Norton & Co., 1932).
34. " 'Towards a New Architecture,' " *World Unity* (September 1928).
35. *The New York Times*, February 26, 1931.
36. "American Architect," *Outlook and Independent* 157 (March 11, 1931): 358; Douglas Haskell, "Frank Lloyd Wright and the Chicago Fair," *The Nation* 131 (December 3, 1930): 605; C. K. Bauer, "The Americanization of Europe," *The New Republic* 67 (June 24, 1931): 153–154. Note also Lewis Mumford, "Two Chicago Fairs," ibid. 65 (January 21, 1931): 271–272.
37. *Baraboo Weekly News*, November 27, 1930; ibid., November 10, 1932; ibid., January 5, 1933; *The New York Times*, December 19, 1930; ibid., November 29, 1931; ibid., November 16, 1932; *The Capital Times*, November 1, 3, 4, 8, 30, 1932.
38. Hitchcock and Johnson, *The International Style* . . . (1966 ed.), p. 26; Wright to Kimball, April 30, 1928, in "American Architecture . . . ," *The Architectural Record* 65 (May 1929): 434.

CHAPTER SEVEN: LITTLE EXPERIMENT STATIONS IN OUT
OF THE WAY PLACES [1932–1938]

1. *Modern Architecture: Being the Kahn Lectures for 1930* (Princeton, N.J.: Princeton University Press, 1931), reprinted in Frank Lloyd Wright, *The Future of Architecture* (New York: Horizon Press, 1953), pp. 108–111.

2. "An Extension of the Work in Architecture at Taliesin to Include Apprentices in Residence," announcement brochure reprinted in Frank Lloyd Wright, *An Autobiography* (1932; new ed., New York: Duell, Sloan and Pearce, 1943), pp. 390–394; *The Capital Times* (Madison, Wis.), August 7, 1932; *The New York Times*, August 19, November 6, 1932. See also Wright's pamphlet, *The Hillside Home School of the Allied Arts: Why We Want This School* (1931).

3. On the opening, building, and activities of the Fellowship see: *The Capital Times*, April 9, November 1, 2, 1933; ibid., May 18, 1934; ibid., November 13, 1936; *Baraboo Weekly News* (Baraboo, Wis.), September 8, November 3, 1932; ibid., October 12, 19, 1933; ibid., March 8, June 7, 14, 1934; *The Weekly Home News* (Spring Green, Wis.), April 13, 1933; ibid., January 4, May 24, July 12, 1934; ibid., May 11, October 5, 1939; *The Milwaukee Journal*, April 9, 1933, quoting *The Nation*; John Gloag, "Frank Lloyd Wright and the Significance of the Taliesin Fellowship," *The Architectural Record* 77 (January 1935): 1–2; Letter by James Watrous to *American Magazine of Art* 26 (December 1933).

4. Financial contributors called "Friends of the Fellowship" were listed in *The Taliesin Fellowship* (Spring Green, Wis., 1933), a descriptive pamphlet including membership application.

5. Hans M. Wingler, *The Bauhaus* (1962; new ed., Cambridge, Mass.: MIT Press, 1969).

6. Mark L. Peisch, *The Chicago School of Architecture: Early Followers of Sullivan and Wright* (New York: Random House, 1964), chap. 3, "The Oak Park Studio"; Don L. Morgan, "A

Wright House on the Prairie," *The Prairie School Review* 2 (3rd Quarter, 1965).

7. *The Capital Times*, August 26, 1934.

8. Of the many books by and about Gurdjieff, see Fritz Peters, *Boyhood with Gurdjieff* (New York: E. P. Dutton, 1964) for a feel of the place.

9. Mrs. Frank Lloyd Wright, "Our House," *The Capital Times*, February 9, 1959; and her book, *The Shining Brow: Frank Lloyd Wright* (New York: Horizon Press, 1960), pp. 85–86.

10. See the application for membership in The Taliesin Fellowship (1933); "An Extension of the Work in Architecture . . . ," Wright, *An Autobiography*, pp. 392–393, 416; Sterling Sorensen, "Wright's Taliesin Is League of Nations in Miniature," *The Capital Times*, September 28, 1947; Bruce Bliven, Jr., "Frank Lloyd Wright," *The New Republic* 103 (December 9, 1940).

11. Wright, *An Autobiography*, p. 399.

12. Ibid.; *The Capital Times*, April 13, December 23, 1934. See the bibliography for additional information.

13. *The Capital Times*, March 2, 1934; ibid., September 6, 1935; *The Weekly Home News*, March 29, 1934.

14. *The Capital Times*, May 4, 1935.

15. Ibid., November 11, 1936; ibid., August 17, 1938; ibid., July 19, 1939; ibid., October 19, 1940; ibid., October 30, 1950; ibid., November 7, 1951; *The Weekly Home News*, June 30, July 28, 1938; ibid., August 28, 1941.

16. A Madison architect who visited Taliesin frequently in the 1950s has described to me the activities there.

17. *The New York Times*, March 27, 1935; *The Capital Times*, April 19, 1935. Olgivanna Wright mistakenly asserts that the Fellowship began its annual winter trips to Arizona in 1933, the year it started work, she says, on the Broadacre model (*Frank Lloyd Wright: His Life, His Work, His Word* [New York: Horizon Press, 1967], p. 214). Preparation of the model actually got underway in the second half of 1934 (*The Capital Times*, December 9, 1934), while the first Fellowship cross-country trek took place in January, 1935 (*The Weekly Home News*, January 10, 1935; *Baraboo Weekly News*, January 24, February 28, March 28, 1935;

and especially the *Wisconsin State Journal* [Madison], February 10, 1935).

Both Olgivanna (*Frank Lloyd Wright . . .*, p. 213) and Henry-Russell Hitchcock, *In the Nature of Materials: The Buildings of Frank Lloyd Wright, 1887–1941* (New York: Duell, Sloan and Pearce, 1942), p. 124, plates 276–280, give incorrect dates for the construction of "Ocatillo Camp." Wright and his assistants left for the San Marcos Desert near Chandler in January 1929 and designed the camp when they got there (*Baraboo Weekly News*, January 17, 1929; *The Weekly Home News*, January 24, March 7, 1929). On "Broad Acre Ranch" see ibid., April 18, 1929.

18. The discussion of Broadacre City is based on these and other sources listed in the bibliography.

19. In the analysis of the quadruple block, and of Como Orchards below, I have relied heavily on Norris Kelly Smith, *Frank Lloyd Wright: A Study in Architectural Content* (Englewood Cliffs, N.J.: Prentice-Hall, 1966), pp. 87–90.

20. On Taliesin West see *The Capital Times*, December 26, 1937; *The Weekly Home News*, April 27, 1939; *Chillicothe News Advertiser* (Chillicothe, Tex.), May 1, 1940, clipping in Frank Lloyd Wright Collection (FLW Coll.), Avery Library, Columbia University, New York; Vincent Scully, *Frank Lloyd Wright* (New York: George Braziller, 1960), pp. 28–29.

21. For some curious parallels between Wright's yearly migrations to Arizona and the trek of the agricultural dispossessed during the 1930s see Eugene Masselink, "At Taliesin," *The Capital Times*, January 24, 1936.

CHAPTER EIGHT: BACK ON TOP [1936–1945]

1. On the Jacobs House see Frank Lloyd Wright, *The Natural House* (New York: Horizon Press, 1954), pp. 81–91; *The Architectural Forum* 68 (January 1938); *The Capital Times* (Madison, Wis.), November 20, 1936; ibid., January 23, 1938.

2. *The New York Times*, December 8, 1940; Herbert Jacobs, *Frank Lloyd Wright: America's Greatest Architect* (New York: Harcourt, Brace & World, 1965), pp. 127–133.

3. Peter Blake, *Frank Lloyd Wright: Architecture and Space* (1960; new ed., Baltimore: Penguin Books, 1964), 106.

4. "A Little Private Club," *Life* 5 (September 26, 1938); *The Living City* (New York: Horizon Press, 1958), p. 96; *Two Lectures on Architecture* (Chicago: University of Chicago Press, 1931), reprinted in Frank Lloyd Wright, in *The Future of Architecture* (New York: Horizon Press, 1953), p. 189.

5. *Sixty Years of Living Architecture: The Work of Frank Lloyd Wright*, exhibition brochure, Guggenheim Museum, New York, 1953.

6. Marjorie F. Leighey, "A Testimony to Beauty" in Terry B. Morton, ed., *The Pope-Leighey House* (Washington, D.C.: National Trust for Historic Preservation, 1969), p. 60, emphasis added, illustrates the subtle ways a Usonian home increased informality and changed old habits. Originally designed for Loren Pope in Falls Church, Virginia, Mrs. Leighey's house is the most thoroughly documented of all Wright's residences in this period.

7. Transcript of "Frank Lloyd Wright," *Biography in Sound*, National Broadcasting Company, August 7, 1956, copy in Frank Lloyd Wright Collection (FLW Coll.), Avery Library, Columbia University, New York; conversation with William R. Taylor, former owner of the second Jacobs House, in Madison, Wisconsin, May 14, 1967. Wright's remarks are in *The Natural House*, pp. 165–66, 169. See also Herbert Jacobs in *The New York Times*, December 8, 1940.

8. Statistics are computed from Olgivanna Lloyd Wright, *Frank Lloyd Wright: His Life, His Work, His Word* (New York: Horizon Press, 1967), pp. 214–216. Wright's comment is in *An Autobiography* (1932; new ed., New York: Duell, Sloan and Pearce, 1943), p. 494.

9. Wayne Andrews, *Architecture, Ambition and Americans: A Social History of American Architecture* (Glencoe, Ill.: The Free Press, 1964), p. 243; Vincent Scully, *Frank Lloyd Wright* (New York: George Braziller, 1960), pp. 26–27.

10. Henry-Russell Hitchcock, *In the Nature of Materials: The Buildings of Frank Lloyd Wright, 1887–1941* (New York: Duell, Sloan and Pearce, 1942), p. 91.

11. *The Architectural Forum* 68 (January 1938): 36.

12. *In the Nature of Materials*, p. 90.
13. For the original rendering, description, and architect's comments see *The Racine Journal-Times* (Racine, Wis.), December 31, 1936. Its construction and engineering are excellently appraised in Carl W. Condit, *American Building Art: The Twentieth Century* (New York: Oxford University Press, 1961), pp. 172–176. The famous demonstration, in which Wright proved to the State Industrial Commission that his "mushroom" columns could support over sixty tons of dead weight each, though only required to hold from two to twelve tons, was reported in *The Capital Times*, June 9, 1937, and *The Architectural Record* 82 (July 1937): 38.
14. Wright, *An Autobiography*, p. 474; William Wesley Peters compared the two in *The Capital Times*, March 5, 1937.
15. Wright's comment is in *The Racine Journal-Times*, December 31, 1936. On the social consequences of the building see *The Capital Times*, July 23, 1955, and Wright's "Conversation" with Hugh Downs on NBC-TV, May 17, 1953, in Wright, *The Future of Architecture*, pp. 25–26. In 1939 Wright insisted that the Johnson Building was technically one of the world's best, and as a plastic structure was closest to the ideal of organic architecture of anything he had thus far built (*An Organic Architecture: The Architecture of Democracy* [London: Lund, Humphries & Co., Ltd., 1939], reprinted in Wright, in *The Future of Architecture*, p. 282).
16. Wright and "Hib" (Herbert F.) Johnson, president of the company, certainly seemed simpatico: *An Autobiography*, pp. 467–478.
17. See Blake, *Frank Lloyd Wright* . . ., pp. 106, 108; *Business Week* (May 6, 1939).
18. Maxine Block, ed., *Current Biography 1941* (New York: H. H. Wilson Co., 1941), pp. 938–940, quoting "A City for the Future," *Time* 36 (November 25, 1940).
19. On his honors, exhibitions, laudatory attention, and speaking engagements see: O. L. Wright, *Frank Lloyd Wright* . . ., pp. 214–216; *The Washington Post*, October 26, 1938, sec. 2; *The New York Times*, January 25, June 20, 1938; *The Weekly Home News*, June 17, 1937; ibid., June 15, 1939; *The Capital Times*, June 6, 1937; ibid., January 14, May 23, October 31, 1938; ibid.,

January 2, 1941. For a provocative review of *An Autobiography* see Talbot Hamlin in *The Wisconsin Magazine of History* 27 (December 1943).

20. *The Capital Times*, June 8, 1938; ibid., January 23, 25, 1940; *The Washington Post*, October 26, 1938, sec. 2.

21. *The Milwaukee Journal*, December 6, 1934.

22. For Wright's views on Russia and the flap with the University of Wisconsin Communists see: *The Capital Times*, May 29, 1936; ibid., June 6, July 22, August 1, 3, 5, 13, October 22, 1937; *The Weekly Home News*, June 17, 1937; *The Iowa County Democrat* (Mineral Point, Wis.), August 12, 19, 1937; "Architecture and Life in the USSR," *The Architectural Record* 82 (October 1937).

23. *The Capital Times*, September 19, 21, 1937.

24. Wright expressed his views on Roosevelt and the military buildup in *The Capital Times*, August 11, 1938; ibid., August 4, 1940; ibid., March 29, June 6, 1941; *The Weekly Home News*, July 13, 1939; "The American Quality," *Scribner's Commentator* 10 (October 1941); and in *Taliesin Square-Paper*, an irregular publication of Wright's speeches and newspaper articles, May 27, 1941, and no. 5 (July 1941).

25. The conscientious objection controversy is recorded in *The Capital Times*, April 1, 6, 1941; ibid., December 17, 20, 1942; ibid., January 3, 14, February 26, April 14, 1943; and in FLW to August Derleth, December 22, 1942, Derleth MSS., State Historical Society of Wisconsin, Madison, quoted by permission.

26. "Usonia, Usonia South, and New England: A Declaration of Independence . . . 1941," *Taliesin Square-Paper* no. 6 (August 24, 1941).

27. *The Capital Times*, December 28, 1941; ibid., January 23, 1942; *The New York Times*, January 22, 1942.

28. *The New York Times*, July 10, September 21, 1945; *The Capital Times*, July 10, 1945; "The Modern Gallery," *The Architectural Forum* 84 (January 1946): 81–88; *Time* 46 (July 23, October 1, 1945); *Life* 29 (October 8, 1945).

CHAPTER NINE: MAKING STRUCTURE EXPRESS IDEAS [1930–1959]

1. Frank Lloyd Wright, *An Organic Architecture: The Architecture of Democracy* (London: Lund, Humphries & Co., Ltd., 1939),

reprinted in *The Future of Architecture* (New York: Horizon Press, 1953), p. 245.

2. Santiago del Campo, "An Afternoon with Frank Lloyd Wright," *Americas* 6 (April 1954): 11; preface to the 1951 brochure, *Meeting House of the First Unitarian Society of Madison, Wisconsin*.

3. Frank Lloyd Wright, *The Living City* (New York: Horizon Press, 1958), p. 113.

4. On the "new freedom" of glass and steel see Frank Lloyd Wright, *The Natural House* (New York: Horizon Press, 1954), p. 155.

5. *The Natural House*, p. 139; second interview on "The Mike Wallace Show," Westinghouse Television, reprinted in *The Capital Times* (Madison, Wis.), September 30, 1957.

6. Carl W. Condit, *American Building Art: The Twentieth Century* (New York: Oxford University Press, 1961), pp. 173–176.

7. Of Wright's many comments on nature see particularly, in addition to *The Japanese Print*, "Nature," *Taliesin Square-Paper* no. 9, August 1945; *Modern Architecture: Being the Kahn Lectures for 1930* (Princeton, N.J.: Princeton University Press, 1931), reprinted in *The Future of Architecture* (New York: Horizon Press, 1953), p. 91; and *An Autobiography* (1932; new ed., New York: Duell, Sloan and Pearce, 1943), p. 89.

8. *Genius and the Mobocracy* (New York: Duell, Sloan and Pearce, 1949), p. 28; *An Autobiography*, pp. 158, 451; *The Natural House*, pp. 167–168.

9. On architectural reality as inside space see *The Natural House*, pp. 31, 220; *Modern Architecture . . .*, in *The Future of Architecture*, p. 125; "Conversation," in *The Future of Architecture*, pp. 12–13; *A Testament* (New York: Horizon Press, 1957), p. 224; *An Autobiography*, pp. 338–339. For the creation of Unity Temple see ibid., pp. 153–160.

10. Raymond Williams, *Culture and Society, 1780–1950* (New York: Anchor Books, 1959), p. xiv.

11. Frank Lloyd Wright, *Two Lectures on Architecture* (Chicago: The Art Institute, 1931), reprinted in *The Future of Architecture*, p. 193; "Conversation" in ibid., pp. 12–13; "Recollections—The United States, 1893–1920," *The Architectural Journal* (London), 84 (July 18–August 6, 1936), reprinted in *The Natural House*, p. 24.

12. "Recollections . . . ," in *The Natural House*, p. 20; *An Autobiography*, pp. 146–147; *Two Lectures on Architecture*, in *The Future of Architecture*, p. 191; *Modern Architecture* . . . , in ibid., pp. 95, 128; *Genius and the Mobocracy*, p. 109.

13. *Genius and the Mobocracy*, p. 109; "The Logic of Contemporary Architecture as an Expression of This Age," *The Architectural Forum* 52 (May 1930): 637–638.

14. *An Organic Architecture* . . . , in *The Future of Architecture*, pp. 248–249; "To My Neighbors," *The Weekly Home News* (Spring Green, Wis.), August 20, 1914; FLW to Catherine and Kenneth Baxter, February 7, 1921, Frank Lloyd Wright Collection (FLW Coll.), Avery Library, Columbia University, New York.

15. *An Autobiography*, p. 366; "Louis H. Sullivan—His Work," *The Architectural Record*, 56 (July 1924): 30.

16. *An Organic Architecture* . . . , in *The Future of Architecture*, pp. 225–226, 234; "Frank Lloyd Wright Talks on His Art," *The New York Times Magazine*, October 4, 1953; *The Living City*, p. 138.

17. *The Capital Times*, January 1, 1959; *The Natural House*, p. 21, quoting "Recollections" (1936).

18. *The Natural House*, pp. 135–136; *The Living City*, pp. 25–26, 102–104; *An Organic Architecture* . . . , in *The Future of Architecture*, pp. 225, 288; *An Autobiography*, pp. 351, 450; "The Art and Craft of the Machine," in Edgar Kaufmann and Ben Raeburn, eds., *Frank Lloyd Wright: Writings and Buildings* (Cleveland: World Pub. Co., 1960), p. 57; *The Capital Times*, November 2, 1951.

19. *The Natural House*, p. 187; *An Organic Architecture* . . . , in *The Future of Architecture*, pp. 230, 264; *The Taliesin Fellowship* (Spring Green: Frank Lloyd Wright, 1933); *An Autobiography*, p. 338.

20. *An Autobiography*, p. 332; *An Organic Architecture* . . . , in *The Future of Architecture*, p. 225; Speech to the New York Chamber of Commerce, *The New York Times*, January 10, 1958; *The Living City*, p. 203; *Modern Architecture* . . . , in *The Future of Architecture*, p. 127; Speech to the Institute of Art, *The Providence Journal* (Providence, R.I.), November 12, 1932.

21. *Two Lectures on Architecture*, in *The Future of Architecture*, p. 186; *An Autobiography*, pp. 380, 460; *The Living City*, pp. 31–37,

39; "The Architect" in Robert B. Heywood, ed., *The Works of the Mind* (Chicago: University of Chicago Press, 1947); "Mr. Big," *The Capital Times*, July 18, 1952; Address to a Conference on "Planning Man's Physical Environment" at Princeton University, reprinted in *The Capital Times*, August 17, 1947.

22. The 1893 announcement of independent practice is reproduced in John Lloyd Wright, *My Father Who Is on Earth* (New York: G. P. Putnam's Sons, 1946), p. 22; FLW to William C. Gannett, January 30, 1899, Gannett MSS., Rush Rhees Library, University of Rochester, Rochester, New York.

23. "Chicago Culture," a speech to the Chicago Women's Aid, in Frederick Gutheim, ed., *Frank Lloyd Wright on Architecture: Selected Writings, 1894-1940* (New York: Duell, Sloan and Pearce, 1941), pp. 85-97.

24. "The Art and Craft of the Machine," in Kaufmann and Raeburn, eds., *Writings and Buildings*, pp. 72-73 especially; Wright's later remark is in *Modern Architecture* . . ., in *The Future of Architecture*, p. 157.

25. For Wright's comments on the city see Speech to the Chicago Real Estate Board, *The Capital Times*, June 8, 1938; *An Autobiography*, p. 325; *Modern Architecture* . . ., in *The Future of Architecture*, pp. 148-182, particularly 156, 175; Speech to the American Municipal Association, Saint Louis, *The New York Times*, November 27, 1956; also ibid., November 11, 1940; Speech to the Chamber of Commerce, Bethesda-Chevy Chase, Maryland, *The Washington Post*, October 3, 1958; *The Natural House*, p. 141; *The Living City*, pp. 21-22, 49-50, 60-67.

26. *The New York Times*, November 14, 1931; ibid., November 11, 1940; *The Capital Times*, August 17, 1947; his speech urging a small town to remain that way, *The Reedsburg* (Wis.) *Times-Press*, September 24, 1953; Letter to the editor, *London News Chronicle*, reproduced as *Taliesin Square-Paper* no. 1, January 1941; "Highlights," *The Architectural Forum* 55 (October 1931): 409; *Modern Architecture* . . ., in *The Future of Architecture*, pp. 176-177; *An Autobiography*, pp. 328-329; *The Natural House*, p. 140; *The Living City*, p. 62.

27. *Modern Architecture* . . ., in *The Future of Architecture*, pp. 148-149.

28. Published in *The Capital Times*, August 29–31, September 5, 6, 1956.
29. Published as the jacket and inside covers of Frank Lloyd Wright, *Architecture: Man in Possession of His Earth* (New York: Doubleday and Co., 1962).
30. Seldon Rodman, *Conversations with Artists* (New York: The Devin-Adair Co., 1957), p. 58; "Frank Lloyd Wright's Last Interview: Why People Create," *School Arts* 58 (June 1959), 30.
31. *An Autobiography*, p. 325; *The Living City*, pp. 34–35, 45, 152; *Genius and the Mobocracy*, pp. 65–66, 89; "When Free Men Fear," *The Nation* 162 (June 2, 1951): 527–528; *The Capital Times*, August 4, 1940, May 11, 1948, and September 30, 1957.
32. *Two Lectures on Architecture*, in *The Future of Architecture*, p. 203; *Modern Architecture* . . . , in ibid., pp. 178–179; Address to the Federal Architects Association, *The Washington Post*, sec. 2, October 26, 1938.

CHAPTER TEN: A GIANT TREE IN A WIDE LANDSCAPE [1946–1959]

1. Computed from Olgivanna Lloyd Wright, *Frank Lloyd Wright: His Life, His Work, His Word* (New York: Horizon Press, 1967), pp. 216–222.
2. *The New York Times*, April 21, 1963, sec. 8; ibid., June 7, 1964, sec. 8.
3. "To the Young Man in Architecture—A Challenge," *The Architectural Forum* 68 (January 1938).
4. *The San Francisco Chronicle*, December 7, 1951, reported his announcement from 319 Grant Street, his West Coast business office. See also *The Capital Times* (Madison, Wis.), December 12, 1951; *The Weekly Home News* (Spring Green, Wis.), December 13, 1951; and Frank Lloyd Wright, *The Natural House* (New York: Horizon Press, 1954), pp. 199–207.
5. *The New York Times*, October 14, 1956, sec. 8; ibid., December 21, 1956; ibid., October 25, 1957, sec. 7; *The Capital Times*, October 4, 1956; ibid., June 12, 1957; ibid., January 9, 1958; *The Chicago Tribune*, January 9, 22, 1958; Erdman Company brochure, *Frank Lloyd Wright Prefabricated Homes* (n.p., n.d.).

6. *The New York Times*, February 10, 1957, sec. 8; *The Capital Times*, April 26, 1957.

7. *An Autobiography* (1932; new ed., New York: Duell, Sloan and Pearce, 1943), p. 145.

8. *The New York Times*, October 18, 1955; advertisement, November 18; "New Era for Wright at 86: The Marketplace Redeemed?" *The Architectural Record* 118 (October 1955); Heritage Henredon Fine Furniture brochure (n.p., n.d.); Kenneth R. Volz, Henredon Director of Design, to Author, December 11, 1970. On the theater domes see *The New York Times*, December 11, 1957.

9. *The New York Times*, November 5, 1946; ibid., April 17, 1951; ibid., March 30, April 4, 1952; ibid., July 25, 29, September 3, 1953; ibid., May 7, December 12, 22, 1956; Seldon Rodman, *Conversations with Artists* (New York: Devin-Adair, 1957), p. 73; *Newsweek* 42 (August 10, 1953); ibid. (November 2, 1953); John Haverstock, "To Be or Not To Be," *The Saturday Review* 38 (May 21, 1955); *The New Yorker* 32 (June 16, 1956); ibid., 33 (August 10, 1957); *Time* 62 (August 10, 1953): 70.

10. *The Architectural Record* 116 (July 1954): 20; *The New York Times*, November 15, 1954; ibid., September 13, 1959; *Time* 63 (May 31, 1954): 54; Rabbi Mortimer J. Cohen, *Beth Shalom Synagogue* (Elkins Park, Pa.: n.d.).

11. *The Capital Times*, March 25, 31, 1954; *The New York Times* May 26, 1953; ibid., March 9, March 21 ("A New Debate in Old Venice"), April 22, 1954; ibid., November 16, 1955; *Time* 63 (March 22, 1954): 92.

12. *The New York Times*, August 26, 27, 1956; *The Chicago Tribune*, October 17, 1956; *The Capital Times*, October 16, 1956; Frank Lloyd Wright, *A Testament* (New York: Horizon Press, 1957), pp. 238-248.

13. *The Denver Post*, July 2, 1954; ibid., May 29, 1955; *The Washington Post*, July 8, 1955; *The New York Times*, July 8, 16, 1955; *The Capital Times*, May 27, October 17, 1955 (Pearson column); U.S., Congress, House, *Congressional Record*, 84th Cong., 1st sess., 101, pt. 7: 8781. On Yosemite see *The New York Times*, December 1, 1954; brochure, "Frank Lloyd Wright on Restaurant Architecture," *Food Services Magazine* (November 1958).

14. *The New York Times*, January 27, June 7, 8, 1957; *The Weekly*

Home News, July 17, 1958; *The Capital Times*, May 3, August 20, 1958; ibid., January 8, 1959.

15. *The Capital Times*, April 23, 1951; ibid., July 23, 1956; *The New York Times*, July 22, September 28, 1956; ibid., February 24, April 7, 1957; "Wright Picks a Fight in Arizona," *Life* 42 (May 13, 1957): 59; Wright's own broadside, "Oasis: Plan for Arizona State Capital," February 17, 1957.

16. *The Weekly Home News*, October 2, 9 (including map of proposed highway rerouting), 16, 23, November 13, 1947; ibid., August 2, 16, September 6, October 9, 1951; *The Capital Times*, October 12, 25, 31 (including "Bureaucracy Jumps the Gun"), 1947; ibid., August 1, 15, 24, 28, September 1, 6, 7, 1951.

17. *The Capital Times*, October 16, December 14, 1953; *Baraboo Weekly News* (Baraboo, Wis.), March 18, 1937; *The Weekly Home News*, May 4, 1939; ibid., November 30, 1950; ibid., August 16, 1951; ibid., June 4, September 17, December 10, 1953.

18. *The Weekly Home News*, September 2, November 11, 1954; *The Capital Times*, November 9, 10, 11, 15, 16, 1954; *The New York Times*, September 9, November 10, 12, 1954; *Newsweek* 44 (November 22, 1954): 63.

19. Vernon E. Hill, "They Want Him to Stay," *The Weekly Home News*, November 18, 1954; William T. Evjue, "Wright Will Not Leave State and Will Not Destroy Taliesin," *The Capital Times*, November 23, 1954; *An Autobiography*, p. 118.

20. *The New York Times*, February 12, 1955; *The Capital Times*, February 1, 11, 17, May 18, 1955; *The Weekly Home News*, November 25, 1954; ibid., January 27, February 3, 17, May 19, 1955.

21. *The Weekly Home News*, October 25, November 1, 1956; ibid., January 30, February 5, 1958; *The New York Times*, August 3, 1957; *The Capital Times*, October 17, 1957; ibid., April 7, 1959.

22. For a partial history of the Monona Terrace project see *The Capital Times*, September 28, November 2, 3, December 5, 1938; ibid., June 4, October 15, 1941; ibid., May 31, 1946; ibid., July 7-10, September 15, 21, 1953; July 10, October 4, November 3, 1954; February 7, 8, April 21, August 12, 1955; ibid., May 23, July 6, August 17, 25, 29-31, September 5, 6, 1956; ibid., March 19, May 3, 1957; ibid., June 18, July 19, 1958; ibid., January 21,

March 11, 1959. See also ibid., September 18, 1967, including Wright's 1938 rendering.

23. *The Weekly Home News*, April 12, 1951; *The Capital Times*, April 21, August 21, 1951; "When Free Men Fear," *The Nation* 162 (June 2, 1951): 527–528.

24. "Wake Up Wisconsin," *The Capital Times*, September 22, 1952.

25. *The New York Times*, August 3, 1957; *The San Francisco Chronicle*, August 3, 1957.

26. On the various Spring Green projects, festivals, and relations in general see *The Weekly Home News*, November 3, 10, 1949; ibid., August 7, 1952; ibid., January 31, March 14, 28, May 16, June 27, July 4, 25, September 12, 26, October 31, November 7, December 5, 12, 19, 1957; ibid., January 23, 30, May 15, 22, June 30, July 3, August 7, 1958; *The Capital Times*, October 17, 1957; ibid., April 7, 1959; *The New York Times*, August 3, 1957.

27. Olgivanna Lloyd Wright, *The Shining Brow: Frank Lloyd Wright* (New York: Horizon Press, 1960), p. 242; *Deseret News* (Salt Lake City), April 27, 1953; Rodman, *Conversations with Artists*, pp. 58, 74; "Meeting of the Titans," discussion with Carl Sandburg, *The Capital Times*, June 3, 1957; "Outside the Profession," *The New Yorker* 29 (September 26, 1953): 27.

28. *The New Yorker* 29 (September 26, 1953): 27; text of NBC radio program, "Biography in Sound," in *The Weekly Home News*, August 9, 1956; "A Visit with Frank Lloyd Wright," *Look* 21 (September 17, 1957): 31; *The Capital Times*, January 8, 1958, quoting the February 1958 *Esquire*; Merle Armitage, "Frank Lloyd Wright: An American Original," *Texas Quarterly* 5 (Spring 1962); Maginel Wright Barney, *The Valley of the God-Almighty Joneses* (New York: Appleton-Century, 1965), p. 148; *The Capital Times*, May 5, 1956.

29. Bruce Barton to Otto McFeeley, February 20, 1956, Barton Collection, Manuscripts Division, State Historical Society of Wisconsin, Madison; Peter Blake, *Frank Lloyd Wright: Architecture and Space* (Baltimore: Penguin Books, 1964), p. 118; "The Wright Word," *Time* 64 (August 2, 1954): 61; FLW to Claude Bragdon, May 27, 1932, Bragdon Collection, Rush Rhees Library, University of Rochester, Rochester, New York; Lewis Nichols, "Talk With Mr. Wright," *The New York Times*, November 1,

1953, sec. 7; "Wright Revisited," *The New Yorker* 23 (June 16, 1956): 26–27.

30. Barney, *The Valley* . . . , p. 148.

31. S. J. Woolf, "A Pioneer in Architecture Surveys It," *The New York Times*, January 17, 1932, sec. 5; Harvey Breit, "Talk With Frank Lloyd Wright," ibid., July 24, 1949, sec. 7; Arturo and Janeann Gonzalez, "Life Begins at 40 (x 2)," ibid., June 22, 1958; "Wright Revisited," *The New Yorker* 23 (June 16, 1956); editors of *The Architectural Forum*, "Frank Lloyd Wright 1869–1959," *The Architectural Forum* 110 (May 1959): 112.

32. Ibid., p. 5; *The Capital Times*, April 7, 9, 1959; *The New York Times*, April 8, 10 (editorial and obituary), 1959; Olgivanna Lloyd Wright, *The Shining Brow* . . . , p. 119.

33. *The Capital Times*, April 13, 1959; *The New York Times*, April 13, 1959.

34. *The Architectural Forum* of May 1959 solicited comments from van der Rohe and many other notables. See also "Frank Lloyd Wright Is Gone," *The Weekly Home News*, April 9, 1959, and *The Capital Times*, April 10, 1959, for the impact of the architect's death on his neighbors.

CHAPTER ELEVEN: HOW DO YOU SPEAK TO A DIVINITY?
[AFTER 1959]

1. On the Imperial see *The Capital Times* (Madison, Wis.), April 11, 1937; ibid., August 31, 1945; ibid., September 14, November 7, December 1, 14, 1967; ibid., January 9, 1968; *The Milwaukee Journal*, October 23, November 7, 16, December 1, 1967; ibid., February 16, 1969; *The New York Times*, September 1, 1946; ibid., August 9, 23, 1964; ibid., September 2, 1969; ibid., March 11, 1970; *Time* 47 (September 24, 1945): 46; Frank Riley, "Deathwatch in Tokyo," *The Saturday Review*, December 16, 1967, 40–41.

2. *The New York Times*, February 2, 1963; ibid., March 20, 24, 1964; ibid., September 17, 1968; ibid., June 10, 1970; *Chicago Daily News*, June 12, 1969; *The Capital Times*, February 2, 7, 1963; ibid., July 9, 1964; ibid., September 29, 1965; ibid., July 15, 1966.

3. *The New York Times*, September 7, 1963; *The Milwaukee Journal*, April 14, 1968.
4. For example, see *The Milwaukee Journal*, November 3, 1968, and *Newsweek* 74 (July 14, 1969).
5. *The Capital Times*, September 20, 1967; Ada Louise Huxtable, "An Exercise in Chinese Irony," *The New York Times*, December 1, 1968, for comments on an exhibition of Wright stained glass.
6. For a list of Wright's work in various stages of planning and construction shortly before his death, and for compilations of TAA's projects during its first few years, see *The Capital Times*, January 16, 1959; ibid., August 3, 1960; *The New York Times*, October 20, 1963, sec. 8.
7. On the Fellowship's activities in the mid-1960s see *The Capital Times*, September 13, 1966.
8. On the Lincoln Building see *The Capital Times*, March 15, 1966. For other aspects of life at Taliesin soon after Wright's death see *The Weekly Home News*, June 11, July 2, 1959; ibid., June 9, 1960.
9. *The Capital Times*, September 20, 1967; ibid., March 26, 1968; *The Milwaukee Journal*, August 24, 1967; *Newsweek*, October 23, 1967.
10. Quoted in Stanley Kauffmann, "Art and the Critics' Confusion," *The New Republic* 163 (November 21, 1970): 22.
11. *The Weekly Home News*, April 16, 1959; *The New York Times*, April 19, 1959; ibid., March 18, 1962, sec. 2.
12. Mrs. Wright has also articulated her own philosophy in *The Struggle Within* (1955). Except for *Architecture* (1962), a Doubleday book, her publisher in every instance has been Horizon Press. The analysis in the following paragraphs is based largely on Mrs. Wright's books, and on the architect's autobiographical writings.
13. "Outside the Profession," *The New Yorker* 29 (September 26, 1953): 27; "Conversation" in *The Future of Architecture* (New York: Horizon Press, 1953), 29.
14. Olgivanna Wright compared her husband to Jesus in an address to the Phoenix Art Museum League (*The Roots of Life* [New York: Horizon Press, 1963], pp. 139–140). "The Miracle on Fifth

Avenue" is a chapter title in *Frank Lloyd Wright: His Life, His Work, His Word* (New York: Horizon Press, 1967), and "my father who is on earth" is the title of John Lloyd Wright's book (G. P. Putnam's Sons, 1946). For Reverend Emanuel N. Vergis's comments see "Teacup Dome," *Time* 78 (August 18, 1961): 50.

15. Fred C. Robie, Jr., "Mr. Robie Knew What He Wanted," *The Architectural Forum* 109 (October 1958): 126–127, 206, 210.

16. Frank Lloyd Wright, "In the Cause of Architecture," *The Architectural Record* 23 (March 1908); Norris Kelly Smith, *Frank Lloyd Wright: A Study in Architectural Content* (Englewood Cliffs, N.J.: Prentice-Hall, 1966), chap. 1.

17. *Modern Architecture: Being the Kahn Lectures for 1930* (Princeton, N.J.: Princeton University Press, 1931), reprinted in *The Future of Architecture*, pp. 103, 106.

18. Ibid., p. 107.

19. On Wright's European influence see, for example, Vincent Scully, *Modern Architecture* (New York: George Braziller, 1961), pp. 25–27, plates 56, 59–64; Lewis Mumford, "Frank Lloyd Wright and the New Pioneers," *The Architectural Record* 66 (April 1929); Douglass Haskell, "Frank Lloyd Wright and the Chicago World's Fair," *The Nation* 131 (December 3, 1930): 605; C. K. Bauer, "The Americanization of Europe," *The New Republic* (June 24, 1931): 153–154; Fiske Kimball, "Builder and Poet," *The Architectural Record* 71 (June 1932): 379–380. At an appearance in Madison, Wisconsin, in 1937 Gropius mentioned that he had just met Wright for the first time (*The Capital Times*, November 9, 1937).

20. *An Organic Architecture* (London: Lund, Humphries, Ltd., 1939), reprinted in *The Future of Architecture*, pp. 260, 268.

21. Computed from Olgivanna Wright, *Frank Lloyd Wright . . .*, pp. 206–222.

22. Arthur Drexler, ed., *The Drawings of Frank Lloyd Wright* (New York: Horizon Press, 1962), plate 267, and the editor's comment on p. 315.

23. Winthrop Sargeant, *Geniuses, Goddesses and People* (New York: E. P. Dutton, 1949), p. 229.

BIBLIOGRAPHY

Since no adequate Frank Lloyd Wright bibliography has previously been compiled, I have included sources regardless of their value in this study, indicating when necessary their nature and importance. With the exception of the accounts by relatives, friends, and clients (page 361) and the secondary sources (pages 360–362), the entries in each category are listed in chronological order.

PRIMARY SOURCES

After the executed buildings themselves, the most primary of all sources are anthologies and photographs, drawings, and plans. Wright's earliest illustrations were in *The Inland Architect and News Record* (Chicago), appearing in the following issues:

9 (June 1887); 10 (August 1887); 11 (February 1888); 24 (August 1894); 24 (January 1895); 29 (July 1897); 30 (January 1898); 31 (June 1898); 32 (January 1899); 33 (February 1899); 35 (April 1900); 39 (July 1902); 45 (June 1905); 46 (August 1905); 47 (July 1906); 48 (October 1906); 50 (July 1907); 50 (November 1907); 50 (December 1907); 51 (January 1908); 52 (December 1908). Publication ended in December 1908.

1. Collections of Illustrations (General)

Ausgeführte Bauten und Entwürfe von Frank Lloyd Wright. Berlin: Ernst Wasmuth, 1910. Introduction by Wright.

Frank Lloyd Wright Ausgeführte Bauten. Berlin: Ernst Wasmuth, 1911. Introduction by W. R. Ashbee.

Widjeveld, Hendricus Theodorus, ed. *The Life-Work of the American Architect, Frank Lloyd Wright.* Sanspoort, Holl.: C. A. Mees, 1925 (including essays by Wright and others).

De Vries, H., ed. *Frank Lloyd Wright.* Ernst Pollack, 1926.

Hitchcock, Henry-Russell. *Frank Lloyd Wright.* Paris: "Cahiers d' Art," 1928.

Badovici, Jean, ed. *Frank Lloyd Wright: American Architect.* Paris: Albert Marance, 1932.

The Architectural Forum (special issues) 68 (January 1938); 88 (January 1948); 94 (January 1951).

Hitchcock, Henry-Russell. *In the Nature of Materials: The Buildings of Frank Lloyd Wright, 1887–1941.* New York: Duell, Sloan and Pearce, 1942.

Kaufmann, Edgar, Jr., ed. *Taliesin Drawings: Recent Architecture of Frank Lloyd Wright, Selected from his Drawings.* New York: Wittenborn, Schultz, Inc., 1952.

Moser, Verner M., ed. *Sixty Years of Living Architecture.* Winterthur, Switzerland: Verlag Buchdr., 1952.

House Beautiful (special issue), 97 (November 1955).

"Frank Lloyd Wright: Selection of Current Work," *The Architectural Record* 123 (May 1958): 167–190.

House and Home published a number of color features of Wright's later work that together would make an excellent volume: 2 (December 1952); 3 (March 1953); 3 (June 1953); 4 (November 1953); 5 (March 1954); 6 (November 1954); 7 (January 1955); 7 (April 1955); 10 (September 1956); 10 (December 1956); 14 (August 1958); 15 (February 1959).

Drawings for a Living Architecture. New York: Horizon Press, 1959.

Drexler, Arthur, ed. *The Drawings of Frank Lloyd Wright.* New York: Horizon Press, 1962.

Pawley, Martin, and Futagawa, Yukio. *Frank Lloyd Wright: I. Public Buildings.* New York: Simon and Schuster, 1970.

2. *Particular Buildings*

The Solomon R. Guggenheim Museum. New York: The Solomon R. Guggenheim Foundation and Horizon Press, 1960.

Zevi, Bruno, and Kaufmann, Edgar, Jr. *Frank Lloyd Wright's Fall-ingwater*. Milan: ETAS KOMPASS, 1962.

James, Cary. *The Imperial Hotel: Frank Lloyd Wright and the Architecture of Unity*. Rutland, Vt.: Charles E. Tuttle Co., 1968.

Morton, Mrs. Terry B., ed. *The Pope-Leighy House*. Washington: National Trust for Historic Preservation, 1969.

3. *Books by Frank Lloyd Wright*

The House Beautiful. River Forest, Ill.: Auvergne Press, 1896–1897. Text by William C. Gannett, page decorations by Wright. Privately published.

Ausgeführte Bauten und Entwürfe von Frank Lloyd Wright. Berlin: Ernst Wasmuth, 1910. A portfolio of drawings with an introduction by Wright.

The Japanese Print: An Interpretation. Chicago: Ralph Fletcher Seymour Co., 1912.

Two Lectures on Architecture. Chicago: The Art Institute, 1931. Contains "In the Realm of Ideas" and "To the Young Man in Architecture."

Modern Architecture: Being the Kahn Lectures for 1930. Princeton, N.J.: Princeton University Press, 1931.

The Disappearing City. New York: William Farquar Payson, 1932.

An Autobiography. New York: Longmans, Green, and Co., 1932. Contained three books: "Family-Fellowship," "Work," and "Freedom." In 1943 Wright released an expanded edition (New York: Duell, Sloan and Pearce), which divided the 1932 Book One in two ("Family" and "Fellowship") and added a fifth book, "Form." Subsequent printings included Book Six, "Broadacre City," originally published separately as *An Autobiography: Book Six, Broadacre City* (Spring Green, Wis.: A Taliesin Publication, 1943). Except for changes in paragraphing, the texts of the two editions and later printings are the same.

Architecture and Modern Life. New York: Harper & Brothers, 1938. With Baker Brownell.

An Organic Architecture: The Architecture of Democracy. London: Lund, Humphries & Co., Ltd., 1939. The Sir George Watson Lectures of the Sulgrave Manor Board, 1939.

When Democracy Builds. Chicago: University of Chicago Press, 1945. An expanded version of *The Disappearing City.*

Genius and the Mobocracy. New York: Duell, Sloan and Pearce, 1949. A biography of Louis H. Sullivan.

The Future of Architecture. New York: Horizon Press, 1953. Contains: "A Conversation" with Hugh Downs, NBC-TV, May 17, 1953; *Modern Architecture; Two Lectures on Architecture; Organic Architecture; Architecture and Modern Life,* chaps. 2, 4; "The Language of Organic Architecture," *The Architectural Forum* 98 (May 1953).

The Natural House. New York: Horizon Press, 1954. Contains: "Recollections—The United States, 1893–1920," *The Architectural Journal* (London) 84 (July 16–August 6, 1936); Preface to *Sixty Years of Living Architecture: The Work of Frank Lloyd Wright* (exhibition brochure, Guggenheim Museum, New York, November 1953); sections from *An Autobiography;* and some new material.

The Story of the Tower: The Tree that Escaped the Crowded Forest. New York: Horizon Press, 1956. On the Price Building, Bartlesville, Oklahoma.

A Testament. New York: Horizon Press, 1957. Further autobiographical material.

The Living City. New York: Horizon Press, 1958. An expanded version of *When Democracy Builds.*

Architecture: Man in Possession of His Earth. New York: Doubleday and Co., 1962. A reformulation of the 1927–1928 "In the Cause of Architecture" series in *The Architectural Record* (listed below) with a biography by Iovanna Wright, the architect's daughter.

4. Anthologies of Wright's Writings

Gutheim, Frederick, ed. *Frank Lloyd Wright on Architecture: Selected Writings, 1894–1940.* New York: Duell, Sloan and Pearce, 1941.

Kaufmann, Edgar, Jr., ed. *An American Architecture: Frank Lloyd Wright.* New York: Horizon Press, 1955.

Kaufmann, Edgar, Jr., and Raeburn, Ben, eds. *Frank Lloyd Wright: Writings and Buildings.* Cleveland: World Publishing Company, 1960.

Wright, Olgivanna Lloyd. *Frank Lloyd Wright: His Life, His Work, His Word.* New York: Horizon Press, 1967.

5. *Wright's Shorter Writings* (*Articles, Reviews, Letters, Speeches, and Interviews*)

To the author, George R. Dean, " 'Progress Before Precedent.' " *The Brickbuilder* 9 (May 1900): 96–97.

"The Architect." Ibid. 9 (June 1900): 124–128. Address to the Second Annual Convention of the Architectural League of America.

"A Home in a Prairie Town." *The Ladies' Home Journal* 18 (February 1901): 17.

"A Small House with 'Lots of Room in It.' " Ibid. 18 (July 1901): 15.

"The 'Village Bank' Series. V." *The Brickbuilder* 10 (August 1901): 160–161.

Three letters to Mrs. Harvey P. Sutton, July 9, 30, 1906, April 9, 1907. In Morgan, Don. L., and the editors, "A Wright House on the Prairie." *The Prairie School Review* 2 (3rd Quarter, 1965): 15–16.

"The New Larkin Administration Building." *The Larkin Idea* (November 1906). Reprinted in *The Prairie School Review* 7 (1st Quarter 1970): 15–19.

"A Fireproof House for $5,000." *The Ladies' Home Journal* 24 (April 1907): 24.

"Tribute" to actor Donald Robertson. *Oak Leaves* (Oak Park, Ill.), December 14, 1907.

"In the Cause of Architecture," *The Architectural Record* 23 (March 1908): 155–222.

"Ethics of Ornament." Speech to the Nineteenth Century Club, *Oak Leaves*, February 16, 1909. Reprinted in *The Prairie School Review* 4 (1st Quarter 1967): 16–17.

Press statements regarding his affair with Mamah Cheney. In *The Chicago Tribune*, December 26–31, 1911; ibid., January 4, 1912.

Letter to the editor. In *The Weekly Home News* (Spring Green, Wis.), January 4, 1912.

Eulogy for Daniel H. Burnham. In *The Architectural Record* 32 (August 1912): 184.

"In the Cause of Architecture, II." Ibid. 34 (May 1914): 405–413.

"To My Neighbors." *The Weekly Home News.* August 20, 1914.

Press interview. In Sell, Henry Blackman. "Interpretation not Imitation: The Work of Frank Lloyd Wright." *The International Studio* 55 (May 1915): 79–83.

"Love Truce at Wright Cote; Live in Fear." Interview by Walter Noble Burns, *The Chicago Tribune,* November 8, 1915.

Press statement regarding his affair with Miriam Noel. In *The Chicago Herald,* November 11, 1915.

Speech in Chicago on the "American System" houses. In *The Western Architect* 24 (September 1916): 121–123.

"Non-Competitive Plan for Development of Quarter Section of Land." In Yeomans, Alfred B., ed. *City Residential Land Development. Competitive Plans for Subdividing a Typical Quarter Section of Land in the Outskirts of Chicago.* Chicago: University of Chicago Press, 1916. Also in *The Western Architect* 25 (January 1917).

"In the Cause of Architecture: The New Imperial Hotel, Tokio." Ibid. 32 (April 1923): 39–46.

"In the Cause of Architecture: In the Wake of the Quake, Concerning the Imperial Hotel, Tokio." Ibid. 32 (November 1923): 129–132; 33 (February 1924): 17–20.

"Louis H. Sullivan: Beloved Master." Ibid. 33 (June 1924): 64–66.

"Louis H. Sullivan–His Work." *The Architectural Record* 56 (July 1924): 28–32.

Statement on American commercial architecture to *Baraboo Weekly News* (Baraboo, Wis.), December 4, 1924.

Speech to Baraboo Kiwanis Club. Partly reprinted in ibid., December 4, 1924.

"To the Countryside." *The Weekly Home News,* June 10, 1926.

"Frank Lloyd Wright Tells Story of Life; Years of Work, Love, and Despair." *The Capital Times* (Madison, Wis.), November 1, 1926.

"In the Cause of Architecture: I. The Architect and the Machine." *The Architectural Record* 61 (May 1927): 394–396.

"In the Cause of Architecture: II. Standardization, The Soul of the Machine." Ibid. 61 (June 1927): 478–480.

"In the Cause of Architecture: Part III. Steel." Ibid. 62 (August 1927): 163–166.

"In the Cause of Architecture: Part IV. Fabrication and the Imagination" and "Part V. The New World." Ibid. 62 (October 1927): 318–324.

"Why the Japanese Earthquake Did Not Destroy the Imperial Hotel." Liberty, December 3, 1927.

Letter to the editor. In The Weekly Home News, December 15, 1927.

"In the Cause of Architecture: I. The Logic of the Plan." The Architectural Record 63 (January 1928): 49–57.

"In the Cause of Architecture: II. What 'Styles' Mean to the Architect." Ibid. 63 (February 1928): 145–151.

"In the Cause of Architecture: III. The Meaning of Materials—Stone." Ibid. 63 (April 1928): 350–356.

"In the Cause of Architecture: IV. The Meaning of Materials—Wood." Ibid. 63 (May 1928): 481–488.

"In the Cause of Architecture: V. The Meaning of Materials—The Kiln." Ibid. 63 (June 1928): 555–561.

"In the Cause of Architecture: VI. The Meaning of Materials—Glass." Ibid. 64 (July 1928): 11–16.

"In the Cause of Architecture: VII. The Meaning of Materials—Concrete." Ibid. 64 (August 1928): 99–104.

"In the Cause of Architecture: VIII. Sheet Metal and a Modern Instance." Ibid. 64 (October 1928): 334–342.

"In the Cause of Architecture: IX. The Terms." Ibid. 64 (December 1928): 507–514.

"Fiske Kimball's New Book." Ibid. 64 (August 1928): 172–173.

" 'Towards a New Architecture.' " World Unity, September 1928.

"Taliesin: The Chronicle of a House with a Heart." Liberty, March 23, 1929. Later included in An Autobiography.

"American Architecture: Correspondence of Walter Pach, Paul Cret, Frank Lloyd Wright and Erich Mendelsohn with Fiske Kimball." The Architectural Record 65 (May 1929): 431–434.

"A Building Adventure in Modernism: A Successful Adventure in Concrete." Country Life 56 (May 1929): 40–41. On "La Miniatura," later included in An Autobiography.

"Surface and Mass,—Again." The Architectural Record 56 (July 1929): 92–94.

"The Logic of Contemporary Architecture as an Expression of this Age." *The Architectural Forum* 52 (May 1930): 637–638.

"Frank Lloyd Wright and Hugh Ferris Discuss the Modern Architect." Ibid. 53 (November 1930): 535–538.

"Architecture as a Profession Is Wrong." *The American Architect* 138 (December 1930): 22–23, 84, 86, 88.

"Principles of Design." *Annual of American Design*, 1931.

"Highlights" of a speech to the Michigan Architectural Society. In *The Architectural Forum* 55 (October 1931): 409–410.

Interview. In *The New York Times*, January 17, 1932.

"To the Students of the Beaux-Arts Institute of Design, All Departments" (January 1932). *Architecture* 66 (October 1932). Also in *An Autobiography*, pp. 296–298.

"For All May Raise the Flowers Now For All Have Got the Seed." *The T-Square Journal* 2 (February 1932): 6–8.

Letter to the editor. In ibid. p. 32.

" 'Broadacre City': An Architect's Vision." *The New York Times Magazine* (March 20, 1932), pp. 8–9.

"Why the Great Earthquake Did Not Destroy the Imperial Hotel." *Creative Art* 10 (April 1932): 269–277. Later included in *An Autobiography*.

"Of Thee I Sing." *Shelter* 2 (April 1932): 10–12.

"America Tomorrow." *The American Architect* 141 (May 1932): 16–17, 76.

"A Treatise on Ornament." *The Saturday Review of Literature* 8 (May 21, 1932): 744.

"An Extension of the Work in Architecture at Taliesin to Include Apprenticeship in Residence." Circular letter, Summer 1932. Reprinted in *An Autobiography*, pp. 390–394.

"The House of the Future." Excerpts from an address to the Cincinnati Convention of the National Association of Real Estate Boards. *National Real Estate Journal* 33 (July 1932): 25–26.

"Caravel or Motorship?" *The Architectural Forum* 52 (August 1932): 90.

"What Does the Machine Mean to Life in a Democracy?" *The Pictorial Review*, September 1932. Reprinted in Gutheim, ed., *Selected Writings*, pp. 167–171.

"Why I Love Wisconsin," which Gutheim lists as appearing in *Wisconsin Magazine* in 1932, did not appear before February, when the journal ceased publication. See *Selected Writings*, pp. 157–160.

"Another Pseudo." *The Architectural Forum* 59 (July 1933): 25.

"The Chicago World's Fair." *The Architect's Journal* 78 (July 13, 1933).

"In the Show Window at Macy's." *The Architectural Forum* 59 (November 1933): 419–420.

Letter to the editor. In *The Capital Times*, February 6, 1934.

Letter to the editor. In *The Weekly Home News*, February 22, 1934.

"The Architecture of Individualism." *Trend*, March–April 1934.

"What Is the Modern Idea?" *Physical Culture*, June 24, 1934.

"At Taliesin," sometimes called "Taliesin," was a sporadic weekly column written by Wright's apprentices and occasionally by the Master himself, running in four Wisconsin newspapers: *The Capital Times* and *Wisconsin State Journal* in Madison from February 2, 1934 to October 1937; *The Weekly Home News* in Spring Green from March 1934 to July 1935; and *The Iowa County Democrat* in Mineral Point from May 20 to September 30 and December 2, 1937. Wright's articles, all in *The Capital Times*, were: 1934 (February 13, July 13, 20, August 26, November 23, December 14); 1935 (April 26, August 9, October 4, 11, 18, November 7); 1936 (May 29, July 11, 31, September 18, November 20, December 18); 1937 (January 3, February 26, April 2, July 30, August 13, September 17, 24, October 1).

"Louis Sullivan's Words and Work." *The Architectural Review* 77 (March 1935): 116–117.

"Broadacre City: A New Community Plan." *The Architectural Record* 77 (April 1935): 243–254.

"Broadacre City." *The American Architect* 146 (May 1935): 55–63.

"Form and Function." *The Saturday Review* 13 (December 14, 1935): 6.

"Skyscrapers Doomed? Yes!" *The Rotarian*, March 1936.

"Taliesin: Our Cause." *Professional Arts Quarterly*, March 1936.

"Recollections—The United States, 1893–1920." *The Architect's Journal* 84 (July 16–August 6, 1936).

"Apprenticeship-Training for the Architect." *The Architectural Record* 80 (September 1936): 207–210.

"What the Cause of Architecture Needs Most." *The Architectural Review* 81 (March 1937): 99–100.

"Wright Regrets Russia Is Using US as Model for Architecture. Raps Communists of University as Racketeers after Trip." Interview in *The Capital Times*, July 22, 1937.

"US, USSR are the Two Greatest Hopes for Better Life and Democracy, FLW Declares." Ibid., August 1, 1937.

"Wright Lists 'Testament' of Beliefs after Visit to Russia; Lauds Stalin." Talk to Taliesin Fellowship in ibid., August 3, 1937.

"Wright Denies He Said Communists Racketeers." Ibid., August 5, 1937.

"Building Against Doomsday." *The Reader's Digest* 31 (September 1937). On the Imperial Hotel, also in *An Autobiography*.

"Architecture and Life in the U.S.S.R." *The Architectural Record* 82 (October 1937): 59–63. Originally published in *Soviet Russia Today* and included in *An Autobiography*.

"To the Young Man in Architecture—A Challenge." *The Architectural Forum* 68 (January 1938).

"Architect Wright Boosts Tom Amlie for Senate; Calls Him 'Like FDR.' " *The Capital Times*, August 11, 1938.

"Ideas for the Future." *The Saturday Review* 18 (September 17, 1938): 14–15.

"A Little Private Club." *Life* 5 (September 26, 1938). Reprinted in *The Architectural Forum* 69 (November 1938): 331–340.

Letter to the Blackburn family. In "Houses for $5,000–$6,000." Ibid.

"FLW Offers Lake Monona Development Plan for Public Buildings." *The Capital Times*, November 2, 1938.

"Williamsburg as a Museum Piece." *The New York Herald Tribune*, November 6, 1938.

"Frank Lloyd Wright Again." *Architect and Engineer*, March 1939.

"To the 58th." *Journal of the Royal Institute of British Architects*, October 16, 1939.

"Let's Discover America." *The Capital Times*, August 4, 1940.

"Chicago's Auditorium Is Fifty Years Old." *The Architectural Forum* 73 (September 1940): 10, 12.

"From Frank Lloyd Wright." *The Christian Century* 57 (November 13, 1940): 1419–1420.

Taliesin: The Taliesin Fellowship Publication (Spring Green, Wis.), October 1940, February 1941. Wright edited and contributed articles to the only two issues of his projected quarterly to appear.

"FLW Hits Conscription; Says U.S. Has Five Years to Build Defense Machine." *The Capital Times*, June 6, 1941.

"The American Quality." *Scribner's Commentator* 10 (October 1941): 25–46.

"FLW Denounces Stone for Judgment Hearsay." *The Capital Times*, December 20, 1942.

"FLW in Tribute to Will,–and Sally [Allen White]." Ibid., February 1, 1944.

"Viewpoints: To the Mole." *Magazine of Art* 37 (December 1944): 310, 312–315. A reply, which *The Times* declined to print, to an article by Robert M. Moses in *The New York Times Magazine* (June 18, 1944).

"The Modern Gallery: For the Solomon R. Guggenheim Foundation: New York City." *Magazine of Art* 39 (January 1946): 24–26.

Speech to the Herald Tribune Forum, New York. In the *New York Herald Tribune*, November 10, 1946.

"We Must Shape True Inspiration." *The New York Times Magazine* (April 20, 1947): 59.

"Frank Lloyd Wright Replies: . . . to Robert Moses' Attack on 'Functionalism.' " *New York Herald Tribune*, June 30, 1947.

"Let Us Go Now and Mimic No More." Speech at Princeton University. In *The Capital Times*, August 7, 1947.

"Bureaucracy Jumps the Gun." *The Weekly Home News*, October 30, 1947.

"The Architect." Lecture at the University of Chicago in 1946. In Heywood, Robert B., ed. *The Works of the Mind*. Chicago: University of Chicago Press, 1947.

"FLW Sees Hypocrisy as a Taint in All American Life." *The Capital Times*, May 11, 1948.

"Begin with a Hoe: An interview with Frank Lloyd Wright." *The Nation's Schools* 42 (November 1948): 20–24.

"State Road Commissioner's Use of High-Truss Steel Bridges Flayed by Wright." *The Capital Times*, November 25, 1948.

Breit, Harvey. "Talk with Frank Lloyd Wright." *The New York Times*, sec. 7, July 24, 1949.

Memorial to Lloyd Lewis. In Lewis, Lloyd, "The New Theatre." *Theatre Arts* 33 (July 1949): 32–34.

Roche, Mary. "Chairs Designed for Sitting." Interview in *The New York Times*, sec. 6, August 21, 1949.

"To Arizona." *Arizona Highways* 25 (October 1949): 10–11.

"Living in the Desert." Ibid., pp. 12–15.

"A Birthday Message." *The Capital Times*, June 10, 1950.

"An Adventure in the Human Spirit." Address at Florida Southern College. In *Motive*, journal of the Methodist Student Movement (November 1950): 30–31.

"Force Is a Heresy." *Wisconsin Athenean* 11 (Spring 1951): 10–11.

"Reply of FLW to House Un-American Activities Group Charge." *The Capital Times*, April 21, 1951.

"When Free Men Fear." *The Nation* 167 (June 2, 1951): 527–528. Same as "Force Is a Heresy," above.

"Listen to . . . Frank Lloyd Wright." Interview in *Collier's* 138 (August 3, 1951): 21.

"FLW Hits McCarthyism: Sees Need for a New Third Party," *The Capital Times*, August 21, 1951.

"Unitarian Building 'Makes Music—Is Itself a Form of Prayer,' Wright Says." Ibid., August 22, 1951.

"Wright Asks US Build Truck Routes Along Rail Lines as Safety Measure." Open letter to Wisconsin Highway Commission. In ibid., September 10, 1951.

Press statement on the Guggenheim Museum and organic architecture. In *The New York Times*, March 30, 1952.

Comments on the Guggenheim Museum. In *The Architectural Forum* 96 (April 1952): 141–144.

"Organic Architecture Looks at Modern Architecture." *The Architectural Record* 119 (June 1952): 149–154.

Address at Meeting of Student Members, AIA, June 25, 1952. In Coles, William A., and Reed, Henry Hope, Jr., eds. *Architecture in America: A Battle of Styles*. New York: Appleton-Century-Crofts, 1961.

"Nautilus's Prune." Interview in *The New Yorker* 28 (July 12, 1952): 20–21.

"Mr. Big." *The Capital Times,* July 18, 1952.

"Wake Up Wisconsin." Ibid., September 22, 1952.

Comments on Florida Southern College. In *The Architectural Forum* 97 (September 1952): 120.

Contributor to "The Future: Four Views." In *The New York Times,* sec. 6, pt. 2, February 1, 1953.

Interview. In *New York Herald Tribune,* May 14, 1953.

"The Language of Organic Architecture." *The Architectural Forum* 98 (May 1953): 106–107.

"Against the Steamroller." *The Architectural Review* 113 (May 1953): 283–284.

"Frank Lloyd Wright Speaks Up." *House Beautiful* 95 (July 1953): 86–88, 90.

"U.N. Stands Like Slab in a Graveyard." *The Capital Times,* July 13, 1953.

"Wright Now Ashamed of Town of His Boyhood." Ibid., August 25, 1953.

Letter to the editor. In ibid., September 22, 1953.

"FLW Protests Court Rule on Tax Exemption." Ibid., September 24, 1953.

"A Letter from Frank Lloyd Wright." *The Weekly Home News,* September 24, 1953.

"Outside the Profession." Interview in *The New Yorker* 29 (September 26, 1953): 26–27.

"Frank Lloyd Wright Talks of His Art." *The New York Times Magazine,* October 4, 1953.

"Wright, Continued." Interview in *The New Yorker* 29 (October 21, 1953): 25–27.

Nichols, Lewis. "Talk With Mr. Wright." *The New York Times,* sec. 7, November 1, 1953.

"Frank Lloyd Wright Talks About Photography." *Photography* 34 (February 1954): 40–41, 118.

"A New Debate in Old Venice." *The New York Times,* sec. 6, pt. 1, March 21, 1954.

Del Campo, Santiago. "An Afternoon with Frank Lloyd Wright." *Americas* 6 (April 1954): 9–12, 44–46.

"Man." *AIA* 28 (April 1954): 34–35.

"FLW Discusses Plan for New Civic Center." *The Capital Times*, May 27, 1954.

"Madison to be Commonplace?" Ibid., October 4, 1954.

"Wright Tells the Capital Times What He Had in Mind for Taliesin." Ibid., November 20, 1954.

Interview with I. Monte Radlovic. In *The Diplomat*, March, April 1955. Reprinted in U.S. Congress *Congressional Record*, 84th cong., 1st sess. (1955) 101, pt. 4: 4892–4894.

"Wright Says Civic Auditorium Can Be Built in 2 Years." *The Capital Times*, April 21, 1955.

Letter to the editor. In Colorado Springs *Free Press*, May 27, 1955. Reprinted in *The Denver Post*, May 29, and in U.S. Congress, *Congressional Record*, 84th cong., 1st sess., 1955, 101, pt. 7:8781.

"The Future of the City." *The Saturday Review* 32 (May 21, 1955): 10–13.

"FLW Explains His Views on [Air Force] Academy Design." *The Capital Times*, August 16, 1955.

"Wright Replies to Architectural Record Article." Ibid., September 6, 1955.

"Wright Denies Air Academy Link to 'Interests.'" Ibid., October 21, 1955.

" 'I Believe a House Is More a Home by Being a Work of Art.' " *House Beautiful* 97 (November 1955): 258–263, 358, 361–363.

"Faith in Your Own Individuality." Ibid., pp. 270–271, 302, 304.

"Architecture: Organic Expression of the Nature of Architecture." *Arizona Highways* 32 (February 1956): 12–18.

Wright and others on the Price Tower. In *The Architectural Record* 119 (February 1956).

"Wright Revisited." Interview in *The New Yorker* 32 (June 16, 1956): 26–27.

Two interviews. In *The Capital Times*, August 27, 28, 1956.

Three interviews. In Rodman, Seldon. *Conversations With Artists*. New York: The Devin-Adair Co., 1957.

"U.S. Architecture to be Greatest in World—Wright." *The Wisconsin Architect* (February 1957): 5, 11.

"Meeting of the Titans: Frank Lloyd Wright, Carl Sandburg Talk of Life, Work, Happiness." *The Capital Times*, June 3, 1957. Reprinted from *Newsday*.

Partial transcript from "The Mike Wallace Show," Westinghouse TV. In *The Capital Times*, September 2, 1957.

"A Visit with Frank Lloyd Wright." *Look* 21 (September 17, 1957): 28–34.

Saarinen, Aline B. "Tour with Mr. Wright." *The New York Times Magazine*, September 22, 1957.

"Wright Asks Court Test of Metzner Law's Validity." *The Capital Times*, September 27, 1957.

"Architecture and Music." *The Saturday Review* 40 (September 28, 1957): 72–73.

Complete transcript of the second interview on "The Mike Wallace Show," Westinghouse TV. In *The Capital Times*, September 30, 1957.

"Education and Art in Behalf of Life." Interview, *Arts in Society* 1 (January 1958): 5–10.

Letter to the University of Wichita, May 28, 1958. In Wright, Olgivanna Lloyd. *The Shining Brow: Frank Lloyd Wright*. New York: Horizon Press, 1960.

Brandon, Henry. "A Conversation with Frank Lloyd Wright: 'Flat on Our Faces.' " *The New Republic* 139 (September 8, 1958): 14–15.

"Frank Lloyd Wright on Restaurant Architecture: An Exclusive Interview of the Month." *Food Services Magazine*, November 1958.

Interview with representative of "Wide, Wide World," NBC-TV. In Wright, Olgivanna Lloyd. "Our House." *The Capital Times*, January 19, 1959.

Letter to the editor. In ibid., February 12, 1959.

"Frank Lloyd Wright's Last Interview: Why People Create (April 3, 1959)" in *School Arts* 58 (June 1959): 27–30.

"Wright Replies to Group Seeking to Stall on Terrace." *The Capital Times*, April 6, 1959.

6. Pamphlets, Catalogues, and Brochures

Wright often wrote introductions to his exhibition catalogues, as, for example, the preface to *Sixty Years of Living Architecture: The Work of Frank Lloyd Wright*, a 1951 to 1953 tour of several American and European cities, which varied slightly from place to place but was in essence the same. Other pamphlets of particular note are:

Hiroshige: An Exhibition of Colour Prints from the Collection of Frank Lloyd Wright. Chicago: The Art Institute, 1906.

Antique Color Prints. Chicago: The Arts Club, 1917.

Experimenting With Human Lives. Hollywood: The Fine Arts Society, 1923.

The Frank Lloyd Wright Collection of Japanese Prints. New York: The Anderson Galleries, 1927.

The Hillside Home School of the Allied Arts. Why We Want This School. Spring Green, Wis.: Frank Lloyd Wright, October 1931.

The Taliesin Fellowship. Spring Green, Wis.: Frank Lloyd Wright, 1933. Descriptive pamphlet and application for membership.

Taliesin. Spring Green, Wis.: Frank Lloyd Wright, 1934, 1935. A twenty-eight-page magazine that survived for only two issues.

Taliesin: The Taliesin Fellowship Publication. Spring Green, Wis.: Frank Lloyd Wright, October 1940, February 1941. Lasted for only two issues.

A Taliesin Square-Paper. A Non-Political Voice from Our Democratic Minority. Spring Green, Wis.: Taliesin Press, 1941–1951. A one-sheet, quarter-fold, unnumbered before three, then numbered to fifteen, publication, appearing occasionally from January 1941 to January 1951.

7. Manuscript Collections

The Frank Lloyd Wright Foundation denies access to the voluminous files stored at Taliesin West, pending construction, it says, of a library to house his still uncatalogued papers. Although William Wesley Peters has publicly stated that researchers are welcome, no one is permitted entrance, and there is no indication that proper library facilities will be made available. There are a few Wright letters in the public domain. The largest collection, some forty pieces, is at Northwestern University Library, Evanston, Illinois, but is not particularly useful, dealing mostly with abortive plans in the 1930s and 1940s to build mobile homes. There are other letters scattered in the Claude Bragdon and the William Channing Gannett Collections, the Rush Rhees Library, the University of Rochester; The American Council for Judaism, Jane Lloyd Jones, Bruce Barton, and August Derleth (restricted) Collections at the State Historical Society of Wisconsin, Madison; and the Frank Lloyd Wright Collection at Avery Library, Columbia University, New York. There are four excellent letters in the Harriet Monroe Poetry Collection, the University of Chicago Library.

8. Accounts by Relatives, Friends, and Clients

Armitage, Merle. "Frank Lloyd Wright: An American Original." *Texas Quarterly* 5 (Spring 1962): 85–90.

Barney, Maginel Wright. *The Valley of the God-Almighty Joneses.* New York: Appleton-Century, 1965.

"Honeycomb House." *The Architectural Record* 84 (July 1938): 58–84. Including comments by the Paul Hannas.

Jacobs, Herbert. *Frank Lloyd Wright: America's Greatest Architect.* New York: Harcourt, Brace and World, 1965.

Robie, Frederick C., Jr. "Mr. Robie Knew What He Wanted." *The Architectural Forum* 109 (October 1958): 126–127, 206, 210.

Jeannette Wilber Schofield to FLW. In Lloyd Wright, Olgivanna. "Our House." *The Capital Times*, September 22, 1958. The Schofields owned the Robie House from 1912 to 1926.

Woollcott, Alexander. "The Prodigal Father." *While Rome Burns.* New York: Grossett & Dunlap, 1934.

Wright, John Lloyd. "In My Father's Shadow." *Esquire*, February 1958: 55–57.

———. *My Father Who Is on Earth.* New York: G. P. Putnam's Sons, 1946.

Wright, Olgivanna Lloyd. *Our House.* New York: Horizon Press, 1959.

———. *The Roots of Life.* New York: Horizon Press, 1963. Also contains undated FLW talks and speeches.

———. *The Shining Brow: Frank Lloyd Wright.* New York: Horizon Press, 1960.

9. Miscellaneous Primary Sources

Johonnot, Rodney F. *The New Edifice of Unity Church.* Oak Park, Ill.: The Unity Church Club, 1906. Descriptive material and renderings.

The several versions of Monona Terrace were published in *The Capital Times*: November 2, 1938; June 4, 1941; July 7–10, 1953; August 29–31, September 5, 6, 1956; September 18, 1967 (1938 rendering).

"General Plan of Highway and Bridge Relocation" for the Spring Green area. In *The Weekly Home News*, October 9, 1947.

Talk in Chicago (1955?) at opening of Heritage Henredon furniture exhibition. Copy of tape in author's possession.

Frank Lloyd Wright On Record. New York: Caedmon Records, 1961. Recordings made in June 1956.

10. A Note on the Use of Newspapers

For Wright's Oak Park years, *The Reporter*, *The Vindicator*, and the *Argus* (all weeklies) were surpassed in quality and extent of coverage by *Oak Leaves*, inaugurated in 1902. *The Weekly Home News* in Spring Green is indispensable for any Wright biographer, and along with its predecessors was researched for the years 1879–1968. With the exception of the several newspapers cited in Chapter 1, other Wisconsin weeklies—*The Sauk County Democrat* (Baraboo), *The Iowa County Democrat* (Mineral Point), and the *Baraboo Weekly News*— were most useful from 1911 into the 1930s. *The New York Times*, which in Wright's case did not print all the fit news, was consistently the most inaccurate newspaper source, but after the 1930s was useful as an index to Wright's national impact. *The Chicago Tribune* was unfriendly to Wright but a valuable source after September 1909. Clearly the best and most important press coverage came from *The Capital Times* in Madison, whose editor, William T. Evjue, interviewed Wright upon his final return from Japan in 1922, beginning a warm friendship that lasted until the architect's death in 1959. Evjue opened his pages to Wright, and carried news of his most trivial activities.

SECONDARY SOURCES

As a group, the book-length studies of Wright are disastrous. Finis Farr's is the best of a bad lot of popular biographies. His inside information suggests that his book was in some sense "official," although like the other journalists, and like Blake and Zevi of the more scholarly authors, he leans rather heavily on *An Autobiography*. Hitchcock and Manson make no attempt at synthesis, but their heavily detailed works are valuable compilations of raw data. Eaton's comparative analysis is not a full biography, but his fruitful approach should serve as a model for further studies. The most stimulating approaches to Wright have been taken by Scully and Smith. Scully locates Wright in the process of architectural history, tracing the influences upon him and the pool of ideas upon which he drew. Unfortunately, Scully's brilliant and incisive text is only twenty-one pages long. Smith defines the intellectual milieu in which Wright functioned, shows the sociopolitical problems he confronted, and analyzes the solutions he proposed. Since Scully has unearthed the architectural, and Smith the intellectual, influences upon Wright, I have attempted to explicate his work rather than argue with them or retrace their steps, but to both I am indebted.

1. Popular Biographies

Farr, Finis. *Frank Lloyd Wright*. New York: Charles Scribner's Sons, 1961.

Foresee, Alysea. *Frank Lloyd Wright: Rebel in Concrete*. Philadelphia: Macrae Smith Co., 1959.

Jacobs, Herbert. *Frank Lloyd Wright: America's Greatest Architect*. New York: Harcourt, Brace and World, 1965.

Ransohoff, Doris. *Frank Lloyd Wright: Living Architecture*. Chicago: Britannica Books, 1962.

2. Scholarly and Professional Studies

Blake, Peter. *Frank Lloyd Wright: Architecture and Space* (Baltimore: Penguin Pelican, 1964). Originally one-third of *The Master Builders* (New York: Alfred A. Knopf, 1960).

Eaton, Leonard K. *Two Chicago Architects and Their Clients: Frank Lloyd Wright and Howard Van Doren Shaw*. Cambridge, Mass.: MIT Press, 1969.

Hitchcock, Henry-Russell. *In the Nature of Materials: The Buildings of Frank Lloyd Wright, 1887–1941*. New York: Duell, Sloan and Pearce, 1942.

Manson, Grant C. *Frank Lloyd Wright to 1910: the First Golden Age.* New York: Reinhold Publishing Corp., 1958.

Scully, Vincent, Jr. *Frank Lloyd Wright.* New York: George Braziller, 1960.

Smith, Norris Kelly. *Frank Lloyd Wright: A Study in Architectural Content.* Englewood Cliffs, N.J.: Prentice-Hall, 1966.

Zevi, Bruno. *Frank Lloyd Wright.* Milan: Il Balcone, 1954.

INDEX

Page numbers in **boldface** denote illustrations.

73 74 75 76 77 10 9 8 7 6 5 4 3 2 1